Learn Robotics Programming

Build and control autonomous robots using Raspberry Pi 3
and Python

Danny Staple

BIRMINGHAM - MUMBAI

Learn Robotics Programming

Commissioning Editor: Gebin George
Acquisition Editor: Akshay Jethani
Content Development Editor: Priyanka Deshpande
Technical Editor: Mohit Hassija
Copy Editor: Safis Editing
Project Coordinator: Drashti Panchal
Proofreader: Safis Editing
Indexer: Pratik Shirodkar
Graphics: Tom Scaria
Production Coordinator: Jyoti Chauhan

First published: November 2018

Production reference: 1281118

Published by Packt Publishing Ltd.
Livery Place
35 Livery Street
Birmingham
B3 2PB, UK.

ISBN 978-1-78934-074-7

www.packtpub.com

To my dear wife, Carol, for her love, her inspiration, and her unwavering support.

`mapt.io`

Mapt is an online digital library that gives you full access to over 5,000 books and videos, as well as industry leading tools to help you plan your personal development and advance your career. For more information, please visit our website.

Why subscribe?

- Spend less time learning and more time coding with practical eBooks and Videos from over 4,000 industry professionals

- Improve your learning with Skill Plans built especially for you

- Get a free eBook or video every month

- Mapt is fully searchable

- Copy and paste, print, and bookmark content

PacktPub.com

Did you know that Packt offers eBook versions of every book published, with PDF and ePub files available? You can upgrade to the eBook version at `www.Packt.com` and as a print book customer, you are entitled to a discount on the eBook copy. Get in touch with us at `customercare@packtpub.com` for more details.

At `www.Packt.com`, you can also read a collection of free technical articles, sign up for a range of free newsletters, and receive exclusive discounts and offers on Packt books and eBooks.

Contributors

About the author

Danny Staple builds robots and gadgets as a hobbyist, makes videos about his work with robots, and attends community events such as PiWars and Arduino Day. He has been a professional Python programmer, later moving into DevOps, since 2009, and a software engineer since 2000. He has worked with embedded systems, including embedded Linux systems, throughout the majority of his career. He has been a mentor at a local CoderDojo, where he taught how to code with Python. He has run Lego Robotics clubs with Mindstorms. He has also developed Bounce!, a visual programming language targeted at teaching code using the NodeMCU IoT platform.

The robots he has built with his children include TankBot, SkittleBot (now the Pi Wars robot), ArmBot, and SpiderBot.

I would like to thank David Anderson for being a great person to bounce ideas off and for his motivational energy. I would like to thank Ben Nuttall and Dave Jones for GPIOZero, and for helping me out countless times on twitter. Dave Jones kickstarted my journey into computer vision in a restaurant in Cardiff and is the author of the PiCamera Library. Finally, I would like to thank my children, Helena and Jonathan, for their support and patience, even occasionally reviewing diagrams for me.

About the reviewer

Leo White is a professional software engineer, and a graduate of the University of Kent. His interests include electronics, 3D printing, and robotics. He first started programming on the Commodore 64, later wrote several applications for the Acorn Archimedes, and currently programs set-top boxes for his day job. Utilizing the Raspberry Pi as a base, he has mechanized children's toys and driven robot arms, blogging about his experiences and processes along the way, has given presentations at Raspberry Jams, and entered a variety of robots in the Pi Wars competition.

Packt is searching for authors like you

If you're interested in becoming an author for Packt, please visit `authors.packtpub.com` and apply today. We have worked with thousands of developers and tech professionals, just like you, to help them share their insight with the global tech community. You can make a general application, apply for a specific hot topic that we are recruiting an author for, or submit your own idea.

Table of Contents

Preface

Learn Robotics is about building and programming a robot with smart behaviors. It covers the skills required to makes, and build, a gadget from parts, including how to choose them. This book follows with how to make the code to make those parts do something interesting. The book uses Python, together with a little bit of HTML/CSS and JS.

The technology shown here is intended to include things that are available and affordable, and the code intended to demonstrate concepts, so that these can be used and combined to create even more interesting code and robots.

It combines aspects of being a programmer, with aspects of being a robot maker, with a number of specialist topics such as computer vision and voice assistants thrown in.

Who this book is for

This book is intended for someone with a little programming experience. They do not need to be an expert-level programmer, but to have written some lines of code and be comfortable with looping, conditionals, and functions. Object oriented (class and object)-based programming isn't necessary, but is introduced in the book.

The book does not require a specialist workshop, although there will be a little soldering. This will be introduced later in the book.

The reader does not need to have any experience at all of electronics or making things, but hopefully a healthy interest in learning more, since some very basic concepts are introduced throughout the book. Being keen to build a robot, get it to do stuff, and find out what to do with it next is probably the most important aspect of the book.

What this book covers

Chapter 1, *Introduction to Robotics*, introduces what a robot is, together with examples.

Chapter 2, *Exploring Robot Building Blocks – Code and Electronics*, starts looking at the components of a robot. This is where we will start making choices about the robot's parts and it also introduces the block diagrams for both systems and code.

Chapter 3, *Introducing the Raspberry Pi - Starting with Raspbian*, introduces the Raspberry Pi and its connections, the Raspbian Linux operating system we'll use on it, and also covers the preparation of an SD card for use in a robot.

Chapter 4, *Preparing a Raspberry Pi for a Robot - Headless by Default*, looks at what a "headless" Raspberry Pi means and getting the Pi ready to run without a keyboard or screen.

Chapter 5, *Backing Up the Code with Git and SD Card Copies*, outlines how to restore things when they go wrong. This establishes habits to prevent you from losing your work.

Chapter 6, *Building Robot Basics - Wheels, Power, and Wiring*, introduces the choices and trade-offs for building the robot base, finding out what to buy, and taking your first steps in assembling it.

Chapter 7, *Drive and Turn - Moving Motors with Python*, covers how to connect our robot to the Raspberry Pi and write code to make the robot move, laying down the foundations for the code in subsequent chapters.

Chapter 8, *Programming Line-Following Sensors Using Python*, adds line sensors to the robot, explains how to fit them, and explains then how to use them to make line-following code.

Chapter 9, *Programming RGB Strips in Python*, demonstrates how to add an LED strip to the robot and write code to drive it, which the reader can then use to extend behaviors with colorful lights, for aesthetics, debugging, and information. This chapter also introduces soldering.

Chapter 10, *Using Python to Control Servo Motors*, gives our robot a set of servo motors, for the purpose of moving a "head" around, and shows the principles by which servo motors can be programmed.

Chapter 11, *Programming Distance Sensors with Python*, introduces distance sensors. Through the addition of a pair of variable inputs, we can make our robot avoid walls and obstacles autonomously.

Chapter 12, *Programming Encoders with Python*, demonstrates the concepts of odometry, measuring how far the robot has traveled according to wheel rotations, and uses it to compensate for motor variations and make accurate turns using a proportional-integral controller.

Chapter 13, *Robot Vision - Using a Pi Camera and OpenCV*, connects our robot to a camera mounted on the servo driven pan and tilt head. We program the robot to follow colored objects, or track faces in the camera, while allowing us to view its activity on a computer or phone.

Chapter 14, *Voice Communication with a Robot Using Mycroft*, introduces a voice assistant running on a second Pi, Mycroft, which we can program in Python to communicate with our robot and ask it to do things.

Chapter 15, *Programming a Gamepad on Raspberry Pi with Python*, is where we use HTML/CSS and JS to turn a phone into a smart game-like controller for our robot so that we can manually drive it, and launch autonomous behaviors at a touch, while seeing through the robot's camera.

Chapter 16, *Taking Your Robot Programming Skills Further*, looks at the wider world of robotics, what communities there are, how to get in touch with other robot builders and makers, potential development areas, and where to compete with a robot.

Chapter 17, *Planning Your Next Robot Project - Putting It All Together*, is the final chapter, where we summarize what you have seen in the book, while encouraging you to plan the construction of your next robot.

Chapter 18, *Appendix*, will cover extra information to help build your robot.

To get the most out of this book

Before you begin with this book, you need to have programmed a little in a text programming language. I am assuming some familiarity with variables, conditional statements, looping, and functions.

In terms of manual skills, I assume that you can use a screwdriver, that you can deal with occasional fiddly operations, and that you won't be too scared off by the possibility of soldering things.

Please find a well-lit work surface to build the robot on when those sections come, and somewhere to store it where it won't get dropped or damaged.

Download the example code files

You can download the example code files for this book from your account at www.packt.com. If you purchased this book elsewhere, you can visit www.packt.com/support and register to have the files emailed directly to you.

You can download the code files by following these steps:

1. Log in or register at `www.packtpub.com`.
2. Select the **SUPPORT** tab.
3. Click on **Code Downloads & Errata**.
4. Enter the name of the book in the **Search** box and follow the onscreen instructions.

Once the file is downloaded, please make sure that you unzip or extract the folder using the latest version of:

- WinRAR/7-Zip for Windows
- Zipeg/iZip/UnRarX for Mac
- 7-Zip/PeaZip for Linux

The code bundle for the book is also hosted on GitHub at `https://github.com/PacktPublishing/Learn-Robotics-Programming`. In case there's an update to the code, it will be updated on the existing GitHub repository.

We also have other code bundles from our rich catalog of books and videos available at `https://github.com/PacktPublishing/`. Check them out!

Download the color images

We also provide a PDF file that has color images of the screenshots/diagrams used in this book. You can download it here: `https://www.packtpub.com/sites/default/files/downloads/9781789340747_ColorImages.pdf`.

Code in Action

Visit the following link to check out videos of the code being run:

`http://bit.ly/2FLWiIr`

Conventions used

There are a number of text conventions used throughout this book.

`CodeInText`: Indicates code words in text, database table names, folder names, filenames, file extensions, pathnames, dummy URLs, user input, and Twitter handles. Here is an example: "This creates the `myrobot.img` file as a clone of the whole SD card in your home directory."

A block of code is set as follows:

```
import socket
print('%s is alive!' % socket.gethostname())
```

Any command-line input or output is written as follows:

```
C:\Users\danny>ping raspberrypi.local
```

Bold: Indicates a new term, an important word, or words that you see on screen. For example, words in menus or dialog boxes appear in the text like this. Here is an example: "You'll see two download links, **Download Torrent** and **Download Zip**. Click the **Download Zip** button and save this file."

Warnings or important notes appear like this.

Tips and tricks appear like this.

Get in touch

Feedback from our readers is always welcome.

General feedback: Email `customercare@packtpub.com` and mention the book title in the subject of your message. If you have questions about any aspect of this book, please email us at `customercare@packtpub.com`.

Errata: Although we have taken every care to ensure the accuracy of our content, mistakes do happen. If you have found a mistake in this book, we would be grateful if you would report this to us. Please visit www.packt.com/submit-errata, selecting your book, clicking on the Errata Submission Form link, and entering the details.

Piracy: If you come across any illegal copies of our works in any form on the internet, we would be grateful if you would provide us with the location address or website name. Please contact us at copyright@packt.com with a link to the material.

If you are interested in becoming an author: If there is a topic that you have expertise in, and you are interested in either writing or contributing to a book, please visit authors.packtpub.com.

Reviews

Please leave a review. Once you have read and used this book, why not leave a review on the site that you purchased it from? Potential readers can then see and use your unbiased opinion to make purchase decisions, we at Packt can understand what you think about our products, and our authors can see your feedback on their book. Thank you!

For more information about Packt, please visit packtpub.com.

Introduction to Robotics 1

Throughout this book, we will build a robot and create programs for it that give the robot behaviors that make it feel intelligent and able to make decisions. We will write code to use sensors to observe the robot's surroundings, and build real-world examples of advanced topics such as vision, speech recognition, and talking.

You will see how the simple build techniques, when combined with a little bit of code, will result in a machine that feels like some kind of pet. You will also see how to debug it when things go wrong, which they will, and how to give the robot ways to indicate problems back to you, along with selecting the behavior you would like to demonstrate. We will connect a joypad to it, give it voice control, and finally show you how to plan a further robot build.

Before we start building a robot, it's worth spending a little time on an introduction to what robotics really is, or what a robot is. We can explore some of the types of robots, along with the basic principles that distinguish a robot from another type of machine. We will think a little about where the line between robot and non-robot machines are, then perhaps muddy that line a little bit with the somewhat fuzzy truth. We will then look at the types of robots that people start building in the hobbyist and amateur robotics scene.

In this chapter, we will be covering the following topics:

- What does robot mean? Where the word comes from, and what exactly defines a robot.
- Top robots, where we'll take a look at some amazing real robots.
- Robots in industry, to explore robots seen in factories and warehouses.
- Robots in the home, to show how robots are already with us in our lives.
- We'll look at competitive, educational, and hobby robots where people are using robots for fun, learning, and showing off.

What does robot mean?

A **robot** is a machine that is able to make autonomous decisions based on input from sensors. A software agent is a program that is designed to automatically process input and produce output. Perhaps a robot can be best described as an autonomous software agent with sensors and moving outputs. Or, it could be described as an electromechanical platform with software running on it. Either way, a robot requires electronics, mechanical parts, and code.

The word robot conjures up images of fantastic sci-fi creations, devices with legendary strength and intelligence. These often follow the human body plan, making them an **android**, the term for a human-like robot. They are often given a personality and behave like a person who is in some simple way naive. Refer to the following diagram:

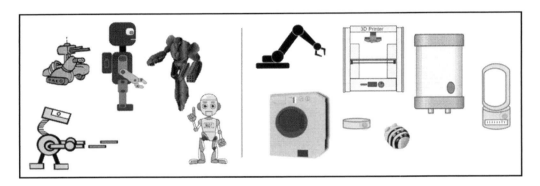

Science fiction and real-world robots. Images used are from the public domain OpenClipArt library

The word robot comes from sci-fi. The word is derived from the Czech for slave, and was first used in the 1921 Karel Capek play, *Rossums Universal Robots*. The science fiction author Isaac Asimov coined the word robotics as he explored intelligent robot behavior.

Most real robots in our homes and industries have a few cutting edge and eye catching examples standing out. Most do not stand on two legs, or indeed any legs at all. Some are on wheels, and some are not mobile but still have many moving parts and sensors.

Robots like washing machines, autonomous vacuum cleaners, fully self regulating boilers, and air sampling fans have infiltrated our homes and are part of everyday life. They aren't threatening, and have became just another machine around us. The 3D printer, robot arm, and learning toys are a bit more exciting though. Take a look at the following diagram:

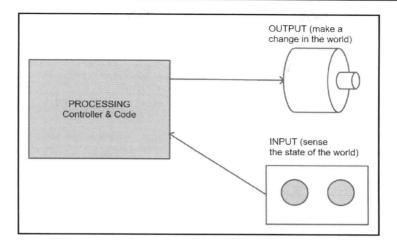

The robot, reduced

At their core, robots can all be simplified down to what is represented in the preceding diagram with outputs, such as a motor, inputs, and a controller for processing or running code. So, the basis of a robot, represented as a list, would look something like this:

- A robot has inputs, and sensors to measure, and sample a property of its environment
- A robot has outputs, motors, lights, sounds, valves, sounds, heaters, or other types of output to alter it's environment
- A robot will use the data from its inputs to make autonomous decisions about how it controls its outputs

Advanced and impressive robots

Now you have an overview of robots in general, I'll introduce some specific examples that represent the most impressive robots around, and what they are capable of. These robots are technical demonstrations, and with the exception of the Mars robots, have favored their closeness to human or animal adaptability and form over their practical and repeated use.

Robots that look like humans and animals

Take a look at the following picture and understand the similarities between robots and humans/animals:

A selection of human and animal-like robots. Cog: an Mit Project, Honda ASIMO By Morio, Nao From Softbank Robotic, Boston Dynamics Atlas, Boston Dynamics BigDog (https://commons.wikimedia.org/)

What these robots have in common is that they try to emulate humans and animals in the following ways:

- The first robot on the left is Cog, from the Massachusetts Institute of Technology. Cog attempted to be human-like in its movements and sensors.
- The second robot is the Honda ASIMO, which walks and talks a little like a human. ASIMO's two cameras perform object avoidance, and gestures and face recognition, and have a laser distance sensor to sense the floor. It can follow marks on the floor with infrared sensors. ASIMO is able to accept voice commands in English and Japanese.
- The third robot in this selection is the Nao robot from Softbank Robotics. This rather cute, 58 cm tall robot was designed as a learning and play robot for users to program. It has sensors to detect its motion, including if it is falling, and ultrasonic distance sensors to avoid bumps. Nao uses speakers and a microphone for voice processing. Nao includes multiple cameras to perform similar feats to the ASIMO.
- The fourth robot is Atlas from Boston Dynamics. This robot is speedy on two legs and is capable of natural looking movement. It has a laser radar (LIDAR) array, which it uses to sense what is around it to plan and avoid collisions.

- The right-most robot is the Boston Dynamics BigDog, a four legged robot, or quadruped, which is able to run and is one of the most stable four legged robots, capable of being pushed, shoved, and walking in icy conditions while remaining stable.

We will incorporate some features like these in the robot we will build, using distance sensors to avoid obstacles, a camera for visual processing, line sensors to follow marks on the floor, and voice processing to follow and respond to spoken commands. We will use ultrasonic distance sensors like Nao, and experiment with distance sensors a little like Asimo. We will also look at pan and tilt mechanisms for camera a little like the head used in Cog.

The Mars rovers

The **Mars rover robots** are designed to function on a different planet, where there is no chance of human intervention if something goes wrong. They are robust by design. New code can only be sent to a Mars rover via a remote connection as it is not practical to send up a person with a screen and keyboard. The Mars rover is **headless by design**. Refer to the following photo:

The Curiosity Mars rover by NASA

Mars rovers depend on wheels instead of legs, since this is far simpler to make a robot stable, and there is far less that can go wrong. Each wheel on the Mars rovers has it's own motor. They are arranged to provide maximum grip and stability to tackle the rocky terrain and reduced gravity on Mars.

The Curiosity rover was deposited on Mars with its sensitive camera folded up. After landing, the camera was unfolded and positioned with servo motors. The camera package can be positioned using a **pan and tilt** mechanism so it can take in as much of the Mars landscape as it can, sending back footage and pictures to NASA for analysis.

Like the Mars robot, the robot we will build in this book will use motor-driven wheels. Our robot will also be designed to run without a keyboard and mouse, being **headless by design.** As we expand the capabilities of our robot in this book, we will also use servo motors to drive a pan and tilt mechanism.

Robots in the home

Many robots have already infiltrated our homes. They are overlooked as robots because on first glance they appear commonplace and mundane. However, they are more sophisticated than they seem.

The washing machine

Let's start with the washing machine. This is used every day in some homes, with a constant stream of clothes to wash, spin, and dry. But how is this a robot? Let us understand this by referring to the following diagram:

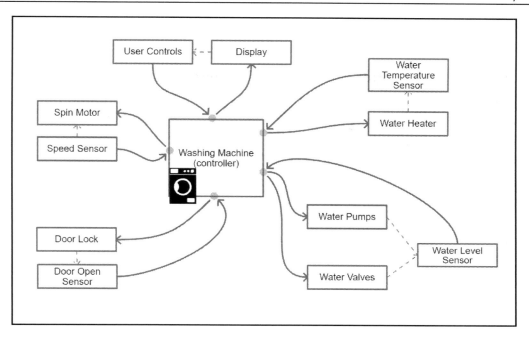

The humble washing machine as a robot

The preceding diagram represents a washing machine as a block diagram. There is a central controller connected to the display, and with controls to select a program. The lines going out of the controller are outputs, and the lines going into the controller are data coming in from sensors. The dashed lines from outputs to the sensors show a closed loop of output actions in the real world causing sensor changes; this is feedback, an essential concept in robotics.

The washing machine uses the display and buttons to let the user choose the settings and see the status. After the start button is pressed, the machine will check the door sensor and sensibly refuse to start if the door is open. Once the door is closed and the start button is pressed, it will output to lock the door. After this, it uses heaters, valves, and pumps to fill the drum with heated water, using sensor feedback to regulate the water level and temperature.

Each process could be represented by a set of statements like these, which simultaneously fill the drum and keep it heated:

```
start water pump
turn on water heater
while water is not filled and water is not at the right temperature:
  if water filled then
    stop water pump
  if water is at the right temperature then
    turn off heater
  else
    turn on water heater
```

Note the `else` there, which is in case the water temperature drops below the right temperature a bit. The washing machine then starts the drum spinning sequence: slow turns, fast spins, sensing the speed to meet the criteria. It will drain the drum, spin the clothes dry, release the door lock, and stop.

This washing machine is in every respect a robot. A washing machine has sensors and outputs to affect its environment. Processing allows it to follow a program and use sensors with feedback to reach and maintain conditions. A washing machine repair person may be more of a roboticist than I.

Other household robots

A gas central heating boiler has sensors, pumps, and valves and uses feedback mechanisms to maintain the temperature of the house, water flow through heating, gas flow, and ensure that the pilot light stays lit.

Smart fans use sensors to detect room temperature, humidity, and air quality, then output through the fan speed and heating elements.

A computer printer is also a robot, with moving part outputs and sensors to detect all those pesky paper jams.

Perhaps the most obvious home robot is the robot vacuum cleaner. Refer to the following diagram:

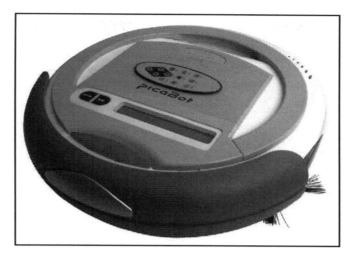

A robotic vacuum cleaner (PicaBot By Handitec)

This wheeled mobile robot is like the one we will build here, but prettier. They are packed with sensors to detect walls, bag levels, and barrier zones, and avoid collisions. They most represent the type of robot we are looking at.

As we build our robot, we will explore how to use its sensors to detect things and react to them, forming the same feedback loops we saw in the washing machine.

Robots in industry

Another place robots are commonly seen is in industry. The first useful robots have been used in factories, and have been there for a long time.

Robot arms

Robot arms range from very tiny and delicate robots for turning eggs, to colossal monsters moving shipping containers. Robot arms tend to use stepper and servo motors. We will look at servo motors in the pan and tilt mechanism used in this book. An impressive current industrial arm robot is **Baxter** from Rethink Robotics:

The Rethink Robotics Baxter Robot

Many robot arms are unsafe to work next to and could result in accidents. Not so with Baxter; it can sense a human and work around or pause for safety. In the preceding image, these sensors can be seen around the "head." The arm sensors and soft joints also allow Baxter to sense and react to collisions.

Baxter also has a training and repeat mechanism for workers to adapt it to work, using sensors in the joints to detect their position when being trained or playing back motions. Our robot will use encoder sensors so we can precisely program wheel movements.

Warehouse robots

Another common type of robot used in industry is those that move items around a factory floor or warehouse.

There are giant robotic crane systems capable of shifting pallets in storage complexes. They receive instructions on where goods need to be moved from and to within shelving systems:

Intellicart Line Following Robot

Smaller item-moving robot vehicles often employ line sensing technology, by following lines on the floor, wire underneath the floor via magnetic sensing, or marker beacons like ASIMO does. Our robot will follow lines like these. These line-following carts frequently use wheeled arrangements because these are simple to maintain and can form stable platforms.

Competitive, educational, and hobby robots

The most fun robots can be those built by amateur robot builders. This is an extremely innovative space.

Robotics always had a home in education, with academic builders using them for learning and experimentation platforms. Many commercial ventures have started in this setting. University robots tend to be group efforts, with access to increasingly hi-tech academic equipment to create them, as shown in the following picture:

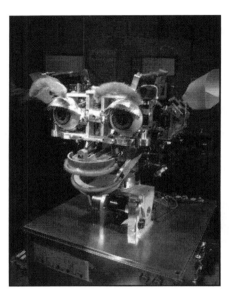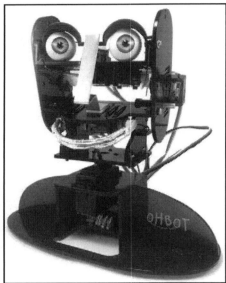

Kismet and OhBot

Kismet was created at MIT in the late 90s. There are a number of hobbyist robots that are derived from it. It was groundbreaking at the time, using servo motors to drive face movements intended to mimic human expressions. This has been followed in the community with OhBot, an inexpensive hobbyist kit using servo motors, which can be linked with a Raspberry Pi, using voice recognition and facial camera processing to make a convincing display.

Hobby robotics is strongly linked with open source and blogging, sharing designs, and code, leading to further ideas. Hobbyist robots can be created from kits available on the internet, with modifications and additions. The kits cover a wide range of complexity from simple three-wheeled bases to drone kits and hexapods. They come with or without the electronics included. An investigation of kits will be covered in Chapter 6, *Building Robot Basics - Wheels, Power, and Wiring*. I used a hexapod kit to build SpiderBot to explore walking motion. Refer to the following photo:

Spiderbot - built by me, based on a kit. Controller is an esp8266 + Adafruit 16 Servo Controller

Skittlebot was my Pi Wars 2018 entry, built using toy hacking, repurposing a remote control excavator toy into a robot platform. **Pi Wars** is an autonomous robotics challenge for Raspberry Pi-based robots, which has both manual and autonomous challenges. There were entries with decorative cases and interesting engineering principles. **Skittlebot** uses three distance sensors to avoid walls, and we will investigate this kind of sensor in Chapter 11, *Programming Distance Sensors with Python*. Skittlebot uses a camera to seek out colored objects, as we will see in Chapter 13, *Robot Vision - Using A Pi Camera And OpenCV*. Here is a photo of Skittlebot:

Skittlebot - My PiWars 2018 Robot - based on a toy

Some hobbyist robots are built from scratch, using 3D printing, laser cutting, vacuum forming, woodwork, CNC, and other techniques to construct the chassis and parts. Refer to the following set of photos:

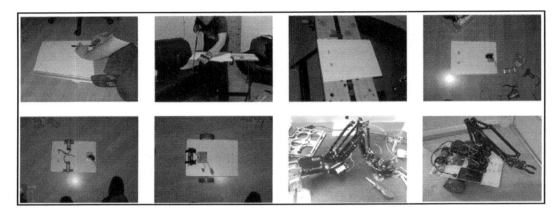

Building Armbot

I built the robot from scratch, for the London robotics group the Aurorans, in 2009. The robot was known as eeeBot in 2009, since it was intended to be driven by an Eee PC laptop. The Aurorans were a community who met to discuss robotics. The robot was later given a Raspberry Pi, and a robot arm kit seemed to fit it, earning it the name **Armbot**. In the current market, there are many chassis kits and a beginner will not need to measure and cut materials in this way to make a functioning robot. This was not built to compete, but to inspire other robot builders and kids to code. Towards the end of the book, we will cover some of the communities where robots are being built and shared, along with starting points on using construction techniques to build them from scratch.

The television series *Robot Wars* is a well known competitive robot event with impressive construction and engineering skills. There is no autonomous behavior in Robot Wars though; these are all manually driven, like remote control cars. Washing machines, although less exciting, are smarter, so they could be more strictly considered robots.

Summary

In this chapter, we have looked at what the word robot means, and the facts and fiction with robots. We have defined what a real robot is, and gained some idea of what a machine needs to do to be considered a robot.

We've investigated the robots seen in the home, and in industry, and those that are designed to amaze or have traveled to other planets. We've also looked at hobbyist and education robots, and how some of these are just built for fun. You've seen some block diagrams of real-world devices that may not have been considered robots, and have seen how our homes may already have a number of robots present.

Now we know what robots are, let's move on to the next chapter, in which we'll look at how to plan a robot so we can build it.

Questions

Based on the topics covered in this chapter, answer the following questions:

1. What element of a robot is used to monitor its environment?
2. What type of robot element do motors represent?
3. What are the three elements of a robotic system?
4. Where have robots been operating the longest in regular usage?
5. Why are wheels used more often than legs?
6. What is the principle connecting output, input, and control in a loop?
7. Why might a household washing machine be considered more robotic than a UK Robot Wars entry?

Further reading

Refer to the following links:

- Honda Asimo: http://asimo.honda.com/
- Baxter at Rethink Robotics: https://www.rethinkrobotics.com/baxter/
- Kistmet at MIT: http://www.ai.mit.edu/projects/humanoid-robotics-group/kismet/kismet.html
- The OhBot: http://www.ohbot.co.uk/
- The Mars Science Laboratory at NASA: https://mars.nasa.gov/msl/

2
Exploring Robot Building Blocks - Code and Electronics

In this chapter, we will go over the parts and systems that make up robots. What are the parts of a robot? These parts will be both software (code, and other) and hardware. How do they go together? When starting to make a robot, it's valuable to think about the parts you want and how they relate to each other. I recommend you sketch a plan of your robot—a block diagram as a guide to the connected code and parts.

In this chapter, we will be covering the following topics:

- What is inside a robot? We will take apart a robot and examine its parts
- Types of motors, sensors, and actuators - details on these robot parts
- Controllers and IO - we will look at the main controllers and input/output functions
- Planning components and code structure—we will make block diagrams to describe code, and components anywhere
- A plan of our robot—example plans of the robot we will build in this book

Technical requirements

For this chapter, you will require basic drawing materials, such as a pen and paper. While software such as Draw.io, Dia, Pencil, Inkscape, or Visio could be used, a back-of-an envelope sketch of a block diagram is a great start to robot planning. Most of my robots start that way.

What is inside a robot?

We can start by looking at a robot as a physical system. However, instead of looking at it all joined together, you can see how a typical hobby rover looks when totally disassembled in the following diagram:

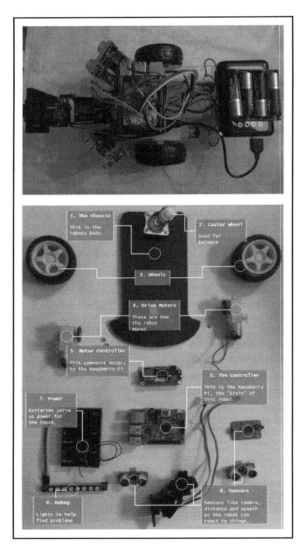

A hobby rover with components laid out

A robot can also be visualized as a block diagram of connected parts. Block diagrams use simple shapes to show a rough idea of how things may be connected. Refer to the following diagram:

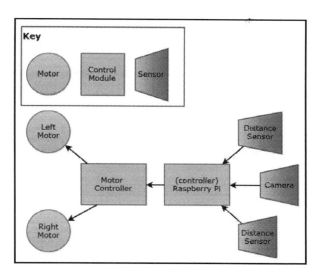

A robot block diagram

The preceding diagram is a block diagram. This is not a formal notation; the important factor is that you can clearly see the blocks of functionality you intend in the hardware, with the high-level flow of data between them. This can be a sketch on the back of a bit of scrap paper. The key I've created is off the top of my head, but it must be something that helps distinguish sensors, outputs, and controllers.

An important thing to note is this is **not** a schematic, nor a scale diagram of a finished robot. It does not even attempt to represent the actual electronic connections, or small details such as having to signal an HCSR04 sensor before it responds; it just gives a general idea of the data flow. This is the right sketch to show how many motors there are, the kinds of motors, how many sensors, and, if known, what additional control circuitry is needed.

It is from this diagram that you can start to flesh out more detail, such as examining the electrical connections, thinking about the power requirements, the actual hardware, and how much space will be needed. For a bit of fun, pick up some paper and sketch a block diagram for a robot you'd like to create. This is the first step toward making it happen.

Types of motors, sensors, and actuators

A **motor** is an output device that results in rotation when power is applied. An **actuator** is an output device, which is any device that creates movements from an electrical signal. Examples of actuators are solenoids, valves, and pneumatic rams. Motors are a subset of actuators too.

A **sensor** is a device that provides input to a robot, allowing it to sense its environment. There are more sensor types than a single book can list, so we'll keep to the commonly available and fun-to-use ones.

Motors and actuators

I've laid out some of the different kinds of motors, all of which are used in robotics. Let's take a look at what each one does, and how we might use them for different kinds of motion, as shown in the following photo:

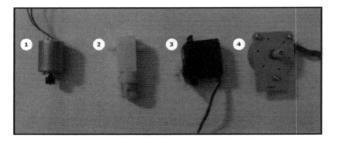

Different motor types

I've shown some common motor types in the preceding photo. Let's understand them in detail:

1. The most common type of motor is the DC motor. This has the property of spinning in proportion to the amount of voltage running through it.
2. A bare DC motor like this tends to spin a little too fast to be useful bare, and is very easily stopped. This is a DC Gear motor—a DC motor fitted with a gearbox, providing a reduction in speed and increase in mechanical advantage so it can move a larger load. Note that this gear motor is missing soldered leads! These types are most useful in the wheels of a robot. We will be attaching gear motors very much like the second image to our robot in chapter 6, *Building Robot Basics - Wheels, Power, and Wiring* and chapter 7, *Drive and Turn - Moving Motors with Python*.

3. This is the servo motor (or servomechanism). A controller sends a signal to this type of motor telling it what angular position to move to, with code working in degrees. The motor will attempt to reach and hold that position using it's own internal feedback loop, which means it can repeatably reach the same position. Servo motors are used in pan and tilt mechanisms to position sensors, robot arms, or other limbs and appendages, where the ease of positioning makes them more suitable than other motor types. We will be programming servo motors in Chapter 10, *Using Python to Control Servo Motors.*

4. This is a stepper motor. These have coils powered in a sequence to allow the motor to step a certain number of degrees, so it can be used for very precise motions. Stepper motors tend to be slower and generate a lot of heat compared with DC motors or servo motors, but are most suitable for fine control, like that needed in 3D printers and high-end robot arms. They are also more expensive than the other types.

All motors will require some sort of hardware so a microcontroller/computer like the Pi can drive them. This hardware allows the Pi to switch power hungry devices without destroying them. Don't connect DC motors, stepper motors, or solenoids directly to a Raspberry Pi!

Linear actuators are devices where electrical signals are converted into motion along a single axis. These can be a stepper motor driving a screw in a fixed enclosure or magnetic systems that work like mag-lev trains and move very smoothly. Refer to the following photo:

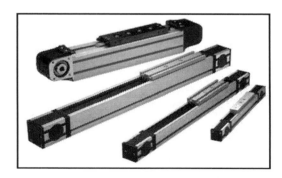

Linear actuators: By Rollon91

A **solenoid** is a simple linear actuator using an electromagnetic coil with a metal core that is pulled or pushed away when power is applied to it. A common use of this type is in a doorbell mechanism. They are also used to operate valves on hydraulic or pneumatic actuators, which can create powerful motions like those seen in excavators and large industrial robotic arms.

Status indicators – displays, lights, and sounds

Another helpful output device is a display—a simple light (or LED) to indicate the status of some part of the robot, or an array of LEDs, a display that can show some text, or a full graphical display like those found on a mobile phone. We will be connecting an LED strip to the robot as a display in `Chapter 9`, *Programming RGB Strips in Python*.

Speakers and beepers can be used for a robot to communicate with humans by making sounds. The sound output from these can range from simple noises up to speech or playing music.

Many robots do not have any mounted status indicators and rely on a connected phone or laptop to display their status for them.

Types of sensors

I have a small selection of common sensors I use—similar to those that will be covered in this book. These have been used in robots I have built. Let's examine each one, and what we would use it for. Note that these may look different from the same sensor types seen before - there is a large variation in sensors that perform the same task, and when we get to adding them into the robot, we will cover their variants in more detail. Refer to the following set of photos:

A selection of sensors from my robots

Let's understand each image in detail:

1. This is a Raspberry Pi Camera module, which connects directly into a Raspberry Pi. We will be using this camera for our visual processing programming in Chapter 13, *Robot Vision - Using A Pi Camera And OpenCV*. This module can capture single images or video sequences. It can generate a lot of data quickly, which is one of the complications for robot vision. It is sensitive to lighting conditions.

2. This is a distance sensor, the VL53L0X Time of Flight laser ranging sensor. It uses an infrared laser to bounce off objects and detect how far away they are. This type of sensor sends a detected range directly to the controller. It can be sensitive to lighting conditions. The VL53L0X sensors use I2C, which means they send information as data directly to the Raspberry Pi, and can share their two communication pins with many other devices. I2C is good for when you have lots of sensors and outputs, and you are starting to run out of places to connect things. I2C sensors are handy, but they tend to be more expensive than sensors without this capability.

3. This is another distance/ranging sensor - the HCSR04 ultrasonic distance sensor - which bounces sound pulses off objects instead. It's more sensitive to the types of material an object is made from and will fail to detect some surfaces, but is impervious to lighting conditions. The HC-SR04 requires the controller to trigger a pulse of sound, and then time the echo, which we will have to manage in our code for it. It has a far greater range than the VL53L0x laser sensor, and is far cheaper, but is also less sensitive at near distances. We will be programming both sound and light-based range sensors in Chapter 11, .

4. This is a set of three line sensors, that use light to detect transitions from light to dark. They can be adjusted to sense in different conditions. There are a few variations of these modules. We will use a set of these sensors for line following in Chapter 8, *Programming Line-Following Sensors Using Python*. These will each provide an on or off signal, depending on light or dark areas beneath it. They are the simplest of the sensors we will use in this book.

5. The fifth sensor is a pair of microphones with some tape to stick them crudely to a robot. These can connect directly to PCM pins on a Pi, but other microphones may need to be connected to electronics to process their signal further, into something the Raspberry Pi uses. There are arrays of four microphones or a single microphones that can be used, and in some contexts can detect the direction of sound as well. Microphones will be used for voice processing in Chapter 14, *Voice Communication With A Robot Using Mycroft*.

6. The last sensor is an optical interrupt sensor, which passes infra-red light through a gap between two posts to detect whether something is between them, interrupting the beam. These are used with notched wheels to sense rotations, which can determine how far a robot has gone and introduce more accuracy into movements. Using an offset pair of these sensors with a wheel can encode the direction of the movement as well as its speed, and such an arrangement is known as an encoder. There are complete encoder assemblies available as sensors too, making it mechanically simpler to use them. We will investigate using encoders in `Chapter 12`, *Programming Encoders with Python*.

There are many more sensors not covered here to detect positions of limbs, light, smoke, heat sources, and magnetic fields. These can all be used to make more advanced robots and add more interesting behavior.

Controllers and IO

At the center of the robot block diagram are the controllers. Robots usually have a main controller, a computer of some kind. They may also have some secondary controllers, and some more unusual robots have many controllers. Sticking with the conventional main controller, this is the system that your code will run. It is the part that connects all the other components together and forms the basis of their interactions.

IO pins

IO pins are used for input and output from the controller; they give the controller its ability to connect to real-world sensors and motors.

The number of IO pins on the controller can be a major limiting factor in what you can connect to a robot without using secondary controllers. You may also see the term **General Purpose Input Output** (**GPIO**). Controller IO pins have different capabilities.

The simplest IO pins are only able to output an on/off signal, or read an on/off signal, like in the following image; these are known as Digital IO pins. However, these can be programmed to perform more complicated tasks by detecting timing between signals, which is exactly the principle used in the HC-SR04 distance sensor. Refer to the following diagram:

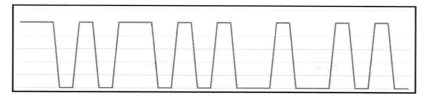

A digital signal

Some IO pins may be able to read varying levels, like that in the following image; these are analog input pins. If a sensor produces a changing resistance or continuous scale of values, then an analog pin may be the suitable place to connect it. Refer to the following diagram:

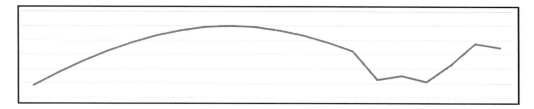

An analog signal

Pulse Width Modulation (PWM) pins are able to output a cycling digital waveform, allowing the code to select the frequency and how much time they are on for. The simple idea is that the length of ontime vs offtime in a cycle will change to vary an output signal and is often used to control the speed of motors. We will spend more time on PWM pins in Chapter 6, *Building Robot Basics - Wheels, Power,* and *Wiring,* and Chapter 7, *Drive and Turn - Moving Motors with Python*. Refer to the following diagram:

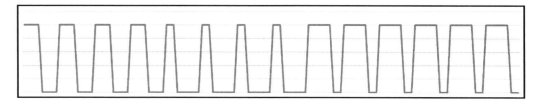

A PWM signal

Some IO pins can be used to form data transmission lines, like serial, I2S, I2C, and SPI buses. They are known as data buses. This can be used to send data to or from other controllers and intelligent sensors. We will encounter these as we program with them in part 2 of the book. Many controllers allow the usage mode of pins to be configured in the software you run on them, but some capabilities are restricted to certain pins.

Controllers

Although it is possible to use bare controller chips with the right skills to create surrounding electronics and your own PCBs, we will keep things simple in this book by using controller modules. These tend to come in packaged and easy-to-use systems. The next set of photos shows a few of them:

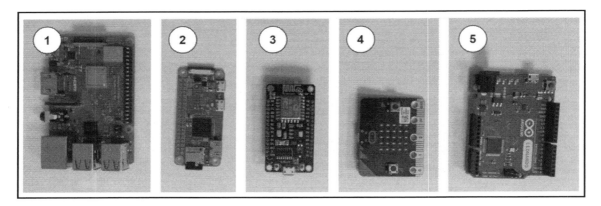

A selection of controller modules

The preceding photo shows a selection of some of my favorite controllers. They can all be powered via a USB connection of some kind, and for all but the Raspberry Pi, programmed over the same connection. They all have easy-to-use connectors for making use of their IO pins. For each of the controllers, what are they, and what are their pros and cons? Let's understand them:

1. The Raspberry Pi 3B+, the latest in the Raspberry Pi line at the time of writing, is the most powerful in this lineup, and is the controller we are using for our robot, as it is the most capable of visual processing from a camera. This fast and capable controller is closer to a phone in complexity. It's IO pins support many of the databus types, and digital IO, but for analog reading and some other IO functions, external controllers are needed. It is also the most expensive in this group and uses the most power.

2. The Raspberry Pi Zero W is an inexpensive, lighter weight alternative to the full Raspberry Pi. It supports a camera and speakers. The Zero WH model includes the headers for IO too. It will perform speech and visual recognition, but will be slower at these than a Raspberry Pi 3. Their small size makes them an interesting option for a remote control pad though.

3. This is the ESP8266 or NodeMCU. This controller has built-in Wi-Fi, and in this NodeMCU format can be programmed very easily from a PC using the same system as the Arduino, with Micropython or in Lua. It has plenty of IO pins, but only one is able to read analog signals. It supports many data bus types. It is somewhat faster and can hold larger programs than the Arduino. It is the cheapest controller in this lineup.

4. The Micro:bit was released in 2015 for use in education, and is ideal for children. Its use in robotics requires a further adapter if you need more than the 3 IO pins shown, but it is still a pretty capable robot controller and comes with a nice built-in LED matrix. This can be programmed in Micropython, C, JavaScript, and a number of other languages.

5. The last panel is an Arduino Leonardo, based around the Atmega 328 chip, and is a controller module that formed the basis of most of my robots around 2010-2012. The Arduino was important for the ease with which it could be connected to a PC via USB and programmed to immediately interact with devices attached to its IO pins. The Arduino is mostly programmed in the C++ language. In terms of IO, it has built-in pins to read analog devices, many digital pins, PWM output pins, and can be set up to handle most data buses. The Arduino is very flexible, but the processor is very simple; it is not capable of visual or speech processing tasks. The Arduino has the lowest power consumption of all the options shown here.

An honorable mention should go to the PIC microcontroller, not pictured here. These were used for hobby robotics long before any of the others, and have a thriving community since they are small, have low power consumption, and are extremely cheap.

Here is a comparison of controllers based on pro's and con's:

Controller Name	Pros	Cons
Arduino	Very low power consumption, very flexible IO.	Quite large, least capable processor, not suitable for visual processing or speech.
Micro:bit	LED Matrix, easy to program.	Needs external adapters for connections, not suitable for visual processing or speech.
ESP8266/NodeMCU	Many programming languages, onboard Wi-Fi, very cheap, flexible IO, can be very small.	Not suitable for visual processing or speech. Only a single analog input pin.
Raspberry Pi Zero W	Small, powerful, suitable for some visual processing and speech recognition, and inexpensive. Runs a full Linux system. Wi-Fi and Bluetooth.	Slower than the Raspberry Pi 3. External devices needed for analog input.

Raspberry Pi 3	Powerful. Easy access to IO pins. Runs a full Linux system. Suitable for visual processing and speech recognition. Wi-Fi and Bluetooth.	Large, power hungry, and expensive. Has some heat issues. External devices needed for analog input.
Raspberry Pi 3B+	Heat issues with Pi 3 are remedied. Otherwise, the same as the Pi 3.	In addition to the Raspberry Pi 3, power over Ethernet pins reduces compatibility with add-on boards (Hats).

Where the other controllers may run a simple interpreter or compiled code, both the Raspberry Pis run complete operating systems. They both have Wi-Fi and Bluetooth capabilities, which we will use to make a robot headless and connect with game controllers. The Raspberry Pi 3B+ also consumes the most power when operating, a trade-off worth making for the behavior we are aiming to program.

Planning components and code structure

You've now briefly seen some components you might use in a robot, and you've encountered a block diagram to put them together. This is where you may start taking the next step and thinking further about how things will be connected, and how the code you write for them will be structured. Code is easier to reason about when taken as logical blocks instead of one large lump. Arranging code in ways that are similar to a hardware functionality diagram will help navigate your way around as it becomes more complicated.

So, let's return to the robot block diagram seen before.

This diagram has three sensors and two outputs. Throughout this book, you will see diagrams like this, and then be adding new modules along with new bits of code to deal with them. Each component (sensor, output, and controller board) may need a few bits of code to deal with it, and then you need some code for the behavior of combined modules.

Motor controllers come in many flavors, they have slightly different ways to output to motors, they may have monitoring for battery levels, and some more sophisticated ones interface with wheel encoders directly to ensure wheels have traveled a specified amount. When we write behavior for a robot, we may not want to rewrite it if we change the motor controller. Even if there are no plans, mixing the direct motor controller code with the behavior code would make it harder to reason about. Making an interface layer, an "abstraction" between the real motor controller code and a common interface, will make that possible; we will see this in practice in Chapter 7, *Drive and Turn - Moving Motors with Python*.

This is similar for each sensor; they will have some code to manage how they get signals and turn them into usable data. All these devices may have setup and teardown code that needs to run when starting or stopping behavior that connects to them. The camera is quite a sophisticated example of this, where a lot of processing is needed to get the data values we can use to perform a task. Refer to the following block diagrams:

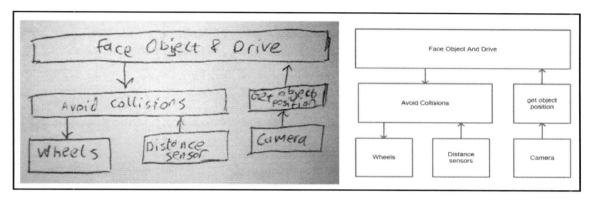

A quick software block diagram, in pen on an envelope, and the same diagram using the Pencil software

Just like the hardware, a simple diagram can represent the software, which can be made in a drawing program or sketched on any paper you have to hand. In the preceding image, I've deliberately chosen a hand-drawn one, so you don't feel that you need a drawing tool to do this. This won't be tidy, but it's easily redrawn, and can even be done on the back of receipt paper if an idea comes to you while out dining. Important here is that if you use pencil, go back over it in a pen or fineliner so it doesn't fade, and if you can, scan this for later reference. Since it may be clearer to me than the reader, I have made this in a computer drawing tool in the right panel, but don't feel you need to do this.

Using a software tool may take longer than a hand-drawn version, and a quick sketch is probably needed then, as it can be easy to be distracted by the quirks and styling of a tool.

In terms of the design itself, this is still a very simplistic view. The Wheels box will be a block of code to deal with asking the wheel motor controller to do things. This may sit on top of code written by the motor controller company, or talk directly to IO pins connected to the controller. Distance sensors would be a block of code to read distances from the sensors, triggering them when necessary. We will be looking at two different kinds of sensors and comparing them. By having a block of code like this, swapping out the sensors at this level means the other code won't have to change.

There is also a block of code for the camera, doing fiddly stuff like setting it up, resolution, white balancing, and other fiddly parts that we will cover. On top of this is a layer that will use the camera images to get the position of a colored object and return this position information to the layer above.

Across the motors and distance sensors is a behavior layer that allows the robot to automatically avoid collisions, perhaps when it is below a threshold on one side; this will override other behavior to turn away from that obstacle and drive off a bit.

The top layer is another behavior that will take the position data from the Get Object Position code, use this position to choose a direction, then instruct the motors to drive to the object. Because this behavior goes through the Avoid Collisions behavior, there will be a complicated interaction that leads the robot to seek the correct object, but avoiding obstacles and going around things. It will also not come close enough to the intended object to collide with it.

Each module is fairly simple, perhaps with the lower layers that are closer to the hardware being more complex, especially in the camera case.

Breaking the code down into blocks like these means that you can approach a single block at a time, test, and tweak its behavior, and then focus on another one. When you have written blocks like this, you can reuse them. It's likely you will need the motor code multiple times, and now will not need to write it multiple times.

Using blocks to describe our software lets us implement the blocks and their interactions in different ways. We can consider whether we will use functions, classes, or services for these blocks. I will spend more time on this as we start writing the code for this and show the different ways.

Planning our robot

Let's put all of this to use, and plan the robot that we are making in this book. Although as we go through chapters we will be adding new components each time, having an overall map in our minds as we go helps us to see where we are. It is quite exciting to start to picture all the things a robot will do. Let's start with a list of what our robot will do and be:

- It will have wheels and be able to drive around the floor
- It will have a Raspberry Pi 3 controller
- It will have a motor controller for the wheels
- It will be able to follow lines with a pair of line following sensors

- It will be able to indicate its status with a set of multicolored LEDs
- The robot will use a pair of servo motors for a pan and tilt mechanism
- It will be able to avoid walls and navigate around obstacles with either ultrasonic or laser distance sensors
- It will have an encoder per wheel to know how far it has moved
- The robot will use a camera to sense colored objects or faces
- The robot will have a microphone and speaker to work with voice commands
- It will have a game pad as a remote control
- It will need power for all of these things

Phew, that is a lot of functionality. Now, we need to draw the hardware blocks. Refer to the following block diagram:

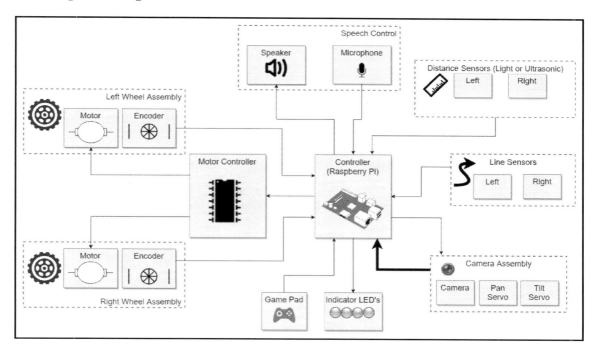

Block diagram of the robot we will build. Created using the draw.io web app

Although this looks like a daunting amount of robot, we will be focusing on an area of functionality in each chapter and building it before moving to other areas. The annotation here is not any formal notation, it is just a way of simply visualizing all the parts that will need to be connected. Along with this, I usually sketch roughly where I would physically place sensors and parts in relation to each other, as follows:

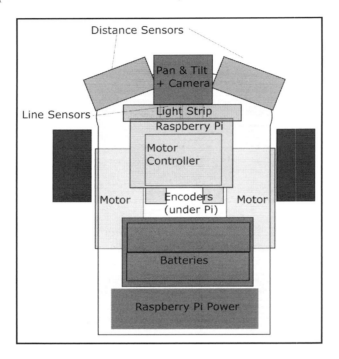

An overview of how the robot could be physically laid out. Created with Inkscape

This sketch is not exhaustive, accurate, or to scale, but just an idea of where I want the parts to end up. Note a few things in this diagram:

- Sensors have a clear field of view, and the distance sensors are pointing out to the sides. I'll cover more in the relevant sensor chapters on why this is important.
- Encoders are placed over the wheels where they will be used; line sensors need to be under the robot where the lines will be.
- Heavy items, specifically batteries, should be kept low to avoid a robot falling.
- Batteries need to be changed, so think about access to them.

- Try to keep components that are directly connected quite close to each other.
- This is a rough plan. It need not be this detailed, and this is **not** the test fit. Real dimensions, design compromises, and hitches will mean that this will change. This is just a starting point.

As we work through the book, we will look at the details in these diagrams, and start to flesh out the real robot, making some of this less fuzzy. Any diagram like this, at the start of a project, should be taken as a bit rough and not to scale, or to be followed blindly, but as a guide, or a quick map to start working from.

Summary

In this chapter, you've been able to see a number of the different component parts that go into a robot, and through a block diagram as a plan, start to visualize how you'd combine those blocks to make a whole robot. You've seen how you can quickly sketch your robot ideas on an envelope, and that drawing tools on a computer can be used for a neater version of the same diagram.

You've had a quick tour of motors, sensors, and controllers, along with a few ways, such as analog, digital, PWM, and databuses, for controllers to communicate with the other devices connected to them.

Following on from this, you've seen a plan of the robot we will build in this book.

Questions

1. What is an IO pin?
2. What tools do you need to make a block diagram?
3. What are the drawbacks of the laser ranging sensor versus the ultrasonic distance sensor?
4. What type of system is a microphone?
5. What kind of IO pin is correct for measuring varying resistance?
6. What type of IO pin would be suitable for detecting an on/off signal?

Further reading

- Raspberry Pi Sensors by Rushi Gajjar: Integrate sensors into your Raspberry Pi projects and let your powerful microcomputer interact with the physical world.

- Make Sensors: A Hands-On Primer for Monitoring the Real World with Arduino and Raspberry Pi by Tero Karvinen, Kimmo Karvinen, and Ville Valtokari. Learn to use sensors to connect a Raspberry Pi or Arduino controller with the real world.

- Make Electronics: Learning by Discovery by Charles Platt: This is useful if you want to find out more about electronic components and dive deeper into individual components.

3
Introducing the Raspberry Pi - Starting with Raspbian

For this book, we will be building a robot using the Raspberry Pi, and at the time of writing, the Raspberry Pi 3B+ is the current model. We will investigate why I've chosen this specific board as a controller, and we will also look at the connections on the Raspberry Pi and how we will use them, the plus Raspbian software we will use on it, and we will finish by preparing Raspbian for use on the Raspberry Pi.

By the end of this chapter, you will know the following:

- What the Raspberry Pi is, what it can do, and why I chose it
- What Raspberry Pi connections we will use for the sensors and actuators in our robot
- What the Raspbian operating system is and why I am using it
- How to prepare an SD card with Raspbian to use in your robot

Technical requirements

For this chapter, you will require the following:

- A microSD card storing 16 GB
- A Raspberry Pi 3B+
- A Windows, Linux, or macOS computer or laptop connected to the internet and able to read/write to SD cards

Check out the following video to see the Code in Action:

http://bit.ly/2QoX2Y4

What can the Raspberry Pi do?

As we saw in Chapter 2, *Exploring Robot Building Blocks - Code And Electronics*, the controllers chosen for a robot can be one of the most important choices you make. This will determine what kinds of inputs and outputs you have, what the power requirements of your electronics will be, what types of sensors you will be able to use, and what code you will run. Changing a controller could mean rewriting the code, redesigning where the controller would fit, and changing the power requirements.

Raspberry Pi is a range of small computers designed for use in education, which have became quickly a favorite of makers due to being a complete computer with the cost and size of a microcontroller, with using IO pins for connecting to custom hardware. All the Raspberry Pi models have abilities such as attaching a camera, display, and keyboard, and some kind of networking. We are specifically working with the Raspberry Pi 3 range.

Speed and power

The Raspberry Pi is powerful enough to handle some visual processing tasks, with later models being able to perform this faster. The same can be said for the voice recognition tasks too. It is for this reason that the faster 3 and 3B+ models are recommended. The Zero and Zero W are much slower, and although the system will still work, the speed may be frustrating.

The Raspberry Pi is powerful enough to run a complete computer operating system, a version of Linux. We will explore this later, but this allows us to use Python to perform the visual processing and voice processing using libraries and tools that are well maintained by others. Other controllers, such as the Arduino, Esp8266, and Micro:bit simply do not have the capabilities to perform these tasks.

There are alternative controllers that run Linux, such as the Beaglebone, C.H.I.P. , OnionIOT, and Gumstix Linux computers, but these are either more costly than the Raspberry Pi or less capable. They also don't come with the camera integration. Although the Beaglebone has superior analog IO connectivity, the Raspberry Pi 3B+ makes for the better all-rounder, and has plenty of options for extending it.

Connectivity and networking

The Raspberry Pi 3B+ comes with USB ports and HDMI ports too. We don't plan on using them in this book, although they are handy for debugging if things go really wrong and you lose contact with a robot using a Raspberry Pi. With that in mind, having an additional screen and keyboard handy is recommended. It has a wired Ethernet port that can be used to connect it to a network, but this would be inconvenient for keeping in touch with a robot, so we will favor the Wi-Fi.

Raspberry Pi 3, 3B+, and Zero W models all have Wi-Fi and Bluetooth on board. Throughout this book, we will be using Wi-Fi to connect to the robot so we recommend a model that has this.

The Raspberry Pi has IO pins to allow you to connect it to the sensors. In the Raspberry Pi 3B+, the GPIO connections are ready to use, due to having the pins (known as headers) already soldered in place. The Raspberry Pi Zero is smaller and cheaper, but usually comes without these headers. The early Raspberry Pi boards had different IO connectors, both of which are reasons to stick with the 3B+.

The recommended Raspberry Pi version

Putting all this together, the Raspberry Pi 3B+ is a complete computer with IO and a special connector for a camera. It is capable of visual and speech processing, has onboard Wi-Fi and Bluetooth, and can run Python code, and has presoldered headers ready for connecting to robot devices, as well as being small and relatively cheap. Later Raspberry Pi versions may supersede these with faster processing and additional capabilities.

What connections will we use?

When building the robot, we will be using a subset of the connections the Raspberry Pi has to offer. Lets take a look at what those connections are and how we will use them. As we connect sensors and parts to the Raspberry Pi, we will cover the connections in detail, so do not feel you need to memorize these now. However, this pin diagram may serve as a reference for these connections.

In the following image, the highlighted areas show the connections in use. Note that on the 3+, there is an additional four-pin connector (POE) that we will not be using. First, we will be using the power connector, located at the top right of the following image; this plugs in via a micro-USB connector similar to that on many phones. We will use this while learning to go headless, and this is one of the options for powering a robot. We can plug USB battery packs into this port if they are able to provide the correct amount of power. Refer to the following diagram:

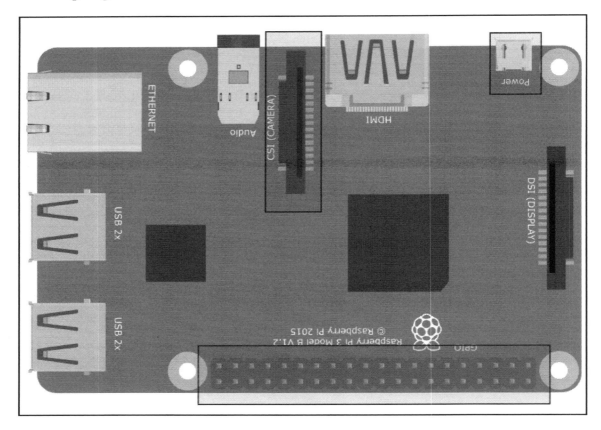

Raspberry Pi connections

The top-middle highlighted port is the CSI port; this is for the Pi Camera, which we will attach when preparing to do visual processing.

We will be using the MicroSD card slot under the Pi to run our code. We will not be using Ethernet or HDMI, as we will be talking to the Raspberry Pi via Wi-Fi.

When we connect a Game Pad to the robot later in the book, we will be using the USB ports to connect to it. Take a look at the following diagram:

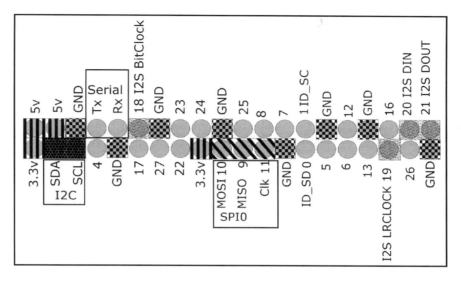

The Raspberry Pi GPIO Port (B+, 2, 3, 3B+, Zero, and Zero W)

The large connector across the bottom of the Raspberry Pi connections image is the GPIO port. The preceding image shows a close-up diagram with the names and uses of some of the pins shown. This is where we will connect most of our sensors and motors. It has SPI, I2C, Serial, and I2S databuses, and digital IO pins to attach external devices to.

SPI, I2C, and Serial are used to send control and sensor data between a controller and smart devices. I2S is used to carry encoded digital audio signals (PCM) to and from the Raspberry PI. The ports for these databuses can be enabled through configuration, or the pins can be used as general digital pins when the databuses are not enabled.

The 5V pins will be used to provide power to the Raspberry Pi while on the robot, along with the pins marked GND, an abbreviation of ground, which is the equivalent of a minus terminal on a battery or power supply. We may be using 3.3V power for sensors that require this supply level.

Although there is an audio port on the Raspberry Pi, this is not really suitable for driving a speaker, so we will be using the I2S pins on the GPIO port for this. The I2S pins are 18, 19, 20, and 21. We will be using this for the voice processing.

The pins marked SDA and SCL are an I2c databus. We will be using this for some sensors, and it is also used by some motor control boards. Instructions are sent over this port.

Pins 9, 10, and 11 form the SPI port, which we will be using to connect RGB LEDs to.

The other pins that are numbered, without a specific word or shading type, are general purpose IO pins, which we can use for digital inputs and outputs with motor controllers, servo motors, line sensors, encoders, and ultrasonic sensors.

You'll note that the numbering here is a little mixed up, and this is because these numbers correspond to the numbering of pins on the Raspberry Pi's main processor chip, and not the pin positions on the GPIO port, which is also sometimes used. This is a quirk of the Pi worth getting used to and is known as the BCM numbering system, as an abbreviation of the Broadcom chip these numbers refer to.

Raspberry Pi Hats

Raspberry Pi Hats (also named Bonnets) are circuit boards designed to plug into the GPIO header and conveniently add capabilities to the Raspberry Pi, such as driving motors or specific sensors. Some allow further use of GPIO pins, and some would require you to use other interface boards to gain access to other pins.

These Hats use GPIO pins for different purposes; for example, audio hats will use the I2s pins for audio interfacing, but some motor controller hats use the same pins as general purpose digital IO pins to control motors instead. Using such hats together would be problematic, so be aware of this when using multiple hats or specific buses. We will explore this more in Chapter 6, *Building Robot Basics - Wheels, Power, and Wiring*, when we choose a motor controller.

What is Raspbian?

Raspbian is the choice of software we will use to drive the Pi, an OS that our code will run in. It is the official operating system recommended by the Raspberry Pi Foundation, and comes with software specifically prepared to make working with the Raspberry Pi easier. Raspbian can be set up to support a full desktop, albeit that, due to the Raspberry Pi's hardware limitations, it would feel a little less powerful and slower than your normal laptop.

Raspbian is based on the Debian Linux distribution, which is a collection of software set up to run together, giving lots of functionality and many possibilities. Linux distributions like this are the basis of many large internet servers, mobile phones, and other devices with apps. Raspbian has the software closest to the Raspberry Pi hardware, namely the kernel and drivers, which are made specifically for the Pi and optimized for them. It also has some neat ways to configure the specialized features that Raspberry Pi users might need.

We will use it in a more minimal way than a desktop, forgoing the keyboard, mouse, and monitor support. This minimal version is known as Raspbian-Lite because it is a much smaller download when desktop software is not required, and because it uses less space on the MicroSD card. Not running a window manager will free up memory and use less of the processing power of the Pi, keeping it free for activities such as visual processing. We will then extend Raspbian-Lite with the software and tools we will use to program our robot.

As you work through the book, you will mostly be interacting with the robot through code and the command line. Linux and Raspbian are written with command-line usage over a network in mind, which is a good fit for the headless nature of programming a robot.

We will make a lot of use of Linux's strong support for the Python programming language and the network tools that Linux provides. Raspbian is widely used in the Raspberry Pi community and is among the easiest to find answers for when help is needed. It is not the only OS for the Pi, but it is the most useful choice for someone starting on the Raspberry Pi.

Preparing an SD card

To use Raspbian on a Raspberry Pi, you will need to put the software onto a micro SD card in a way that the Raspberry Pi can load it.

First, we need to download Raspbian. To do this, take your browser to the Raspberry Pi Raspbian Downloads Page: `https://www.raspberrypi.org/downloads/raspbian/`. On this page, you'll see two distributions: Raspbian With a Desktop and Raspbian Lite. Both these links will be the current version of Raspbian:

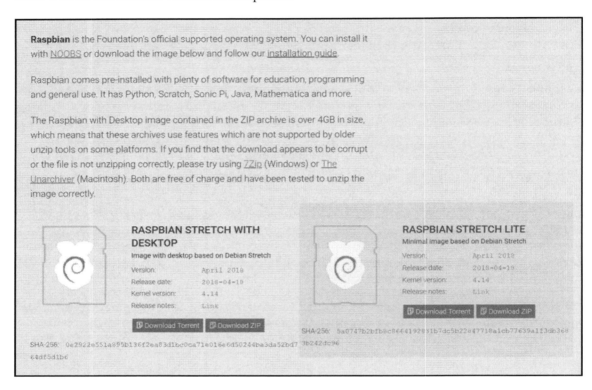

The Raspberry Pi downloads screen

The Raspbian Lite downloads can be seen highlighted in the preceding image. You'll see two download links, **Download Torrent** and **Download Zip**. Click the **Download Zip** button and save this file. Note that the versions do change, so please use the current version. This file is big, at around 400 MB! It will be named something like `2018-06-27-raspbian-stretch-lite.zip`, with a current release data and name in it. You do *not* need to unzip this file.

Flashing the card in Etcher

To put this software onto the SD card in a way the Pi will load it, we cannot just copy the zip onto it. It needs to be stored on the card in a particular way. The Etcher software offers a simple way to do this, and is available for Windows, Mac, and Linux computers.

Getting Etcher

Point your browser at `https://etcher.io/` and then use the download button to choose the version for your computer and download it. The following are the steps for different OSes:

- On Windows, you will have to download an Etcher setup file. Double-click this and give it permission to install Etcher.
- On macOS, you will have to download an Etcher DMG. Open this file and drag the Etcher package into your apps.
- On Linux, you will have to download an appImage. You will need to make this file executable and run it.

Now, start the Etcher app.

Using Etcher to write to the card

To write the image to the SD card with Etcher, follow these steps:

1. At this point, insert your micro SD card into the correct port on your laptop.
2. Click the **Select image** button in Etcher, and than choose the Raspbian Lite zip you downloaded:

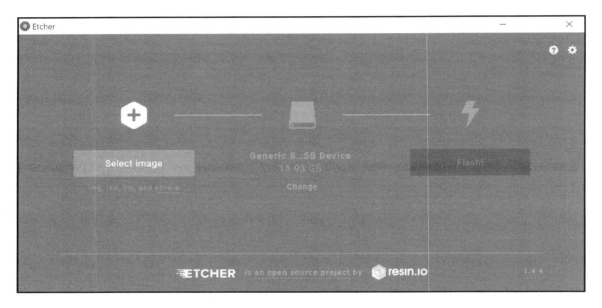

Etcher with Select image highlighted

3. Etcher will automatically detect the SD card unless you have multiple cards present, and the flash button will be highlighted. You can press this button and it will prepare the card. This might take a few minutes. If you are asked by your computer for permission to write to the card, please accept it.
4. You may load this onto a Pi with a screen and keyboard, but before we can use this Raspberry Pi for a robot, we will need to make changes to the SD card on your computer in the next chapter.

Summary

In this chapter, you've seen more of what the Raspberry Pi is, and what connections on the Raspberry Pi we will be using.

We have learned about the Raspbian operating system, which is derived from Linux, how to download it, and how to put this software onto a micro SD card for use in the Raspberry Pi.

In the next chapter, we will make this card headless so that we do not require a screen, keyboard, or mouse to use this Raspberry Pi and contact it from our computer.

Questions

Answer the following questions:

1. What is the name of the software we will be using on our Raspberry Pi?
2. What did we use to make the SD card?
3. What is the CSI connector on the Raspberry Pi for?
4. Which versions of the Raspberry Pi are recommended for use in this book?

Further reading

Refer to the following links:

- The Raspberry Pi Foundation Guide to Installing Raspberry Pi Operating Systems: https://www.raspberrypi.org/documentation/installation/installing-images/README.md.
- Raspberry Pi By Example, Ashwin Pajankar and Arush Kakkar, published by Packt Pblishing, which has a section on alternative operating systems for a Raspberry Pi, along with many interesting Raspberry Pi projects.
- Raspberry PI GPIO Pinout (https://pinout.xyz/): This describes how different boards are connected to the Pi in terms of the pins they actually use. It's useful to know that most boards only use a subset of these pins.

4
Preparing a Raspberry Pi for a Robot - Headless by Default

In this chapter, you will learn why the Raspberry Pi controller on a robot should be wireless, or headless; what headless means; and why it's useful in robotics. You will see how to set up a Raspberry Pi as a headless device from the beginning, and how to connect to this Raspberry Pi once on the network, and then send your first instructions to it.

We will cover the following topics in this chapter:

- What does headless mean and why is it useful?
- How do you make a Raspberry Pi headless?
- Finding your Raspberry Pi on the network
- Connecting to your Raspberry Pi
- Sending your first commands, such as configuring Raspbian and changing the robot's name

Technical requirements

For this chapter, you will require the following:

- A Raspberry Pi preferably a 3B+ (but a Pi 3 will do)
- A USB power supply or port capable of 2.1 amps
- A USB to Micro-USB cable
- The MicroSD card you prepared in the previous chapter
- A Windows, Linux, or macOS computer or laptop connected to the internet and able to read/write to SD cards
- PuTTY software on Windows (SSH software is already available on Mac and Linux desktops)

The GitHub link for the code is as follows:

```
https://github.com/PacktPublishing/Learn-Robotics-Fundamentals-of-Robotics-
Programming/tree/master/chapter4
```

Check out the following video to see the Code in Action:

```
http://bit.ly/2TOLqN5
```

What does headless mean and why?

A **headless system** is a computer designed to be used from another computer via a network, for when keyboard, screen, and mouse access to a device is inconvenient. Headless access is used for server systems and for building robots. Refer to the following diagram:

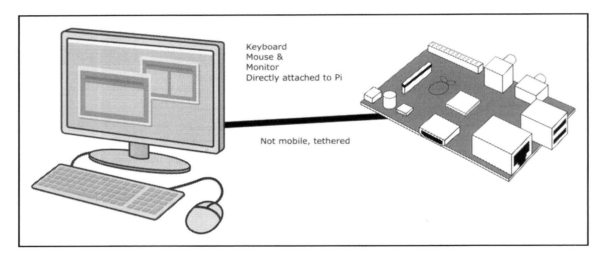

A Raspberry Pi tethered to a screen, keyboard, and mouse

The preceding diagram shows a system with a head where a user can sit in front of the device. You would need to take a screen, keyboard, and mouse with your robot—not very mobile. You may be able to attach/detach them as required, but this is also inconvenient and adds bulk. There are systems designed to dock with Raspberry Pis like this and are portable, but when a robot moves, you'd need to disconnect or move with the robot.

I have seen, at some events, a robot with a tiny screen attached and someone using a wireless keyboard and mouse as an option. However, in this book we are going to focus on using a robot as a headless device. Take a look at the following diagram:

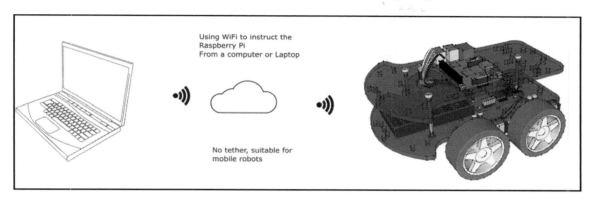

Using WiFi to instruct the
Raspberry Pi
From a computer or Laptop

No tether, suitable for
mobile robots

A Raspberry Pi on a robot in a headless configuration

The Raspberry Pi in the preceding diagram is mounted on a robot as a headless device. This Raspberry Pi is connected to batteries and motors, but not encumbered by a screen and keyboard; those are handled by another computer. The Pi is connected wirelessly to a network, which could be through a laptop. Code, instructions, and information are sent to and from the Raspberry Pi via this wireless network. To interact with it, you use the screen and keyboard on your laptop. However, you would usually expect your robot to function autonomously, so you would only connect to the Pi to modify things or test code. As an alternative to bringing a laptop to control a robot everywhere, it can be more convenient to add a few indicator LEDs (which we will add in Chapter 9, *Programming RGB Strips in Python*) and a wireless Joypad (to be added in Chapter 15, *Programming A Gamepad On Raspberry Pi With Python*) so you can start and stop autonomous behaviors, view the robot's status, or just drive it without needing to hook up the laptop at all. This Raspberry Pi is free from the screen and keyboard.

> Most of the time, a screen and keyboard are not required. However, it is worth having them around for the few cases in which you lose contact with the Raspberry Pi and it refuses to respond via the network. You can then use a screen and keyboard to connect with it and see what is going on.

For our headless access to the Raspberry Pi, we will be using the SSH system, a secure shell. SSH gives you a command line to send instructions to the Pi and a file transfer system to put files onto it. As SSH connects over a network, we need to configure our Raspberry Pi to connect to your own wireless network.

Making a Pi headless makes it free to roam around. It keeps a robot light by not needing to carry or power a screen and keyboard. Being headless makes a robot smaller, since a screen and keyboard are more bulky. It also encourages you, the maker, to think more about autonomous behavior since you can't always type commands to the robot.

Setting up wireless on the Raspberry Pi and enabling SSH

To make your Raspberry Pi headless, we need to set up Wi-Fi. First, you will need to insert the MicroSD card we made earlier back into your computer. If you have come straight here from Etcher, you should remove the card and reinsert it so that the computer can recognize the new state of the drive. You will see the card shows up as two disk drives.

One of the drives is called **boot**; this is the only one that you can read in Windows. Windows will ask if you want to format one of these disks. Click **Cancel** when Windows asks you. This is because part of the SD card holds a Linux-specific filesystem that is not readable by Windows.

In **boot**, you'll need to create two files:

- ssh: Create this as an empty file with no extension
- wpa_supplicant.conf: This file will contain your Wi-Fi network configuration

It is important that the SSH file has no extension, so it is not ssh.txt or some other variation. Windows will hide extensions by default so you may need to reveal them. On Windows, in File Explorer, go to the **View** tab, look for the **Show/Hide** pane, and then tick **File name extensions**. In general, when working with code, having the extensions displayed is important so I recommend leaving this option ticked.

The wpa_supplicant.conf file

The first line you must provide in the `wpa_supplicant.conf` file is a **country** code. These are known as iso/iec alpha2 country codes and you should find the appropriate country code for the country you are in, by going to `https://datahub.io/core/country-list`. This is important, as the Wi-Fi adapter will be disabled by Raspbian if this is not present, to prevent it from operating outside the country's legal standard, and interfering or being interfered with by other equipment. In my case, I am in Great Britain, so my country code is GB. Let's take a look at the code:

```
country=GB
```

Then, add the following lines. `update_config` means that other tools used later are allowed to update the configuration:

```
update_config=1
ctrl_interface=/var/run/wpa_supplicant
```

Now, you can define the Wi-Fi network your robot and Raspberry Pi will connect to:

```
network={
  ssid="<your network ssid>"
  psk="<your network psk>"
}
```

Please be sure to specify your own network details instead of the placeholders here. The **pre-shared key (PSK)** is also known as the Wi-Fi password. These should be the same details you use to connect your laptop or computer to your Wi-Fi network.

The completed `wpa_supplicant.conf` file should look like this:

```
country=GB
update_config=1
ctrl_interface=/var/run/wpa_supplicant

network={
  ssid="<your network ssid>"
  psk="<your network psk>"
}
```

Ensure you use the menus to eject the MicroSD card so the files are fully written before removing it. Now, with these two files in place, you can use the MicroSD Card to boot the Raspberry Pi. Plug the MicroSD card into the slot on the underside of the Raspberry Pi. The contacts of the MicroSD card should be facing the Raspberry Pi in the slot; it will only fit properly into the slot in the correct orientation.

Plug a Micro-USB cable into the side of the Raspberry Pi and connect it to a power supply.

As the technical requirements suggested, you should have a power supply able to provide around 2.1 amps. Lights turning on means that it is starting.

Finding your Pi on the network

Assuming your SSID and PSK are correct, your Raspberry Pi will now have registered on your Wi-Fi network. However, now you need to find it. The Raspberry Pi will use dynamic addresses (DHCP), so every time you connect it to your network, it may get a different address; linking to your router and writing down the IP address can work in the short term, but doing that every time it changes would be quite frustrating.

Luckily, the Raspberry Pi uses a technology known as mDNS to tell nearby computers that it is there. **mDNS** is the **Multicast Domain Name System**, which just means that the Raspberry Pi sends messages to all nearby computers, if they are listening, to say that its name is `raspberrypi.local` and giving the address to find it. This is also known as Zeroconf and Bonjour. So, the first thing you'll need to do is ensure your computer is able to receive this.

Apple macOS

If you are using an Apple Mac computer, it is already running the Bonjour software, which is already mDNS capable.

Microsoft Windows

On Windows, you will need the Bonjour software.

If you have already installed a recent version of Skype or iTunes, you will already have this software. You can use this guide (`https://smallbusiness.chron.com/enable-bonjour-65245.html`) to check that it is already present and enable it.

You can check whether it is already working with the following command in a Command Window:

```
C:\Users\danny>ping raspberrypi.local
```

If you see this, you have Bonjour already:

```
PING raspberrypi.local (192.168.0.53) 56(84) bytes of data.
64 bytes from 192.168.0.53 (192.168.0.53): icmp_seq=1 ttl=64 time=0.113 ms
64 bytes from 192.168.0.53 (192.168.0.53): icmp_seq=2 ttl=64 time=0.079 ms
```

If you see this, you'll need to install it:

```
Ping request could not find host raspberrypi.local. Please check the name
and try again.
```

To do so, browse to the Apple **Bonjour For Windows** site at `https://support.apple.com/downloads/bonjour_for_windows` and download it, then install **Download Bonjour Print Services for Windows**. Once this has run, Windows will now be able to ask for mDNS devices by name.

Linux

Ubuntu and Fedora desktop versions have had mDNS compatibility for a long time. On other Linux desktops, you will need to find their instructions for Zeroconf or Avahi. Many recent ones have this enabled by default.

Testing the setup

The Raspberry Pi's green light should have stopped blinking and only a red power light should be visible.

In Windows, summon a command line by pressing the Windows key and then CMD. In Linux or macOS, summon a Terminal.

From this Terminal, we will try to `ping` the Raspberry Pi, that is, find the Pi on the network and send a small message to elicit a response:

```
ping raspberrypi.local
```

If everything has gone right, the computer will show that it has connected to the Pi:

```
$ ping raspberrypi.local
PING raspberrypi.local (192.168.0.53) 56(84) bytes of data.
64 bytes from 192.168.0.53 (192.168.0.53): icmp_seq=1 ttl=64 time=0.113 ms
64 bytes from 192.168.0.53 (192.168.0.53): icmp_seq=2 ttl=64 time=0.079 ms
64 bytes from 192.168.0.53 (192.168.0.53): icmp_seq=3 ttl=64 time=0.060 ms
64 bytes from 192.168.0.53 (192.168.0.53): icmp_seq=4 ttl=64 time=0.047 ms
```

What if you cannot reach the Raspberry Pi?

If the Raspberry Pi does not appear to be responding to the ping operation, these are some initial steps you can take to try to diagnose and remedy the situation. If it works already, skip to the next heading. Refer to the following steps:

1. First, double-check your connections. You should have seen a few blinks of a green light and a persistent red light. If not, ensure that the SD card is seated firmly and that the power supply can give 2.1 amps.

2. Use your Wi-Fi access point settings with the Pi booted and see if it has taken an IP address there.

3. This may mean that Zeroconf/Bonjour is not running on your computer correctly. If you have not installed it, please go back and do so. If you have and you are on Windows, the different versions of Bonjour print services, Bonjour from Skype, and Bonjour from iTunes can conflict if installed together. Use the Windows add/remove functions to see if there is more than one and remove all Bonjour instances, then install the official one again.

4. Next, turn the power off, take out the SD card, place this back into your computer, and double check that the `wpa_supplicant.conf` file is present and has the right Wi-Fi details and country code. The most common errors in this file are the following:
   - Incorrect Wi-Fi details
   - Missing quotes or missing or incorrect punctuation
   - Incorrect or missing country code
   - Parts being in the wrong case

5. The SSH file is removed when the Pi boots, so if you are certain it was there and has been removed, this a good sign that the Pi actually booted.

6. Finally, this is where you may need to boot the Pi with a screen and keyboard connected, and attempt to diagnose the issue. The screen will tell you whether there are other issues with `wpa_supplicant.conf` or other problems. With these problems, it is important to look at the screen text and use this to search the web for answers. I cannot reproduce all those here, as there are many kinds of problems that could occur here. If you cannot find this, I recommend asking on Twitter using the tag #raspberrypi, on Stack Overflow, or in the Raspberry Pi Forums at `https://www.raspberrypi.org/forums/`.

Using PuTTY or SSH to connect to your Raspberry Pi

Earlier, we added a file to our Raspberry Pi boot named `ssh`. This activated the SSH service on the Pi. As mentioned before, SSH is an abbreviation for a secure shell, intended for secure network access. In this case, we are not specifically targeting the secure encryption capabilities, although those are still a good idea when using the robot in a public place, such as a competition, but are using the remote networking capability of being able to send instructions and files to and from the Raspberry Pi without having physical access to it.

The PuTTY tool is a handy tool for accessing SSH and is available for Windows, Linux, and Mac. If you already have and use an SSH client, please use that, but it is worth noting that not all of the Windows command-line SSH clients support the Zeroconf/Bonjour protocol.

PuTTY installation information can be found at `https://www.ssh.com/ssh/putty/`. This has links under the Download section for Windows, PuTTY For Linux, and PuTTY For Macs.

Once you have PuTTY installed, let's get it connected to your Raspberry Pi. First, start up PuTTY. Here is a screenshot that can help in understanding the configuration:

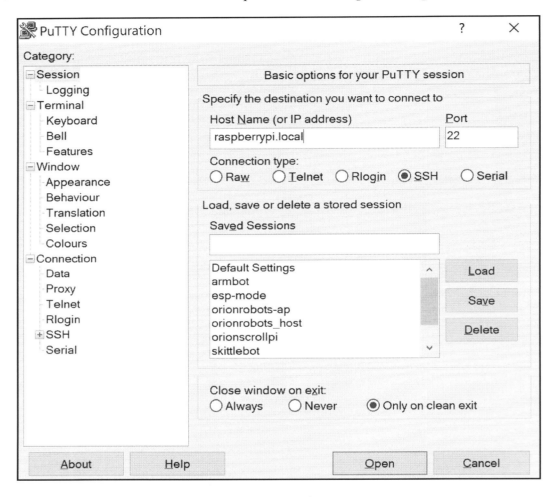

Connecting to the Pi

You will see something like the preceding screenshot, where you can type `raspberrypi.local` and click **Open** to log in to your Pi. It is likely that the first time you do this, PuTTY will show you a security warning and ask you to add the Pi's key if you trust it. Click **Yes**; it will only ask you this again if another device with the same name shows up with a different key. You may also see this if connecting to another fresh Raspberry Pi with the same hostname and different keys.

When you see the **Login as** dialog, type `pi`, press *Enter*, and use the password `raspberry`.

You will now see something like this, and you have connected to the Pi:

Successfully connected

Configuring Raspbian

Now we are connected, let's do a few things to prepare the Raspberry Pi for use: change the user password and change the hostname to make the Pi more secure.

We can perform many of these tasks with the **raspi-config** tool, a menu system to perform common configuration tasks on Raspbian. We start it with another tool, **sudo**, which runs `raspi-config` as root, a master user. Refer to the following command:

```
sudo raspi-config
```

The `raspi-config` interface will appear, as follows:

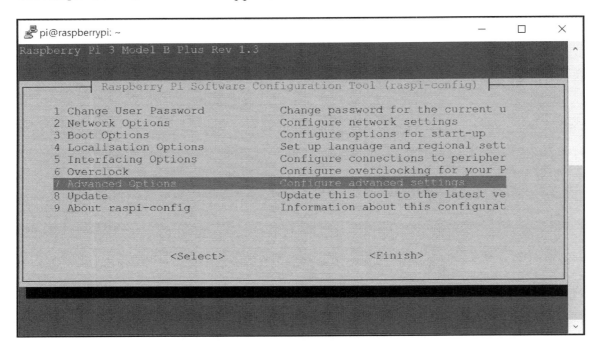

The raspi-config

Renaming your Pi

Every fresh Raspberry Pi image is called **raspberrypi**. This means that if there is more than one of those in a room, your computer will not be able to find yours. It's time to think of a name. For now, I will use myrobot, but I am sure you can think of something better. You can change this later too. It can be letters, numbers, and dash characters only – keep it short though. Perform the following steps:

1. In raspi-config, select **Network Options**, and then, under this, click on **Hostname**:

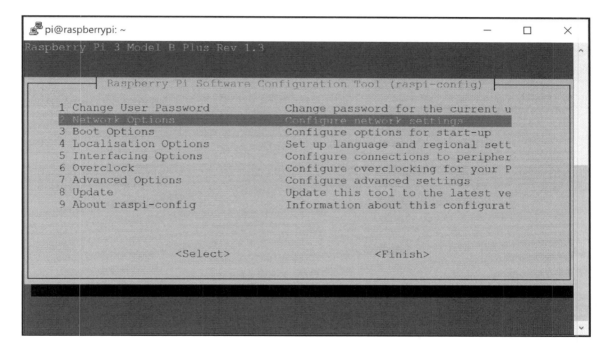

Network options

2. You should be on a screen like this; press *Enter* here and type in your new name, then press *Enter* to set this:

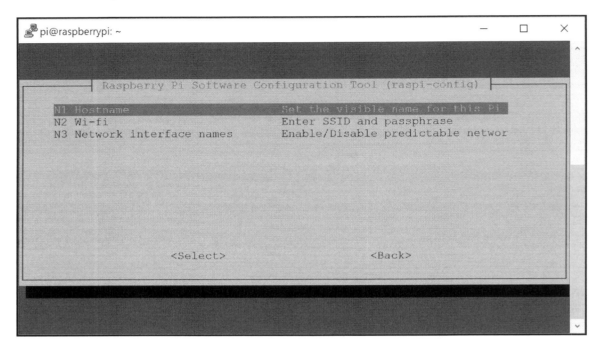

Change the hostname

Securing your Pi (a little bit)

Right now, your Raspberry Pi has the same password as every other Raspberry Pi fresh from an image. This is probably not a great way to keep the robot secure, so it's recommended you change it. Perform the following steps:

1. In the top menu of raspi-config, select **Change User Password**:

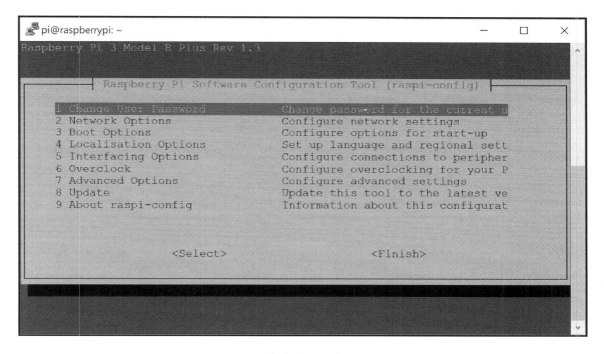

Changing the password

2. When you select this, type a new password for your robot—something you will remember, more unique than `raspberry`, but nothing you would also use for something sensitive such as email or banking.

Reboot and reconnect

It's time to finish configuration and restart the Pi. Refer to the following steps:

1. First, use the *Tab* button to get to the **Finish** item and press *Enter*:

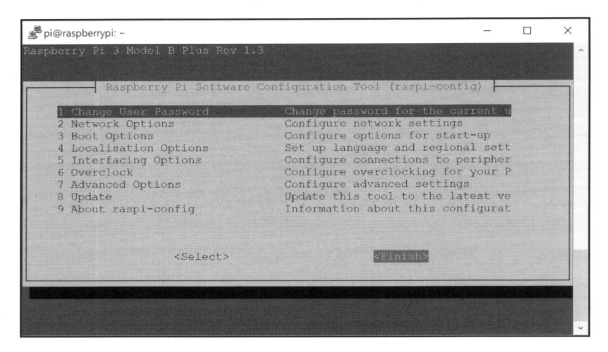

Select Finish

2. The next screen will ask if you want to reboot the Pi. Select **Yes** and press *Enter*. The Raspberry Pi will start to reboot and the PuTTY session will be disconnected as it does so, as shown:

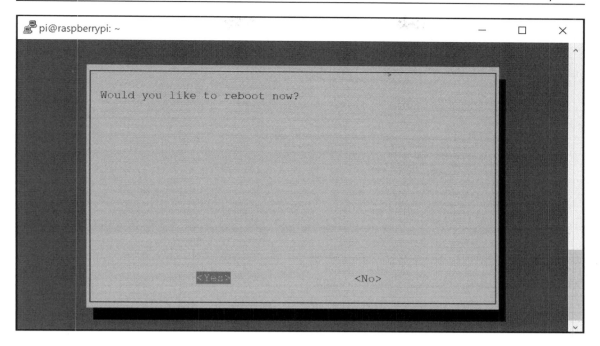

Say Yes to rebooting

Wait for a few minutes; the lights on the Pi should blink a bit and then settle down.

You will see the green activity lights on the Pi stop, and PuTTY will tell you it has lost connection to it (it is now shut down). The red light will stay on until you remove the power supply:

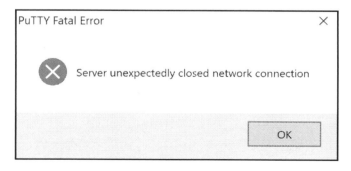

PuTTY telling you the Pi connection has gone

PuTTY only sends commands to and from the robot; it does not understand that this command will shut down the Pi, so it does not expect the connection to then be closed. You and I know better, as we told the Pi to reboot.

3. After this, you will need to connect to it again with PuTTY, but using the new hostname you gave your robot, with the `.local` ending and your new password:

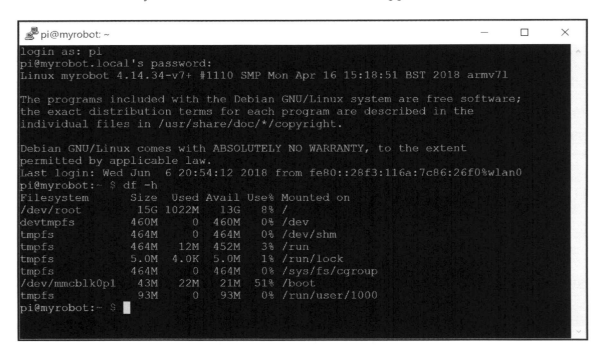

Reconnect to the Raspberry Pi

4. Now, you should be able to log in and see your prompt as `pi@myrobot`, or whatever your robot's name is. Your screen will appear as follows:

```
pi@myrobot: ~                                                    —    □    ×
login as: pi
pi@myrobot.local's password:
Linux myrobot 4.14.34-v7+ #1110 SMP Mon Apr 16 15:18:51 BST 2018 armv7l

The programs included with the Debian GNU/Linux system are free software;
the exact distribution terms for each program are described in the
individual files in /usr/share/doc/*/copyright.

Debian GNU/Linux comes with ABSOLUTELY NO WARRANTY, to the extent
permitted by applicable law.
Last login: Wed Jun  6 20:54:12 2018 from fe80::28f3:116a:7c86:26f0%wlan0
pi@myrobot:~ $ df -h
Filesystem      Size  Used Avail Use% Mounted on
/dev/root        15G 1022M  13G   8% /
devtmpfs        460M     0  460M   0% /dev
tmpfs           464M     0  464M   0% /dev/shm
tmpfs           464M   12M  452M   3% /run
tmpfs           5.0M  4.0K  5.0M   1% /run/lock
tmpfs           464M     0  464M   0% /sys/fs/cgroup
/dev/mmcblk0p1   43M   22M   21M  51% /boot
tmpfs            93M     0   93M   0% /run/user/1000
pi@myrobot:~ $
```

Reconnected to the Raspberry Pi

Now, that we are reconnected to the Raspberry Pi, we can try a simple Linux command to see the size of the filesystem – that is, if we are using the whole SD card. Linux commands are often abbreviations of things you want to ask the computer to do.

The df command in the preceding screenshot shows the device free space, or how much free space there is available in the various storage locations connected to your Raspberry Pi. Adding a -h makes it display this in human-readable numbers, with the G, M, and K suffixes for gigabytes, megabytes, and kilobytes. Type the df -h command, as shown in the previous screenshot, and it will show that /dev/root is close to the full size of the SD card, with some other devices taking up the rest of the space.

Updating the software on your Raspberry Pi

One last thing to do here is to ensure your Raspberry Pi has up-to-date software on it. This is the kind of process you start off and leave going while getting a meal, as it will take a while. Type the sudo apt-get upgrade -y command and you should see the following:

```
pi@myrobot:~ $ sudo apt-get upgrade -y
Reading package lists... Done
Building dependency tree
Reading state information... Done
Calculating upgrade... Done
The following packages will be upgraded:
   bluez-firmware curl libcurl3 libcurl3-gnutls libprocps6 pi-bluetooth
procps
   raspi-config wget
9 upgraded, 0 newly installed, 0 to remove and 0 not upgraded.
Need to get 1,944 kB of archives.
After this operation, 16.4 kB of additional disk space will be used.
Get:1 http://archive.raspberrypi.org/debian stretch/main armhf bluez-
firmware all 1.2-3+rpt6 [126 kB]
   .
   .
   .
```

Please let the Pi continue until it is complete here, and do not interrupt or turn the power off until the pi@myrobot:~ $ prompt has reappeared.

What is sudo?

So, you've probably seen a pattern with typing this `sudo` thing in a few of the commands. This command tells the Raspberry Pi to run the following command (such as `raspbi-config` or `apt-get`) as a **root** user, the Linux administrator/superuser. You can read it as *super user do*. This is needed for software that will make changes to the system or perform updates. It's usually not needed for user programs though.

Shutting down your Raspberry Pi

When you are done with the Pi for a session, it's not very nice to the filesystem to just unplug it.

 Pulling power from the Raspberry Pi when it is not expected can cause loss of files and SD card corruption. You may lose your work on it and you may also damage the SD card enough to need to replace it. Always use the correct shutdown procedure.

It's strongly advised to tell it to shut down. To do this, use the following command:

```
pi@myrobot:~ $ sudo shutdown -h now
```

Wait for the green light activity to stop; PuTTY will detect it has disconnected. You can now safely disconnect the power from the Raspberry Pi.

Summary

In this chapter, you've seen what it means to set a Raspberry Pi free from a screen and keyboard by making it headless. You set up an SD card to connect to your Wi-Fi and to open up the SSH port so you can connect to it.

You've learned how to use raspi-config to personalize your Pi and secure it with your own password. You then made the first small steps in looking around the Linux system it has running on it. You also ensured the Raspberry Pi is up to date and running the most current software.

You then learned how to safely put the Pi into shutdown mode, so that filesystem damage does not occur when you unplug it.

In the next chapter we will look at ensuring you don't loose valuable robot code or configuration when things go wrong. We will learn about what can go wrong, and how to use Git, SFTP and SD Card back ups to protect our hard work.

Questions

Answer the following questions:

1. What are the major items you would not leave attached to a headless computer?
2. If you gave your robot the hostname `awesomegiantrobot`, what address would you use to reach it in PuTTY?
3. Why is it advisable to expand the filesystem on your Raspberry Pi?
4. How do you properly shut down the Raspberry Pi?

Further reading

Refer to the following book:

- *Internet of Things with Raspberry Pi 3* by Maneesh Rao: This book uses a wired headless Raspberry Pi for the demonstrations and experiments inside it

5
Backing Up the Code with Git and SD Card Copies

As you create and customize the code for your robot, you will have invested many hours in getting it to do awesome things that, unless you take precautions, could all suddenly disappear. The programs are also not the whole story, as you've already started configuring Raspbian for use on the robot. You want to keep your programs and config in case of disaster, and be able to go back if you make changes you regret.

In this chapter, we will learn the following:

- **How code can be broken or lost**: The ways that code can be broken and the disasters you might face.
- **Strategy 1—keep the code on a PC and upload it**: How to use your PC/laptop to store the code and upload it to the Pi.
- **Strategy 2—using Git to go back in time**: How you can ensure that you can go back to previous versions, or just compare versions, and protect yourself against changes you might regret.
- **Strategy 3—making SD card backups**: So you can go back to a whole configuration that worked.

Technical requirements

For this chapter, you will require the following:

- The Raspberry Pi and the SD card you prepared in the previous chapter
- The US power supply and cable you used with the Pi

- A Windows, Linux, or macOS computer or laptop, connected to the internet and able to read/write to SD cards
- Software: FileZilla and Git
- On Windows: Win32DiskImager

Here is the GitHub link for the code files:

```
https://github.com/PacktPublishing/Learn-Robotics-Fundamentals-of-Robotics-
Programming/tree/master/chapter5
```

Check out the following video to see the Code in Action:

```
http://bit.ly/2DM9fzh
```

How code can be broken or lost

Code and its close cousin, configuration, take time and hard work. Code needs configuration to run, such as Raspbian configuration, extra software, and necessary data files. Both need research and learning, design, making them, testing, and debugging.

Many bad situations can lead to the loss of code. These have happened to me a week before taking robots to a show, after weeks of work, and I learned the hard way to take this quite seriously. So, what can happen to your code?

SD card data loss and corruption

SD card corruption is when the data on the SD card used to hold your code, Raspbian, and anything you've prepared on it is broken. Files become unreadable or the card becomes unusable. The information on the SD card can be permanently lost.

If a Raspberry Pi unexpectedly loses power, the SD card can be in an poor state, causing data loss. A hot Pi can slowly bake an SD card, damaging it. Visual processing on a Pi is one way it can get hot. SD cards get damaged if something bad happens electrically to the Pi via the GPIO pins or its power supply. MicroSD cards are also very small and easily lost when not in the Pi.

Bad changes to the code or configuration

We all make mistakes. At those times, you'll want to go back and see what you've changed. If you've made a lot of changes, it may no longer be clear which things are different and what differences (if any) have broken the code.

You can render your robot useless with bad configuration, such as the Pi not being on the network or booting anymore. An upgrade to system packages may go wrong and lead to code not working, or needing extensive changes to the code for it to work again.

Combinations

These problems can combine to cause real nightmares. I've seen changes in the code lead a robot to misbehave and damage itself in a way that made the SD card corrupted. I've been updating packages on the operating system when the power cable was knocked out, corrupting the SD card and breaking Raspbian two weeks before a major robot event, and it was painful rebuilding it. This was a lesson learned the hard way.

Back up the code and back up the SD card configuration. Over the rest of this chapter, we'll look at some solutions to keep your robot's software safe from many kinds of disaster.

Strategy 1 - keep the code on the PC and upload it

Secure File Transfer Protocol (SFTP), lets you transfer files from a computer to a Pi. This lets you write code on nice editors on your computer, then upload it to the Raspberry Pi. You can choose your editor and have the safety of more than one copy. SFTP uses SSH to copy files to and from the Raspberry Pi over the network.

First, make yourself a folder on the PC to store your robot code in, then we can make a test file that will just print a bit of text and exit:

hello.py

```
print("Raspberry Pi is alive")
```

We will copy this to the robot and run it.

We will use the SFTP tool FileZilla from `https://filezilla-project.org`. Download this and follow the installation instructions:

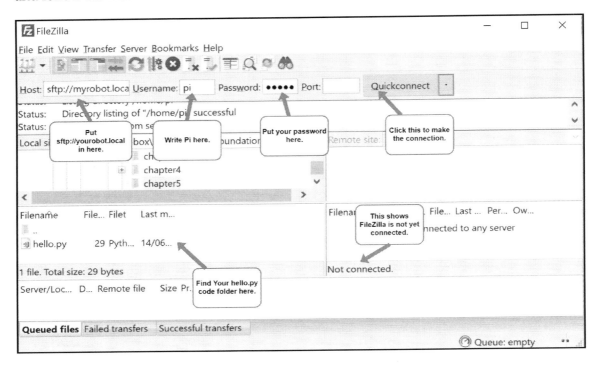

FileZilla

Plug in and power up your Raspberry Pi. Notice in the bottom of the right-hand panel, it says **Not connected**. In the host box, type the local hostname you gave your robot Pi in the headless setup, prefixed with `sftp://`. For example, `sftp://myrobot.local`. In the **Username**, type `pi` and enter the password you set up before. Click the **Quickconnect** button to connect to the Raspberry Pi, as shown:

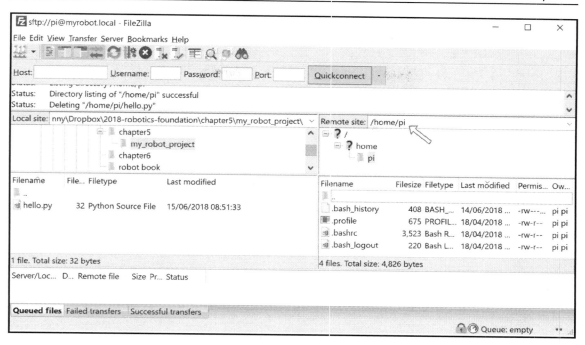

The Raspberry Pi connected

When connected, you'll see files on the Raspberry Pi in the right-hand **Remote Site** panel, like the preceding image. Use the left-hand local site panel to go to your code on your computer. You can click **hello.py**, highlighted in the top-left of the following screenshot, and drag it to the the lower right-hand panel to put it on the Raspberry Pi:

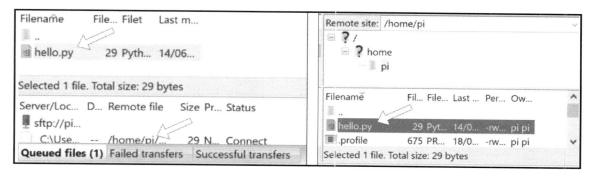

Transferring a file

When you drag the file over, you should see it in the **Queued files** section. Since this file is small, it will only be in this queued state for an instant. You can also use the same system too for larger files and folders. You'll soon see the file over in the remote site (the Raspberry Pi), shown on the right of the preceding screenshot. To run this code, use PuTTY to log in to the Pi and try the following:

```
pi@myrobot:~ $ python hello.py
Raspberry Pi is alive
```

Strategy 2 – using Git to go back in time

Git is a popular form of source control, a way to keep a history of changes you've made to code. You can go back through changes, see what they were, restore older versions, and keep a commented log of why changes were made. Git also lets you store code in more than one location in case your hard drive fails. Git stores code and its history in repositories, or repos. In Git, you can make branches, copies of the whole set of code, to try ideas in parallel with your code and later merge those back to the main branch. I will get you started, but this section can only scratch the surface of what Git is capable of.

To install Git, please follow the instructions at https://git-scm.com/book/en/v2/Getting-Started-Installing-Git for your computer. Windows and Mac users may be able to use the GitHub app for easier setup. Git requires you to set your identity using a command line on your computer:

```
> git config --global user.name "<Your Name>"
> git config --global user.email <your email address>
```

To put this project under source control, we need to initialize it and commit our first bit of code. Make sure you are in the folder for your code (my_robot_project) in a command line on your computer and type the following:

```
> git init .
Initialized empty Git repository in
C:/Users/danny/workspace/my_robot_project/.git/
> git add hello.py
> git commit -m "Adding the starter code"
[master (root-commit) 11cc8dc] Adding the starter code
 1 file changed, 1 insertion(+)
 create mode 100644 hello.py
```

`git init .` tells Git to make the folder into a Git repository. `git add` tells Git you want to store the `hello.py` file in Git. `git commit` stores this change for later, with `-m <message>` putting a message in the journal. Git shows you this commit has been created.

We can now see the journal with `git log`:

```
> git log
commit 11cc8dc0b880b1dd8302ddda8adf63591bf340fe (HEAD -> master)
Author: Your Name <your@email.com>
Date: <todays date>

  Adding the starter code
```

We then modify the code in `hello.py`, changing it to this:

```
import socket
print('%s is alive!' % socket.gethostname())
```

If you copy this to the Pi using SFTP, this will say `myrobot is alive!` or whatever you set the hostname of your robot to be. However, it is the Git behavior we are interested in. Let's see how this code is different from before:

```
> git diff hello.py
diff --git a/hello.py b/hello.py
index 3eab0d8..fa3db7c 100644
--- a/hello.py
+++ b/hello.py
@@ -1 +1,2 @@
-print("Raspberry Pi is alive")
+import socket
+print('%s is alive!' % socket.gethostname())
```

This is Git's way of showing the differences. You've taken away a print line, and in its place added an import and then a print line. We can add this into Git to make a new version, and then use `git log` again to see both versions:

```
> git add hello.py
> git commit -m "Show the robot hostname"
[master 912f4de] Show the robot hostname
 1 file changed, 2 insertions(+), 1 deletion(-)
> git log
commit 912f4de3fa866ecc9d2141e855333514d9468151 (HEAD -> master)
Author: Your Name <your@email.com>
Date: <the time of the next commit>

    Show the robot hostname
```

```
commit 11cc8dc0b880b1dd8302ddda8adf63591bf340fe (HEAD -> master)
Author: Your Name <your@email.com>
Date: <todays date>

    Adding the starter code
```

We have only just scratched the surface of the power of Git. See the reference in the *Further reading* section on how to branch, use remote services, roll back to previous versions, and find tools to browse the code in the Git history.

Strategy 3 – making SD card backups

Git and SFTP are great for keeping code safe, but they don't help you reinstall and reconfigure Raspbian on a card. The procedures for Windows, Linux, and Mac are quite different for this. The basic idea is to insert the SD card and use a tool to clone the whole card to a file known as an image, which you can restore with Etcher when you need recovery. Warning: you should restore images to cards of the same size or larger. First, properly shut down your Raspberry Pi, take its SD card, and put that into your computer. These clean images are large so do not put them in your Git repository. It's beyond the scope of this chapter, but I recommend finding a way to compress these files as they are mostly empty right now. In all cases, expect this operation to take 20-30 minutes due to the image sizes.

Windows

For Windows, we'll use Win32DiskImager. Get an installer for this at `https://sourceforge.net/projects/win32diskimager`. Run this and follow the installation instructions. Since we will use it immediately, I suggest leaving the **Launch immediately** checkbox ticked.

You'll be presented with this screen:

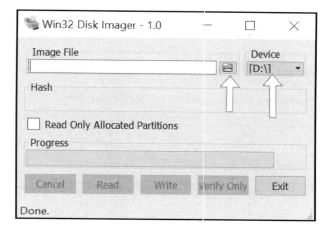

Win32 Disk Imager

Highlighted on the right is the **Device**; this should have automatically found the SD card device. Use the folder icon highlighted to choose where the image file will be stored. Now, refer to the following screenshot:

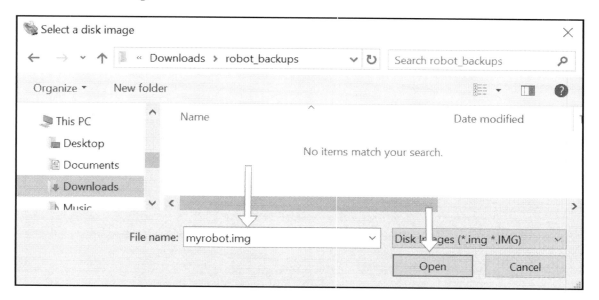

Choose the location

I named my image `myrobot.img` in the **File name** box in the the preceding screenshot, and then clicked the **Open** button to confirm this.

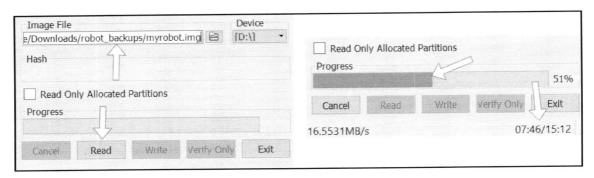

Reading the image

After clicking Open, you'll see a screen like the left side of the preceding screenshot, and your selected location should be in the **Image File** box. Click on the **Read** button to start copying the image. As the image is being read, you'll see the highlighted progress bar. In the bottom right is an estimation of the time remaining. When it's done, Win32 Disk Imager will tell you that the read was successful and you can then exit the software.

Mac and Linux

Backing up SD cards is done on a command line on a Mac and in Linux. After inserting the card, you'll need to find the devices location. This is different on Linux and Mac:

Linux

Type the following:

```
$ dmesg
```

This will output a lot of stuff, but you are interested only in a line near the end that looks like the following:

```
sd 3:0:0:0: [sdb] Attached SCSI removable disk
```

The card is in the square brackets, `[sdb]`, which may be different on your computer. The SD card location will be `/dev/<drive location>`: for example, `/dev/sdb`.

Mac

To list the disk drives on a Mac:

```
$ diskutil list
```

The output should look like this screenshot:

```
/dev/disk0 (internal, physical):
   #:                       TYPE NAME                    SIZE       IDENTIFIER
   0:          GUID_partition_scheme                   *500.1 GB    disk0
   1:                        EFI EFI                    209.7 MB    disk0s1
   2:                  Apple_HFS Macintosh HD           499.2 GB    disk0s2
/dev/disk1 (internal, physical):
   #:                       TYPE NAME                    SIZE       IDENTIFIER
   0:         FDisk_partition_scheme                   *7.9 GB      disk1
   1:            Windows_FAT_32 boot                    45.2 MB     disk1s1
   2:                      Linux                        7.8 GB      disk1s2
```

Diskutil list output with the boot name and device location highlighted

In this list, /dev/disk1 has a device named boot, so in my case /dev/disk1 is the SD card location.

Cloning with DD

On macOS and Linux, once you have the SD location (such as /dev/sdb or /dev/disk1), you can then start the clone with the dd command. This command dumps data to and from drives. Read this section thoroughly and be careful to get the locations right, as you can destroy the contents of an SD card or your computer hard drive. If you are at all unsure, **do not** use this method. The if parameter is the **input file**, which in this case is your SD card. The of parameter is the **output file**, the myrobot.img file you are cloning your card into. The bs parameter is the **block size**, so making this large, such as 32M, will make the operation quicker:

```
$ sudo dd if=/dev/sdb of=~/myrobot.img bs=32M
Password:
474+2 records in
474+2 records out
15931539456 bytes (16 GB, 15 GiB) copied, 4132.13 s, 3.9 MB/s
```

You will need to type your user password for this to start. This creates the `myrobot.img` file as a clone of the whole SD card in your home directory. `dd` will give no output until it is complete, and will then show you stats about the operation.

Summary

In this chapter, you have learned how to look after your code and configuration, which you will spend time on for your robot. You have seen how things can go wrong, and the strategies to protect yourself from them. You have a starting point with Git, SFTP, and SD card backups that can be used together to let you be a bit more experimental and fearless with code changes for your robot.

In the next chapter, we will see how to build a basic robot.

Questions

1. For what reasons would you use source control?
2. What would you use branching for?
3. Why keep SD card copies?
4. What reasons are there for editing files on another computer and uploading them to the Raspberry Pi?

Further reading

- The Git Handbook on GitHub: `https://guides.github.com/introduction/git-handbook/`. This is a comprehensive look at what Git is, and the problems it solves, and a starting point to using its functionality.
- Hands-On Version Control with Git: `https://www.packtpub.com/application-development/hands-version-control-git-video`. This is a video tutorial on using Git.
- The GitHub Guides: `https://guides.github.com/`. A series of guides on getting the best out of Git and GitHub.
- GitLab Basics: `https://docs.gitlab.com/ee/gitlab-basics/`. GitLab is a great alternative to GitHub, with a large community and some excellent guides on using Git.

Building Robot Basics - Wheels, Power, and Wiring

6

In this chapter, we will start building the robot. I'll show you how to choose a robot chassis kit with wheels and motors, a motor controller, and some power for the robot, talking through the trade-offs and things to avoid. I'll show you how to check that everything will fit and then build the robot, showing you how to build yours too.

In this chapter, we will learn the following:

- How to find and buy robot chassis kits
- Understanding the trade-offs when choosing a motor controller
- Understanding battery and power trade-offs
- How to test-fit parts
- How to assemble parts on a robot chassis

Technical requirements

For this chapter, you will require the following:

- A computer with access to the internet.
- A Raspberry Pi 3.
- A set of screwdrivers, M2.5, M3 Posidrive, and some jeweler's screwdrivers are recommended.
- A pair of long nose pliers. Optionally, a set of miniature metric spanners.
- Some electrical tape.
- Hook and loop or Velcro tape.

- Drawing software such as www.draw.io, Inkscape, Visio, or similar software.
- Nylon Standoff Kit with M2.5 and M3 threads. These can be found in many online retailers. (M2 or M2.5 are both fine, but must be M3; you may need more than one kit.)

You will be choosing and purchasing a chassis, motor controller, and battery compartment in this chapter, but do not buy them yet.

Check out the following video to see the Code in Action:

`http://bit.ly/2FS8yYa`

Choosing a chassis kit

The chassis, like the controller, is a fundamental decision when making a robot. Although these can be self-made using 3D printing or toy hacking, the most simple place to start is with a chassis kit. These kits contain sets of parts to start off your robot build. A chassis can be changed, but it would mean rebuilding the robot.

The internet has plenty of chassis kits around. Too many, so how do you choose one?

Size

Getting the size for a robot right matters too. Take a look at the following photos:

Robot chassis sizes compared

Chassis 1 is 11 cm in and just about fits a controller in it, but is too tiny. This will make it hard to build your robot. Squeezing the controller, power, and all the sensors into this small space would need skill and experience beyond the scope of a first robot build.

Chassis 2 is Armbot. This large robot is 33 cm by 30 cm, with an arm reach of another 300 mm. It needs eight AA batteries, big motors, and a big controller. These add to the expense and may cause issues around power handling for a new builder. It has lots of space, but issues around weight and rigidity. Armbot is one of my most expensive robots, excluding the cost of the arm!

Chassis 3 in the preceding image will fit the Pi, batteries, and sensor, but without being large and bulky. It is around the right dimensions, being between 15-20 cm long and 10-15 cm wide. Those that have split levels might be great for this, but only one or two levels, as three or four will make a robot top heavy and may cause it to topple. This has enough space and is relatively easy to build.

Wheel count

Some chassis kits have elaborate movement methods, legs, tank tracks, and tri-star wheels, to name a few. While these are fun and I encourage experimenting with them, this is not the place to start at. So, I recommend a thoroughly sensible, if basic, wheels on motors version.

There are kits with four-wheel drive and six-wheel drive. These can be quite powerful and will require larger motor controllers. They may also chew through batteries, and you are increasingly the likelihood of overloading something. This also makes for trickier wiring, as seen in the following:

Four-wheel drive robot

Two-wheel drive is the simplest to wire in. It usually requires a third wheel for balance. This can be a castor wheel, roller ball, or just a Teflon sled for tiny robots. Two wheels are also the easiest to steer, avoiding some friction issues seen with robots using four or more wheels.

Two wheels won't have the pulling power of four or six-wheel drive, but they are simple and will work. They are also less expensive:

Two wheels with a castor

Wheels and motors

A kit for a beginner should come with the wheels and the motors. The wheels should have simple non-pneumatic rubber tires. The most obvious style for inexpensive robots is shown in the following photo. There are many kits with these in them:

Common inexpensive robot wheels

The kit should also come with two motors, one for each wheel, and include the screws or parts to mount them onto the chassis. I recommend DC Gear motors, as the gearing will keep the speed usable while increasing the mechanical pushing power the robot has.

Importantly, the motors should have the wires connected, like the first motor in the following photo:

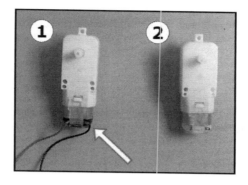

Gear motors with and without wires

It is tricky to solder or attach these wires to the small tags on motors, and poorly attached ones do have a frustrating habit of coming off. The kits you will want to start with have these wires attached, as can be seen in the following:

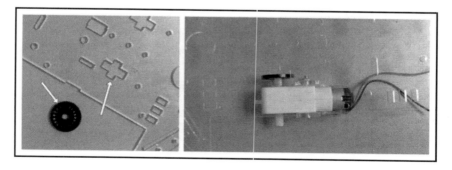

Encoder wheel and slot close up

Another point to note is that where the motors are mounted, the kits should have some encoder wheels, and a slot to read them through. The encoder wheels are also known as odometry, tacho, or tachometer wheels.

Simplicity

You don't want to use a complex or hard-to-assemble kit for your first robot build. I've repeated this throughout with two-wheel drive, two motors with the wires soldered on and steering clear of large robots, or unusual and interesting locomotion systems, not because they are flawed, but because it's better to start simple. There is a limit to this, a robot kit that is a fully built and enclosed robot leaves little room for learning or experimentation and would actually require toy hacking skills to customize.

Cost

Related to simplicity is cost. Robot chassis kits can be brought from around $15, up to thousands of dollars. Larger and more complex robots tend to be far more costly. For this book, I am aiming to keep to the less costly options or at least show where they are possible.

Conclusion

So, now you can choose a chassis kit, with two wheels and a castor, two motors with wires soldered on them, slots, and encoder wheels. These are not expensive, and widely available on popular internet shopping sites as "Smart Car Chassis," with terms like "2WD":

The robot kit I'm using

The kit I'm working with looks like the preceding photo when assembled without the Raspberry Pi.

Choosing a motor controller

The next important part you'll need is a motor controller. Much like the motors, there are a number of trade-offs and considerations before buying one.

Integration level

Motor controllers can be as simple as motor power control driven from GPIO pins directly, such as the L298. This is the cheapest solution: a generic L298N motor controller can be connected to some of the IO pins on the Raspberry Pi. These are reasonably robust and have been easily available for a long time. They are flexible, but using parts like this will take up more space and need to be wired point to point, adding complexity to the build:

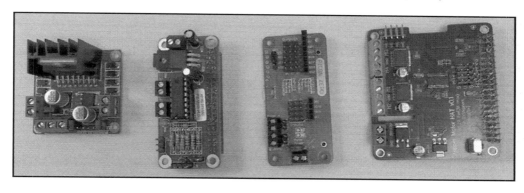

A selection of motor control boards: The L298, PiZMoto, PiConZero, and Full Function Stepper Hat

Others are as complex as whole IO controller boards, many of which hide their own controller similar to an Arduino, along with motor control chips. Although the cheapest and most flexible ways are the most basic controllers, those with higher integration will reduce size, keep the pin usage count low (handy when you are connecting a lot to the robot), and may simplify your robot build.

They often come integrated with a power supply too, but we will look at power in more detail later in this chapter.

Motor controllers can be bought as fully integrated Raspberry Pi hats, boards designed to fit exactly on top of a Raspberry Pi. These tend to have a high level of integration, as discussed before, but may come at the cost of flexibility, especially if you plan to use other accessories.

Pin usage

When buying a motor controller in Raspberry Pi hat form, pin usage is important. If we intend to use microphones (PCM/I2S), servo motors, and I2c and SPI devices with this robot, having boards that make use of these pins is less than ideal.

 Simply being plugged into pins doesn't mean they are all used, so only a subset of the pins is usually actually connected on a hat.

To get an idea of how pins in different boards interact on the Raspberry Pi, take a look at `https://pinout.xyz` , which lets you select Raspberry Pi boards and see the pin configuration for them.

Controllers that use the I2C or serial bus are great because they make efficient use of pins and that bus can be shared.

At the time of writing, PiConZero, the Stepper Motor Hat, and ZeroBorg all use I2C pins. The Full Function Stepper Motor Hat is able to control DC motors and servo motors, is cheap, and is widely available. It also has the pins available straight through on the top and an I2C connector on the side. It's designed to work with other hats and allow more expansion.

Size

The choice of this depends on the chassis, specifically the size of the motors you have. In simple terms, the larger your chassis, the larger a controller you will need. The power handling capacity of a motor controller is specified in amps. For a robot like the *The Robot Kit I'm Using* image, around 1 to 1.5 amps per channel is good. The consequence of too low a rating can be disaster, resulting in a robot that barely moves, while the components cook themselves or violently go bang. Too large a controller has consequences for space, weight, and cost:

An L298n with a Heatsink

The level of integration can also contribute to size. A tiny board that stacks on a Pi would take up less space than separate boards. Related to size is if the board keeps the camera port on the Raspberry Pi accessible.

Soldering

As you choose boards for a robot, you will note that some come as kits themselves, requiring parts to be soldered on. If you are already experienced with this, it may be an option. For experienced builders, this becomes a small cost in time depending on the complexity of the soldering. A small header is going to be a very quick and easy job, and a board that comes as a bag of components with a bare board will be a chunk of an evening.

For this book, I will recommend components that require the least soldering.

Connectors

Closely related to soldering are the connectors for the motors and batteries. I tend to prefer the screw type connectors. Other types may require matching motors or crimping skills:

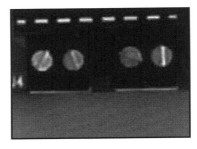

Screw terminals for motor and battery connections

Conclusion

Our robot is space constrained; for this reason, we will be looking at the Raspberry Pi hat type form factor. We are also looking to keep the number of pins it binds to really low. An I2C-based hat will let us do this. The **Full Function Stepper Motor Hat** (also known as the Full Function Robot Expansion Board) gets us access to all the Pi pins while being a powerful motor controller:

The Full Function Stepper Motor Hat

It's available in most countries, has space for the ribbon for the camera, and controls servo motors. I recommend this hat for the robot in this book. As a close second, I recommend the 4tronix PiConZero hat, or assembling a stack of PiBorg hats. These may be harder to source outside of the UK. The reader will need to adapt the code, and consider a tiny shim to retain access to the GPIO pins if using a different board.

Powering the robot

The robot needs power for all its parts. There are two major power systems that need to be considered: the power for all the digital parts, such as the Raspberry Pi and sensors, and then the power for the motors.

Motors need their own power system for a few reasons. First, they consume far more electrical power than most other components on the robot. They may require different voltages; it's not uncommon to have low voltage and high current capacity supplies for motors. The other reason that they need their own power system is that they can cause interference. They can pull enough power that other circuitry has brownouts and loses power long enough to get into an inconsistent or reset state, which would lead to SD card corruption on a Pi, and they can also introduce electrical noise to a power line as they are used, which could cause digital parts to misbehave.

There are two major strategies for powering a robot with motors:

- **Dual batteries**: The motors and the rest of the robot have completely separate sets of batteries, ensuring that their power is independent
- **Battery eliminators**: A battery eliminator circuit (a BEC or uBEC) , switching supply or regulator

This photo shows a UBEC package:

Picture of a Bec

Dual batteries are the most certain option to avoid any brownout, loss of power, or interference issues. This can take up a lot of space; however, a USB power bank is a simple and effective way to do this. Choose one with small outer case dimensions, but a high power rating, such as 10,000mAh, and an output of at least 2.1A.

The power supplies built into motor controller boards can be used, but these often have too low an output rating and can be very inefficient, wasting much battery power. They are very likely to lead to brownouts.

Here is a picture of a USB battery used for the Pi:

The USB power bank from Armbot - slightly old and battered, but still effective

A battery eliminator circuit is lighter and takes up less space, although you may need a bigger set of batteries. However, by sharing a supply with motors it is still vulnerable to the voltage drops that cause controller resets and line noise for the controller. This will affect switching power supply Pi shims like the Wide Input Shim and the power supplies built into some motor controllers.

You will need to ensure that at least 2.1A can be handled, preferably more. It's not uncommon to see 3.4A and 4.2A power banks. UBECs with 5A ratings are also fairly common.

To keep things simple in this robot, and not have to deal with reset issues, we will go with the dual battery approach, and accept the cost in bulk and weight:

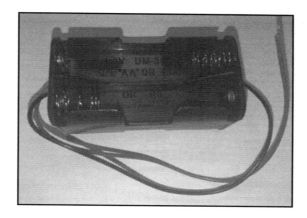

The 4 x AA battery box we will use with the motors

For the motors, 4 x AA batteries will suffice. I recommend using Nickel Metal Hydride rechargeable batteries for them, not just because they can be recharged, but also because they can deliver more current if needed than alkaline batteries. To save space, we can use the *two up/two down* or *back to back* configuration like the battery box shown in the diagram.

Before buying these parts, we will test fit them.

Test fitting the robot

I recommend test fitting before actually ordering parts. This helps me be more confident that they will fit and you know where they will roughly go. This step is optional, but it can save you time and money later.

This is another exercise in which you can use paper and a pen, or an app such as DrawIO on the internet. First, I find the dimensions for all the parts. Here is a screenshot from Amazon showing how to spot product dimensions:

Product details

Colour Name: **Black**

    Product Dimensions: 9.7 x 8 x 2.2 cm ; 240 g

    Boxed-product Weight: 281 g

    Delivery information: We cannot deliver certain products outside mainland UK

Finding product specifications

Some information digging is needed to find these for your parts. For each, first find a shop you can buy them at, such as Amazon, a number of online shops, or eBay. You can then search for, or ask for information about, the dimensions of each board or item. Make sure you are looking at the dimensions of the part and not its packaging. The next diagram shows a datasheet for a battery box and its dimensions:

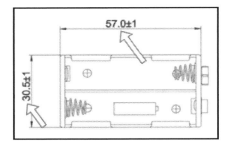

Reading product drawings

Image searches on dimensions or part datasheets can find you diagrams like the preceding image. In this case, the dimensions are in mm. The **±** signs show the manufacturing variation of plus or minus the next number. When test fitting, err on the higher side, so take **57±1** as 58 mm for that dimension.

So, the dimensions I have are as follows:

- The Raspberry Pi: 85 mm x 56 mm.
- The chassis: Mine suggests it is 100 mm x 200 mm. Be aware that the dimensions here are outer dimensions and will include the wheels.

- The motor controller fits over the Pi so is counted here as the Pi. This will make things taller, but is only really a concern for a multi-level robot chassis.
- The 4 x AA battery box: The type I suggested is 58 mm x 31.5 mm.
- The USB power bank: 60 mm x 90 mm.

For this, drawing rectangles to scale is enough detail. In DrawIO, create a new blank diagram. The next screenshot shows what to put in the diagram:

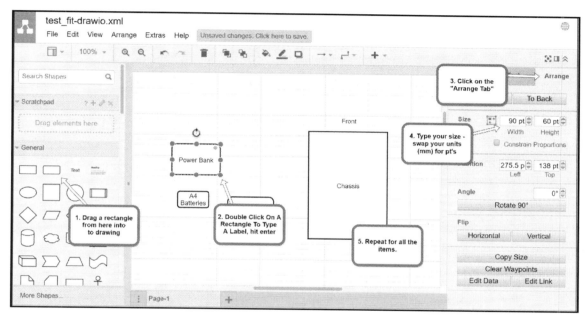

Using Draw.IO to create test fit parts

As shown in the preceding screenshot, use the general palette on the left to drag out rectangles. It helps to clearly label each part; double-click a rectangle and type a label into it. Press *Enter* to accept the label. The item should still have a blue highlight.

Click the tabs in the right to select the "arrange" tab. Here, type your dimensions (swap millimeters for points) into the width and height boxes. Notice I've also put a text label on the "front" of the chassis. The next diagram shows parts brought together to line them up in the chassis:

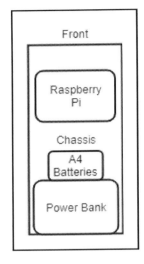

The test fit

Now, you can drag the parts together. The Pi should be near the front of the robot, as we'll later have sensors here, and the motor cables can go forward into it. In the preceding image, I've just dragged the rectangles into place. Draw.io helps you here by showing blue guidelines for centering and aligning objects. I put the power bank at the rear, with the AA batteries closer to the Pi so they can go into the motor controller easily.

This looks like it will fit. It's not 100% accurate, but good enough to say this will probably work.

Now, it's time to buy parts. My shopping list looks like this:

- The chassis kit.
- The Full Function Stepper Motor Hat.
- 4 x AA battery box.
- 4 x metal hydride AA batteries. If you don't have one, you will need a charger for these too.
- 1 x USB power bank able to deliver 3 amps or more.

Assembling the base

Let's build! Assuming you bought a chassis similar to mine, you will be able to assemble it with these steps; for a completely different chassis, I strongly recommend consulting their documentation for assembly instructions. You will have a collection of parts covered in a layer of paper. This is to prevent the plastic from getting scratches, and can be safely removed. You can do this by getting a nail under it, or failing that, a craft knife. It's not essential to remove it, but a robot looks better without it. The next diagram shows how:

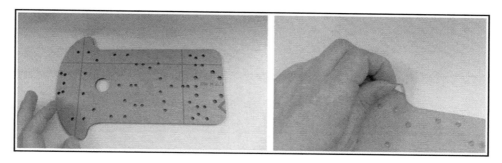

Removing the protective backing from robot parts

For a kit with a plastic motor bracket, you should now have parts like those shown in the following photo:

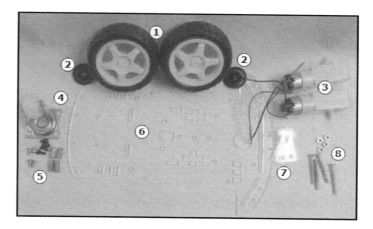

Robot kit parts

In the kit, you should have the following:

- Two wheels.
- Two encoder wheels.
- Two motors, with the wires.
- A castor wheel.
- The screws and brass standoffs to mount the castor wheel. I've replaced one set of screws with a nylon, non-conductive one. You should be able to do the same from the nylon standoff kit.
- In the middle is the chassis plate itself.
- On the right are plastic brackets to mount the motors. Your kit may have metal types, which work slightly differently and come with four extra screws.
- Finally, there are four screws and four nuts to mount the motors.

The following photo shows what parts for a metal motor bracket look like for an alternative kit:

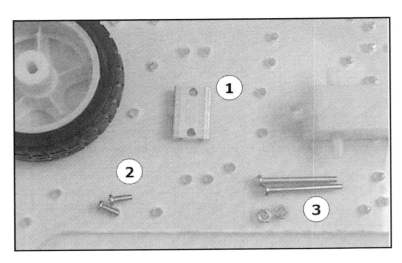

Metal type motor bracket

 The other parts not shown are going to be very similar to this.

Assembling the base, motors, and wheels

We'll start by attaching the encoder wheels onto the motor. It's best done at this stage. When assembling the motor, observe on which side the wires are attached to the motor, as shown in the first panel of the following photos:

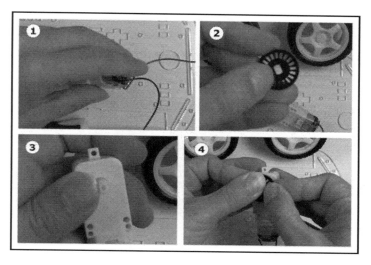

The wires are attached to the motor

Follow these steps:

- The encoder wheel should be attached on the same side as the wires.
- Look at the encoder wheel, and note that it has an axle hole with two flattened sides.
- The axles on the motors have the same shape.
- Line the encoder wheel-shaped hole with the motor axle on the same side as the wires and gently push it on. It should have a little friction. Repeat this for the other motor. You should have two motors with encoder wheels on them, on the same side as their wires. Next, we will fit the motor brackets to the robot.

 If you have the metal type, skip to the section for this.

Plastic motor brackets

To fit the plastic type of bracket, first look for the slots to fit it. Look at the following set of photos:

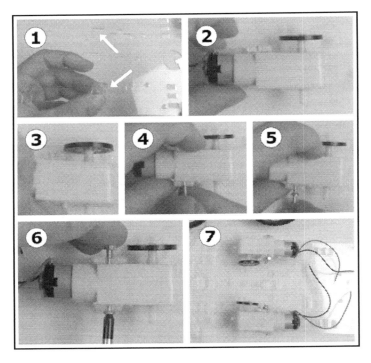

Plastic motor mount

For fitting, follow these steps:

1. The arrows point at the slots. Push the plastic brackets through the slots.
2. With the brackets in place, I've pushed the motor against the bracket; note that the wires and encoder wheel face the inside of the robot, and that the encoder should be under a cutout in the chassis body for it.
3. Here, push an outer bracket onto the outside of the robot; there is another slot in the chassis for this to fit into.
4. Push the long screws through from the outside.

5. Then, push a nut onto the screws and use a screwdriver to screw them in.

6. For the nut closest to the chassis, one of its flattened edges should hold it in place as you tighten the screw. For the outer nut, use a spanner or pliers to hold it.

7. You will need to repeat the same steps for the other side.

Metal motor brackets

The metal type of bracket is slightly different; its assembly is shown in the following photos:

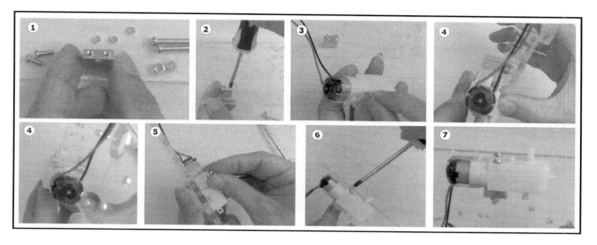

Assembling metal motor brackets

For this, perform the following steps:

1. You should be able to see two small screw holes in the top of the bracket; these are threaded. There will be two short screws per bracket.

2. The chassis will have holes in the wheel mount area that will match these. Line this up, and then screw the short screws through the chassis holes into the bracket.

3. Take the motor, and ensure the wires are facing away from you. Push the long screws through the two holes in the motor.

4. Then, take this motor assembly, and line up the long threads with the holes on the side of the bracket.

5. Now, push nuts onto the threads that stick out the other end of the bracket.

6. You can tighten the ones furthest from the chassis with pliers, or a spanner and a screwdriver. The ones closer will catch on one flat side, so you'll only need a screwdriver.

7. You will now have the completed assembly.

You will need to repeat this assembly for the other side. You should now have a motor mounted on each side.

Adding the castor wheel

Next, it is time to fit the castor wheel, as shown in the following image:

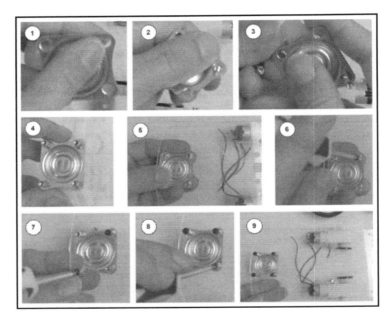

Fitting the castor wheel

Use these steps with the previous image:

1. This is the castor. It has four screw holes.
2. You need to push a metal screw through the hole so the thread is facing away from the wheel.
3. Now, screw one of the brass standoffs into this screw.
4. Repeat this for the four other sides.
5. Line the other side of the standoffs with the four holes on the chassis. Note that this castor wheel is a rectangle, not a square. Make sure the wheel is facing down.
6. Push one of the screws through and screw it down.
7. I suggest you screw the opposite corner.
8. This will make the remaining two screws easier to put in.
9. The cast should now be attached to the robot like this.

Putting the wheels on

The wheels now need to be pushed on, as shown in the following photos:

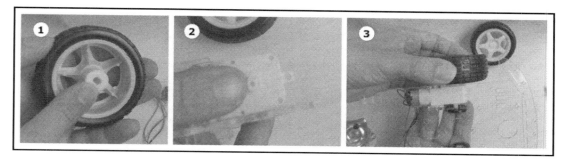

Fitting the wheels

Follow these steps:

1. First, note that they have two flattened sides in their axle hole, like the encoder wheel.
2. Line the wheels up with the axles, taking into account the flat edges, and push them on.
3. Sometimes, rotating the wheels until they push in helps. You should be able to push the wheel on, being sure to support the motor from the other side. After doing this, you may want to realign the encoder wheel with their slots.

Bringing the cables up

A last minor step in chassis assembly is to bring the cables up so you have access to them for later steps. Refer to the following photos, which shows the details:

Bringing the wires up

Perform the following steps:

1. First, gather the two wires from one motor. Locate the small slot in the middle of the chassis.
2. Push the wires through.
3. Gently pull them through to the top of the chassis so they are poking out as shown. Repeat this for the other motor.

We should now have a robot that looks like this (motor brackets will vary):

The assembled chassis

We're now ready to add the electronics.

Fitting the Raspberry Pi

We will not yet fit the motor controller, and will address that in the next chapter, but we can fit the Raspberry Pi now and prepare it to have other boards connected to it. We need to put standoffs on the Pi so it can be bolted onto the chassis, but leave room for the motor bracket mounting, and later sensors that will go under the Pi. The following photos show how:

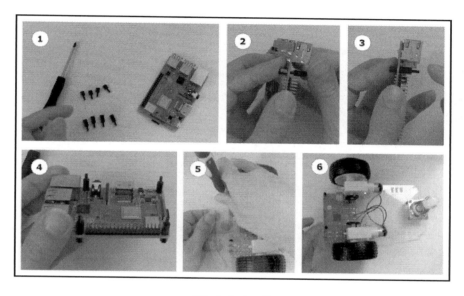

Fitting the Raspberry Pi

Perform the following steps:

1. For this, you will need a small posi screw driver, a small spanner or pliers, 2 x M2.5 screws, 4 x M2.5 16 mm standoffs with threads, 4 x M.25 10 mm standoffs, and the Raspberry Pi.
2. Push a 16 mm standoff thread up through the screw hole from the bottom of the Pi.
3. Then, screw a 10 mm standoff onto the top of these, with the thread facing upwards, using the pliers/spanner to hold the standoff.
4. Repeat for all four corners.
5. Line two of these up with some slots or screw holes on the chassis and screw them in from underneath.
6. On the chassis I used, there were only two holes that line up, so I screwed those in and used the other standoffs to keep the Pi level.

Adding the batteries

There are two sets of batteries that you have bought: the 4 x AA battery holder (with a set of rechargeable metal hydride batteries) and a USB power bank, which will contain a lithium ion cell and USB charging system.

We will mount these on the back of the robot, where they will counterbalance some of the sensors that we will later add.

The USB power bank

Do not connect the power bank to the Raspberry Pi yet (or be sure to log in and shut it down properly before pulling the power out if you have done so). The following photos show how I fitted the USB power bank:

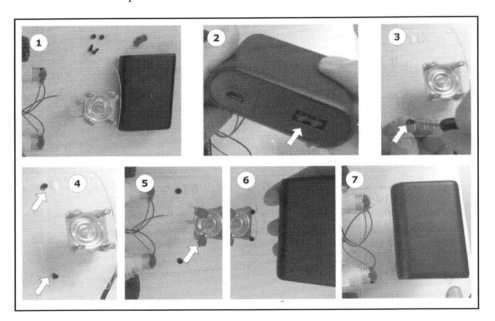

Mounting the power bank

For a chassis and power bank the same size as mine, use the following instructions:

1. For this power bank, we will use some hook and loop tape, two M3 screws and two M3 nuts, a screwdriver, and an M3 spanner or pliers.
2. Take a look at the power bank, and note that one side has the USB connector on it. This should end up on the left of the robot.
3. To mount it on this robot, I used two additional screws with nuts to support it, level with the screws from the castor wheel.
4. I've positioned them in these slots so the power bank is stable, and I used the spanner to tighten them up a little.
5. Measure out two lengths of the hook and loop tape (both sides) and stick them to the power bank.
6. Stick the other side to the robot.
7. Push the power supply down so the hook and loop engages. This connection will hold reasonably well.

Alternatives are to use sticky tack (for a really cheap but flimsy connection), cable ties, double sided tape, or rubber bands to hold the battery in place. These can be used for different sizes of battery.

Mounting the AA battery holder

The AA battery holder is a fairly simple part to add, as shown in the next photos:

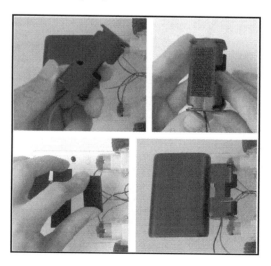

Mounting the AA battery holder

First, stick an adhesive hook and loop strip on the AA battery holder as shown, then stick a strip on the robot so the AA holder can be placed just in front of the power bank. Stick it down. **Do not insert the AA batteries yet.**

At a pinch, sticky tack can be used for this, as the AA battery box needs to be removable to replace the cells in it.

The completed robot base

You will now have a completed the robot base, and in the next chapter we can add the motor controller and start wiring it. It should look something like the following photo:

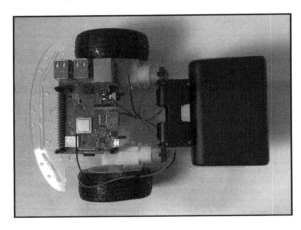

The completed chassis

Summary

You've now learned how to choose the parts for a robot, and some of the reasoning and design decisions that have gone into this one. You've seen how to use a simple tool to test fit these parts and see what will work before buying anything. You've then bought the parts, and built your starting robot platform.

In the next chapter, we will fit the motor controller, then start writing the code to get this platform moving.

Questions

Answer the following questions, based on the topics covered:

- Why is it a good idea when using multiple Raspberry Pi "hats" or "bonnets" to look at the pin usage?
- Why have we chosen to power the Pi separately from the motors?
- What are the consequences of too small a motor controller?
- Why do I recommend test fitting before buying any parts?

Further reading

Refer to the following book:

- More robot chassis designs can be found in *Raspberry Pi Robotic Blueprints* by Dr. Richard Grimmett, including modifying an RC car into a robot.

Drive and Turn - Moving Motors with Python

7

In this chapter, we will take the robot we started building in the last chapter, connect the motors to the Raspberry Pi, and build the Python code to make them move. We will cover programming techniques to create a layer between the physical robot and its behavior code to reduce the impact of hardware changes. The robot will move! We will finish by taking the robot on a small set path.

The following topics will be covered in this chapter:

- How to connect motors to the Raspberry Pi
- How to test motors with simple code
- How to steer the robot—thinking about interfaces
- How to make a robot code object, a layer of code for the motors and chassis
- How to make the robot drive a repeatable path

Technical requirements

For this chapter, you will require the following:

- A computer with access to the internet
- The chassis built in the previous chapter
- The motor controller bought in the last chapter
- Jewelers' screwdrivers
- A USB-to-Micro USB cable (which should have come with the power bank on the assembled chassis)
- Four AA batteries from the last chapter, charged
- A 2-meter-square flat space for the robot to drive on

Be prepared to catch your driving robot going over the edges if you use a table! It's best to use the floor.

Check out the following video to see the Code in Action:

`http://bit.ly/2RcphGM`

Connecting the motors to the Raspberry Pi

In this section, we are trying to connect the motor to the Raspberry Pi. The following is the block diagram that we are aiming for as our output:

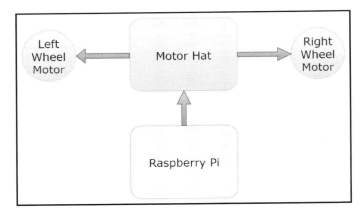

Block diagram of the robot

The first step in connecting the motors is to fit the motor hat onto the Raspberry Pi. The motor hat should look like the following:

The full function stepper motor hat

In this section, we will attach this hat to our robot, and wire it in so we can start programming our robot. The following photo shows how:

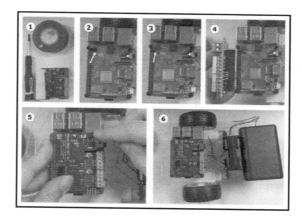

Fitting the motor controller

Perform the following steps :

1. You will need the controller board (remove the foam strip if it has one), insulation tape, and a small screwdriver.
2. The Raspberry Pi 3B+, mounted on the robot chassis, has four pins (indicated by the red arrow in the preceding photo). Other Pi models do not have this. This will need to be insulated from any terminals on the motor board above.

3. On the underside of the motor control board, place a strip of insulating tape, as shown, to cover any metal that could make contact with these four pins.
4. Line up the motor board socket with the Pi header. The four holes in the corners should also line up with the screw threads facing up.
5. Gently and evenly push the motor board onto the Raspberry Pi, guiding the screw threads through until the board is firmly seated on the GPIO header.
6. The robot should now look like image 6 in the preceding photo.

Wiring in

We'll start with a diagram. Right now, we won't wire in the ground (black) wire on the batteries until we are ready to power it up. I suggest using a little insulation tape to tape the tip of it down to a plastic part of the chassis, so it does not catch on anything.

The following diagram is kind of a makeshift switch:

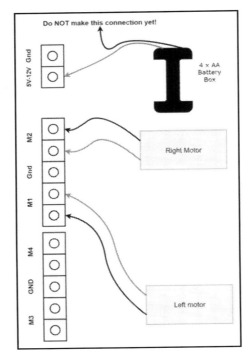

How to wire up the motors and batteries

As you connect up, it should look like the preceding diagram.

The following photo shows the steps for the connections:

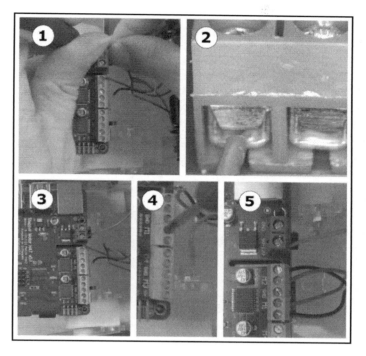

Steps for connecting the wires

Perform the following steps to connect the wires:

1. Loosen up the screw terminals for the 5V-12V terminal (vIn), GND, the two M2 connectors, and the M1 connectors.
2. Push the red wire from the AA battery box into the screw terminal marked 5V-12V, so the metal part of the wire is in the slot formed by the metal cover.
3. Screw it down firmly, it should look like as image 3, the wire should not pull out easily. Ensure that it is the metal part that is being held, and not the plastic part of the wire, its insulation.
4. Repeat for the motor terminals, making the connections shown in image 4.
5. The result should look like image 5.

Independent power

So far, although we have been using a headless display, we have been plugging our Raspberry Pi into the wall. Now it is time to try powering it independently for the next few steps. Refer to the following photo:

Going onto independent power

Perform the following steps:

1. Plug the Micro USB (tiny) end of the cable into the Pi in the USB micro-socket indicated by the arrow in image 1 in the preceding photo.
2. Fit the four AA batteries; you may need to pop the battery box up and push it back down again after this.
3. You can power up the motor board now by wiring the black wire from the motor into the GND terminal indicated by the arrow in image 3, next to 5V-12V. When you do so, a light should appear on the motor board to show it is active.

4. Turn on the Pi by plugging the USB A (wide) end into the power bank. The intention from here is to keep the micro-USB tiny end in, and only connect/disconnect the USB A (wide) end when powering the Pi.

5. The Raspberry Pi and motor board are now powered, as shown in image 5.

Congratulations, your robot is now running on independent power.

 SD cards can become corrupted by removing power from the Pi without shutting it down properly. When you plan to turn it off, please ensure you use the notes from Chapter 4, *Preparing a Raspberry Pi for a Robot - Headless by Default*, to log in with PuTTY and shutdown the Raspberry Pi properly before removing power.

Writing code to test your motors

We will need to download the library to work with the motor board we have chosen. Many robot parts, apart from the simplest ones, have an interface library to control the motors and other devices on the board. It's time to log in to your Pi, using PuTTY again.

Preparing libraries

We will download this code from a project on GitHub using Git, but featuring the Raspberry Pi. So, first, we will need to put Git on the Pi; we are also going to need I2C (i2c-tools and python-smbus) and pip so we can install things into Python. Type the following command:

```
pi@myrobot:~ $ sudo apt-get install -y git python-pip python-smbus i2c-tools
```

It will now install these tools for you.

Now, to get the library, we'll use Git and download it from GitHub, installing it for use in any of your scripts with the following command:

```
pi@myrobot:~ $ pip install git+https://github.com/orionrobots/Raspi_MotorHAT
Collecting git+https://github.com/orionrobots/Raspi_MotorHAT
  Cloning https://github.com/orionrobots/Raspi_MotorHAT to /tmp/pip-c3sFoy-build
Installing collected packages: Raspi-MotorHAT
  Running setup.py install for Raspi-MotorHAT ... done
Successfully installed Raspi-MotorHAT-0.0.1
```

We now have the libraries prepared for starting the robot. Documentation for the `Raspi_MotorHAT` library is sparse, but can be found at `https://github.com/orionrobots/Raspi_MotorHAT` along with some examples of using it.

Test – finding the motor hat

The Raspberry Pi uses I2C to connect to this motor hat. **I2C buses** let you send and receive data, and are flexible in that we can connect many devices to the same bus. To enable I2C, you'll need to use `raspi-config` again. We'll enable SPI while we are here. Type the following command:

```
$ sudo raspi-config
```

Now, we use advanced settings on this. The following screenshot shows how:

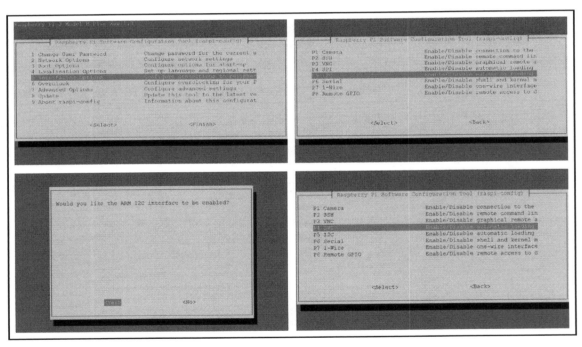

Using raspi-config to enable SPI and I2C

First, select **Interfacing Options**, then **I2C**. The Pi will ask if you want this interface to be enabled. Select **YES**. You will then be back at the **Interfacing Options** screen. Since we will soon need it, select **SPI** and **YES** again. Finally, press Esc twice to finish `raspi-config`. It will ask if you want to reboot. Select **YES**, then wait for the Pi to reboot and reconnect to the Raspberry Pi.

With I2C, we need a way to say which device we are talking to. Just like houses in a street, an address allows us to say which one we specifically want.

We should check that the Raspberry Pi is able to see the motor hat with `sudo i2cdetect -y 1`:

```
pi@myrobot:~ $ sudo i2cdetect -y 1
     0  1  2  3  4  5  6  7  8  9  a  b  c  d  e  f
00: -- -- -- -- -- -- -- -- -- -- -- -- --
10: -- -- -- -- -- -- -- -- -- -- -- -- -- -- -- --
20: -- -- -- -- -- -- -- -- -- -- -- -- -- -- -- --
30: -- -- -- -- -- -- -- -- -- -- -- -- -- -- -- --
40: -- -- -- -- -- -- -- -- -- -- -- -- -- -- -- --
50: -- -- -- -- -- -- -- -- -- -- -- -- -- -- -- --
60: -- -- -- -- -- -- -- -- -- -- -- -- -- -- -- 6f
70: 70 -- -- -- -- -- -- --
```

This scans the I2C bus 1 for devices attached to our Raspberry Pi. It shows numbers at the addresses if something is found. The device found at addresses `6f` and `70` is our motor controller. If you cannot see this, power down the Raspberry Pi, and carefully check that the insulation tape is present over the pins shown in the preceding photo, and that the motor hat has been plugged in, then try again.

The addresses are hexadecimal, so each digit counts to 16 instead of 10. When used in code, these will get an `0x` prefix. Note this is "zero" and then lower case "x".

Test – the motors move

Next, we need a test file to demonstrate that the motors work.

Create the following file, called `test_motors.py`:

```
from Raspi_MotorHAT import Raspi_MotorHAT

import time
import atexit

mh = Raspi_MotorHAT(addr=0x6f)
```

```
lm = mh.getMotor(1)
rm = mh.getMotor(2)

def turn_off_motors():
    lm.run(Raspi_MotorHAT.RELEASE)
    rm.run(Raspi_MotorHAT.RELEASE)

atexit.register(turn_off_motors)

lm.setSpeed(150)
rm.setSpeed(150)

lm.run(Raspi_MotorHAT.FORWARD)
rm.run(Raspi_MotorHAT.FORWARD)
time.sleep(1)
```

Now, upload it to your Raspberry Pi (using the methods found in Chapter 5, *Backing Up the Code with Git and SD Card Copies*).

 Move your robot from your desk and down to the floor for this next step, as it is will move and may not go in the direction you expect it to!

To run this code, through PuTTY on the Pi, type the following:

```
pi@myrobot:~ $ python test_motors.py
```

Your robot should now drive roughly forward. It may move slightly off, but it should not be turning or going backward and both motors should be moving.

Troubleshooting

If you see any problems, try this troubleshooting chart and go back:

Symptom	Likely cause and solution
You see: **ImportError: No module named smbus**	You have missed the step installing the required packages. Ensure you have followed the `apt-get` install steps above.
You see other errors	Please go back and carefully check that you have typed and uploaded the code above to the Raspberry Pi.
One or both sides are going backwards	The motor wires are the wrong way. On the motor terminals only, swap the black and red wire. Refer to the *How to wire up the motors and batteries* photo for help.

The light is on the controller, but one or both motors are not moving.	Please ensure that both motors wires are firmly screwed into the terminals. Please see the steps in the *Wiring in* section.
No light on the motor controller and no movement	Please make sure you have attached both the battery wires into the correct terminals, as shown in the *Independent power* section. Please ensure that your batteries are well charged.
Turning or veering	Some veer will be expected. If it is sever, ensure that both motors' connections are good, and that neither the wheels nor the encoder disks are binding/caught on the chassis.

How does this code work?

The first few lines are imports. Let's take a look at the code:

```
from Raspi_MotorHAT import Raspi_MotorHAT

import time
import atexit
```

The `Raspi_MotorHAT` library is the one we installed for interacting with our motors. The `time` library allows us to work with time; in this case, we will use it for a delay between starting and stopping motors.

The `atexit` library allows us to run code when this file exits.

In the following lines, we will connect to the motor hat and the two motors we have connected:

```
mh = Raspi_MotorHAT(addr=0x6f)
lm = mh.getMotor(1)
rm = mh.getMotor(2)
```

The first line here makes a `Raspi_MotorHAT` object with the I2C address passed in as `addr`, which we saw in the scan, `0x6f`. We call the returned object `mh`, as an abbreviation for **m**otor **h**at.

We then create shortcuts to access the motors, `lm` for **l**eft **m**otor and `rm` for **r**ight **m**otor. We get these motor controls from the `mh` object, using the motor number shown on the board. Motor 1 is left and motor 2 is right.

We will now define a function, `turn_off_motors`, which will run the `Raspi_MotorHAT.RELEASE` on each motor on this board—an instruction to make the motors stop:

```
def turn_off_motors():
    lm.run(Raspi_MotorHAT.RELEASE)
    rm.run(Raspi_MotorHAT.RELEASE)
atexit.register(turn_off_motors)
```

We then pass that into `atexit.register(turn_off_motors)`, a command that will run when this file finishes—when Python exits. This will run even when there are errors. Without this, the code following could break in some interesting way and the robot will keep driving. Robots without this kind of safeguard have a habit of driving off tables and into walls. If they carry on trying to drive when their motors are stuck, it is bad for the motors, motor controllers, and batteries, so it's better to stop.

The speed of the motors for this controller/library ranges from 0 to 255. Our code sets the speed of each motor to just above half speed, and then runs the `Raspi_MotorHAT.FORWARD` mode, which makes each motor drive forward:

```
lm.setSpeed(150)
rm.setSpeed(150)

lm.run(Raspi_MotorHAT.FORWARD)
rm.run(Raspi_MotorHAT.FORWARD)
```

Finally, we ask the code to wait for one second:

```
time.sleep(1)
```

This allows the motors to run in their forward drive mode for one second. The program will then exit. Since we told it to stop motors when the code exits, the motors will stop after this one second.

Steering a robot

Now we've made a robot drive forward. But how do we steer it? How will it turn left or right?

There are a few major forms of steering. We'll take a look at a few, settle on the one our robot actually has available to use, and write some test code to demonstrate it.

Types of steering

The most common techniques for steering a wheeled vehicle (including a robot) fall into two major categories, with a couple of slightly unusual variants.

Steerable wheels

In movable wheels, one or more wheel in a robot can be turned in a different direction from the others. When the robot drives, the differently positioned wheel will make the robot turn. The following diagram shows how:

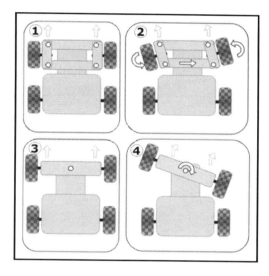

Rack and pinion steering above, and wagon steering below

The preceding diagram shows two common styles of movable wheel steering on a robot. The direction of movement is shown by the green arrows. Changes to the shape of the robot and the angle of the wheels are shown by the white arrows. Refer to these points:

1. Rack and pinion is commonly used in cars. When straight, the car will go forward.
2. When one bar is moved, shown by the black and white arrows, the car will turn.

3. The other common type is wagon style steering, used in homemade racing karts. When straight it goes forward.
4. When the front bar is turned, the vehicle will turn.

Variants include robots with the ability to independently turn each wheel and drive sideways; Ackerman steering, where the proportion by which wheels rotate is different; and rear steering where a front set of wheels and rear set of wheels steer—used in long vehicles. The photo below shows a robot with a turning set of front wheels:

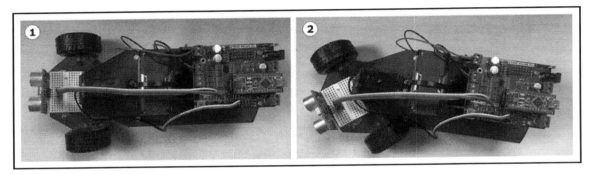

Wagon steering Unotron robot with Arduino Nano controller (built by my son with my assistance)

An example of steering in a robot is the Unotron chassis kit from 4Tronix. The previous photo shows a robot my son built with the Unotron kit. There is a single motor-driven wheel at the back. The two front wheels are steered by a servo motor that turns the whole front plate.

The disadvantages with this type of steering are related to space, weight, and complexity. A chassis set up for movable wheel steering requires more moving parts and space to house them. Unotron is as simple as it gets. There is more complexity, which can lead to required maintenance.

The distance needed to make a turn (known as the turning circle) or for robots with steerable wheel systems tends to be longer, as these must drive forward/backward to steer.

You will require one large motor for the fixed axle, as you will not be able to distribute power across two motors, at least not without complex mechanisms to balance the input. If the mechanism is not completely centered after steering, the robot will veer.

Fixed wheels

More common in robots are fixed-wheel steered robots. This is where the wheels' axes are fixed in relation to the chassis. The relative speed of each wheel or set of wheels sets the direction of the robot. That is, the wheels will not turn from side to side; however, by one side going faster than the other, the robot can make turns. The common use case for this is known as skid steering. Look at the following diagram:

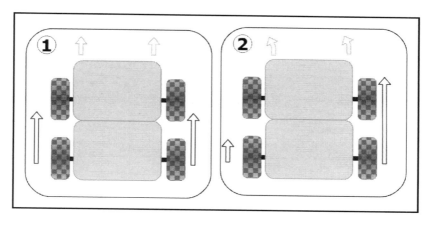

Fixed wheel steering or skid steering

The diagram above shows this in action. In this case, the white arrows show the relative speed of the motors. The green arrows show the direction of the robot:

- In the first image, the motors are going at the the same speed, so the robot is driving straight forward.
- In the second image, the motors on the right are going fast, the motors on the left are going slow. The robot will be driving forward and left.

These have a number of advantages. If you intend to use tank tracks, you will need this type of drive system. It is mechanically simple in that a drive motor per wheel is all that is needed to make turns. The code for this is still simple, where turning can be made by driving one side faster and, in the case of a pair of sensors, sensor feedback can drive motor speeds per side. Skid steering allows a robot to turn on the spot, doing a full 360 degrees—essentially in a turning circle the width of the widest/longest part of the robot.

There are some disadvantages to using this, though. When turning, some wheels are being dragged sideways, causing a lot of friction. Also, as there are motors on each side, with motor controller parts per side, any minor differences in the motors, their gearing, or the controller output can result in a veer.

Other steering systems

The controller we are using on our robot actually allows us to control four motor channels. We are not using it this way in this book, but this can be used for some special wheel types known as Mecanum wheels, which allow skid steering style motions along with crabbing motions where a robot can drive left or right without turning. Technically, this is still fixed wheel steering. The following photo shows a base with Mecanum wheels:

Mecanum wheels on the Uranus Pod by Gwpcmu [CC BY 3.0 (https://creativecommons.org/licenses/by/3.0)]

These are amazingly flexible but mechanically complex, high maintenance, heavy, and expensive. They are fun though.

Steering the robot we are building

Based on the three wheel chassis we have chosen, with one castor wheel, and then a driven wheel on each side, independently controlled, we will be using skid steering. By varying the speed and direction of these, we will steer our robot. We can also spin 360 degrees with it. The castor negates the problem mentioned with the drag seen on four and six wheel skid steer robots.

We can demonstrate how simple the code is by making the robot spin on the spot with one change to the previous code. Spinning is done by making one motor go backward while the other goes forward. We already have motors going forward. If you look at `test_motors.py`, there are the following lines:

```
lm.run(Raspi_MotorHAT.FORWARD)
rm.run(Raspi_MotorHAT.FORWARD)
```

You can modify this so one of them goes BACKWARD:

```
lm.run(Raspi_MotorHAT.FORWARD)
rm.run(Raspi_MotorHAT.BACKWARD)
```

Run this on the Pi with `python turn_motors.py` and your robot will now spin to the right. Swap them so left (lm) is BACKWARD and right (rm) is FORWARD and it will spin the other way.

What about less aggressive turns? In the previous code, before the direction lines, we also set the speed of each motor:

```
lm.setSpeed(150)
rm.setSpeed(150)

lm.run(Raspi_MotorHAT.FORWARD)
rm.run(Raspi_MotorHAT.FORWARD)
```

We can make a gentler turn by resetting lm and rm direction mode to FORWARD, and then making one of the speeds smaller in relation to the other:

```
lm.setSpeed(50)
rm.setSpeed(150)

lm.run(Raspi_MotorHAT.FORWARD)
rm.run(Raspi_MotorHAT.FORWARD)
```

This will make the robot drive forward and turn gently to the left.

The robot object – code for our experiments to talk to the robot

Now we have seen how to move and turn our robot, we come on to a layer of software to group up some of the hardware functions, but isolate them from behavior. Why would we want that? When we chose our motor controller, we made a lot of trade-offs to arrive at one that works for our project. Motor controllers are one of the parts of a robot that can change, because the considerations change or we simply want to build our next robot. Although broadly having two motors and controlling the speed and direction is the same kind of operation, each controller does it slightly differently, so creating a layer in front of it makes a facade—we get to use the same commands to it, even if it changes.

Each controller has a quirks. With this one, we set a run mode and speed. Many controllers use zero to mean stop, but this one uses a RELEASE mode, which is slightly different from speed 0 where the motors are held. Controllers often use negative numbers to mean to go backward; this one has a BACKWARD mode. The speed values on this controller go from 0-255. Some go from -128 to 128, or 0-10. What we can do is to create an object with an interface to hide quirks specific to this controller.

Why make this object?

An interface is designed to give you a way to interact with some other code. It creates a way to simplify, or make more consistent, different underlying systems to make them behave the same way, like all of the types of motor controller mentioned. Refer to the following block diagram:

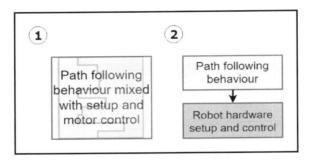

Software layers

It also provides a way to cleanly separate parts of code into layers. Different layers means that you are able to change one part of some code, without it making huge changes in another. In the previous diagram, panel 1 shows a block of code that has different systems mixed together. It will be hard to change; adding a new behavior or swapping the motor controller in this code would be quite tricky.

The code represented by panel 2 shows two separate systems interacting. They have a relationship where the **Path Following Behavior** is in control of the **Robot hardware setup and control** code.

If we write a new behavior, we can use the hardware control library again. We will be writing many behaviors, and we will be able to reuse the robot object throughout, perhaps extending it occasionally. After all, who wants to keep writing the same code?

This common interface means we could make an object that looks the same from the outside on other robots, and our behaviors will still work. So, if the motor board changes, we won't need to modify the behavior code.

The **Robot hardware setup/control** block in the second panel of the previous photo and *Mecanum wheels on the Uranus Pod by Gwpcmu* will be our `Robot` object. It is a real version of our interface. It will hide the quirks of our "full function Stepper Hat" board.

What will we put in the robot object?

The following code will do the following:

- We need to have the motor hat set up
- We want it to deal with the `exit` state
- We want a `stop_motors` function that will stop motors
- Let's use percentages to mean speeds—values of 0 to 100. We can map this to what the controller really wants
- The modes are particular to this controller or it's library. We can use negative values to mean going backward
- It will also later act as a "gatekeeper" to data buses that require code to hold exclusive locks on them and some of the hardware
- Our interface (therefore our object) will not contain the behavior, other than the stopping on exit safeguard

We will put it in a new file, named `robot.py`:

```python
from Raspi_MotorHAT import Raspi_MotorHAT

import atexit

class Robot(object):
    def __init__(self, motorhat_addr=0x6f):
        # Setup the motorhat with the passed in address
        self._mh = Raspi_MotorHAT(addr=motorhat_addr)

        # get local variable for each motor
        self.left_motor = self._mh.getMotor(1)
        self.right_motor  = self._mh.getMotor(2)

        # ensure the motors get stopped when the code exits
        atexit.register(self.stop_motors)
```

```
def stop_motors(self):
    self.left_motor.run(Raspi_MotorHAT.RELEASE)
    self.right_motor.run(Raspi_MotorHAT.RELEASE)
```

Note there are comments in the init, stating what these fragments of code do. So far, our `Robot` object has set up our motor hat and has a way to stop the motors. The code is the same setup code we have seen before, but structured slightly differently. When we create a `Robot` object, this code will set up the motor hat, get the left and right motors, and register a stop system.

We can test this in another file named `behavior_path.py`:

```
import robot
from Raspi_MotorHAT import Raspi_MotorHAT
from time import sleep

r = robot.Robot()
r.left_motor.setSpeed(150)
r.right_motor.setSpeed(150)
r.left_motor.run(Raspi_MotorHAT.FORWARD)
r.right_motor.run(Raspi_MotorHAT.FORWARD)
sleep(1)
```

This starts by pulling in the `robot.py` file we just created with an import. It will go forward for one second and stop. But we still have to set speeds specific to this board (not out of 100). Let's fix that in **robot.py** (new code will be in bold):

```
from Raspi_MotorHAT import Raspi_MotorHAT

import atexit

class Robot(object):
    def __init__(self, motorhat_addr=0x6f):
        self._mh = Raspi_MotorHAT(addr=motorhat_addr)

        self.left_motor = self._mh.getMotor(1)
        self.right_motor = self._mh.getMotor(2)
        atexit.register(self.stop_motors)

    def convert_speed(self, speed):
        return (speed * 255) / 100

    def stop_motors(self):
        self.left_motor.run(Raspi_MotorHAT.RELEASE)
        self.right_motor.run(Raspi_MotorHAT.RELEASE)
```

We can now use `convert_speed`, to use speeds from 0 to 100. This will return us speeds from 0 to 255 for this motor hat. For other motor hats, this would return something else.

We do this by multiplying the speed by 255 and dividing by 100—this is a standard way of turning a percentage into a fraction of the 255. We multiply first because we are doing integer (whole number) maths, and dividing 80/100 with whole numbers will give 0, but dividing (80*255) by 100 will give 204.

This is still unwieldy though—to use it, we need this in `behavior_line.py`:

```
import robot
from Raspi_MotorHAT import Raspi_MotorHAT
from time import sleep

r = robot.Robot()
r.left_motor.setSpeed(r.convert_speed(80))
r.right_motor.setSpeed(r.convert_speed(80))
r.left_motor.run(Raspi_MotorHAT.FORWARD)
r.right_motor.run(Raspi_MotorHAT.FORWARD)
sleep(1)
```

This still uses the `run` and `setSpeed` methods of the `motorHat` code, which are specific to this control board. Other boards don't work the same way. So, let's wrap it further:

```
from Raspi_MotorHAT import Raspi_MotorHAT

import atexit

class Robot(object):
    def __init__(self, motorhat_addr=0x6f):
        # Setup the motorhat with the passed in address
        self._mh = Raspi_MotorHAT(addr=motorhat_addr)

        # get local variable for each motor
        self.left_motor = self._mh.getMotor(1)
        self.right_motor  = self._mh.getMotor(2)

        # ensure the motors get stopped when the code exits
        atexit.register(self.stop_motors)

    def convert_speed(self, speed):
        return (speed * 255) / 100

    def set_left(self, speed):
        self.left_motor.setSpeed(self.convert_speed(speed))

    def set_right(self, speed):
```

```
        self.right_motor.setSpeed(self.convert_speed(speed))
def stop_motors(self):
        self.left_motor.run(Raspi_MotorHAT.RELEASE)
        self.right_motor.run(Raspi_MotorHAT.RELEASE)
```

In this update, I've added the `set_left` and `set_right` methods. These take a speed as a percentage and set the speed using the `motor.setSpeed` method internally. This still leaves us with the motor `run` function. In many of my robots, as mentioned previously, I use negative values to mean the motor goes backward.

This is a bit trickier. We need to do two things:

- Determine if the speed is above, below, or equal to zero and set the mode for the `run` function
- Remove the sign from the speed for `setSpeed` so it's always a positive value

We can use a simple `if` logic to get the `run` command. We can replace the `convert_speed` method in the class to return a mode and positive value. I've used comments to show the two sections to this function:

```
def convert_speed(self, speed):
    # Choose the running mode
    mode = Raspi_MotorHAT.RELEASE
    if speed > 0:
        mode = Raspi_MotorHAT.FORWARD
    elif speed < 0:
        mode = Raspi_MotorHAT.BACKWARD

    # Scale the speed
    output_speed = (abs(speed) * 255) / 100
    return mode, int(output_speed)
```

So, the default mode that we will get at zero is RELEASE, or stop. If the speed is above 0, we return the FORWARD mode, and if it's below 0, we return BACKWARD.

We then add one more operation to our speed calculation: `abs(number)`. This returns the absolute value, which removes the sign from a number. For example, -80 and 80 will both come out as 80.

We then need to change our motor movement methods to use this speed conversion:

```
def set_left(self, speed):
    mode, output_speed = self.convert_speed(speed)
    self.left_motor.setSpeed(output_speed)
    self.left_motor.run(mode)
```

```
    def set_right(self, speed):
        mode, output_speed = self.convert_speed(speed)
        self.right_motor.setSpeed(output_speed)
        self.right_motor.run(mode)
```

So, for each motor, we will get the mode, output speed from the passed-in speed, then call setSpeed and run.

The whole of robot.py should now look like this the following:

```
from Raspi_MotorHAT import Raspi_MotorHAT

import atexit

class Robot(object):
    def __init__(self, motorhat_addr=0x6f):
        # Setup the motorhat with the passed in address
        self._mh = Raspi_MotorHAT(addr=motorhat_addr)

        # get local variable for each motor
        self.left_motor = self._mh.getMotor(1)
        self.right_motor = self._mh.getMotor(2)

        # ensure the motors get stopped when the code exits
        atexit.register(self.stop_motors)

    def convert_speed(self, speed):
        # Choose the running mode
        mode = Raspi_MotorHAT.RELEASE
        if speed > 0:
            mode = Raspi_MotorHAT.FORWARD
        elif speed < 0:
            mode = Raspi_MotorHAT.BACKWARD
        # Scale the speed
        output_speed = (abs(speed) * 255) / 100
        return mode, int(output_speed)

    def set_left(self, speed):
        mode, output_speed = self.convert_speed(speed)
        self.left_motor.setSpeed(output_speed)
        self.left_motor.run(mode)

    def set_right(self, speed):
        mode, output_speed = self.convert_speed(speed)
        self.right_motor.setSpeed(output_speed)
        self.right_motor.run(mode)
```

```
def stop_motors(self):
        self.left_motor.run(Raspi_MotorHAT.RELEASE)
        self.right_motor.run(Raspi_MotorHAT.RELEASE)
```

Our simple behavior in `behaviour_line.py` is now only a few lines:

```
import robot
from time import sleep

r = robot.Robot()
r.set_left(80)
r.set_right(80)
sleep(1)
```

This simplification means we can build on this code to create more behaviors. What is more fun, is because I have a common interface Robot object for my big robot, ArmBot, or my other Raspberry Pi robots, I could take this `behavior_lines.py` and run the same code on them. They would all go forward for one second at 80% of their motor speed.

Write a script to follow a predetermined path

So, we now get to the first behavior that feels like a robot.

Let's make a quick sketch of a path for us to get our robot to follow:

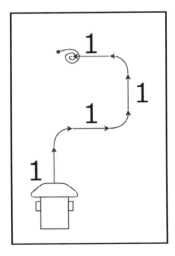

Path for our robot

In the previous diagram, I've drawn a path. The straight lines are for driving forward, the 1s mean one second. We don't yet have a way to consider distance traveled, only time. We may be able to guess at times relative to distances, but they will not be very precise. The gentle curves are a turn where we slow one motor down with respect to the other.

The final spiral means a victory spin on the spot when the path is complete—we can do this by putting one motor in reverse while the other drives forward.

Let's write this code. First, we want the imports, sleep and robot. But before we do anything, let's make some helper functions for this behavior. I called my file behavior_path.py:

```python
import robot
from time import import sleep

def straight(bot, seconds):
    bot.set_left(80)
    bot.set_right(80)
    sleep(seconds)

def turn_left(bot, seconds):
    bot.set_left(20)
    bot.set_right(80)
    sleep(seconds)

def turn_right(bot, seconds):
    bot.set_left(80)
    bot.set_right(20)
    sleep(seconds)

def spin_left(bot, seconds):
    bot.set_left(-80)
    bot.set_right(80)
    sleep(seconds)
```

The helpers use much the same language we described the behavior in. We have straight, turn_left, turn_right and spin_left. These are not in the robot object because other behaviors may use more continuous behavior than this. I've called the robot object bot now, because one letter variable names such as r become less easy to find, read, or reason about when there is more code.

These helpers each set the motor speeds, then sleep for a determined number of seconds. We can then create the robot object and sequence them by adding this to `behavior_path.py`:

```
bot = robot.Robot()
straight(bot, 1)
turn_right(bot, 1)
straight(bot, 1)
turn_left(bot, 1)
straight(bot, 1)
turn_left(bot, 1)
straight(bot, 1)
spin_left(bot, 1)
```

Now, we can upload this to the Raspberry Pi and run it via PuTTY with the following:

```
$ python behavior_path.py
```

Now, if your robot is anything like mine, you saw it drive and make turns, but the turns have overshot by some way and the robot may be veering to one side. We can fix the overshoot here by reducing the amount of time in the turn steps:

```
bot = robot.Robot()
straight(bot, 1)
turn_right(bot, 0.6)
straight(bot, 1)
turn_left(bot, 0.6)
straight(bot, 1)
turn_left(bot, 0.6)
straight(bot, 1)
spin_left(bot, 1)
```

You will need to tweak these values to get close to 90 degree turns. This takes patience: change them and upload them. This is a crude form of **calibration**—tuning values in our code to match the quirks of our robot.

You may be able to account for some of the veer by tuning one motor to be slower in the straight function:

```
def straight(bot, seconds):
    bot.set_left(80)
    bot.set_right(70)
    sleep(seconds)
```

But this will hold up for a while and may be hard to fine tune. Why do we get this veer?

Motor speeds can vary, even those from the same manufacturers. Add to this variations in wheel diameters, axle positioning, weight distribution, slippery or uneven surfaces, and motor controller sides (less likely) and it's easy to see that you are actually unlikely to get a perfectly straight line from a robot this way. Depending on what sensors we are following, this may or may not be a problem. To account for this problem, we will introduce encoders/speed sensors in a later chapter and calibrate those sensors to get a more accurate version of a path behavior.

Without sensors, a robot is not able to determine where it is or if it has bumped into anything, so if it ran into a wall, you probably had to go and move it to where it had room to move.

Summary

In this chapter, we've learned how to connect the motors to the Raspberry Pi via the motor control board. We've then powered it up and downloaded, then installed the libraries for it. We've demonstrated our motors work, and then started building a first layer of code for our behaviors to use, while seeing how a layer like that could be made for different robots. We saw our robot move in a path and tuned it, while finding out some of the shortcomings from using motors without any sensors.

In the following chapters, we will start adding sensors and building behaviors using these sensors.

Questions

Answer the following questions:

1. Why do we use the `atexit.register` mechanism?
2. How can we correct a motor going the wrong way?
3. What are the main advantages of a common interface for a `Robot` object?
4. How must the motors move relative to each other to make this robot turn?

Further reading

- For more information on the style used for the `Robot` object, along with the use of similar interfaces and classes, I recommend *Learning Object-Oriented Programming* by Gastón C. Hillar, which not only works through these concepts in Python, but takes them more generally and show them how they apply also to C# and JavaScript languages.

8
Programming Line-Following Sensors Using Python

This is the first chapter where you will be using sensors. Sensors allow a robot to react to its environment in some way, which allows the start of real robot-like behavior. We will be adding line sensors to our robot, and then creating line-sensing behavior, as seen in robots used in industries such as warehouses. Line sensing can be performed using hidden lines such as wires under a floor, but it's far easier to use visible lines. Visible lines can be detected using either a camera or simple optical sensors bouncing light off the floor below and detecting the level of light coming back.

In this chapter, we'll learn the following:

- How to attach line sensors to your robot and wire them to the Pi
- How to paint yourself a line follower test track
- How to write code to test sensors and tune them to see them working
- How to use sensors to write a line-following behavior in Python

Technical requirements

For this chapter, you will require the following:

- A computer with access to the internet.
- A robot fitted with the Raspberry Pi.
- The robot code object from Chapter 7, *Drive and Turn – Moving Motors with Python*.
- A screwdriver (pozi, for 2 or 2.5M).
- A pair of long nose pliers.
- Some male to female jumper cables—also known as Jumper Jerky and DuPont cables. The male-to-female bit is really important!

- A **Small Plus** size 400 tie point breadboard.
- 3M nylon standoff and bolts kit
- Two line tracking/following/tracing digital sensor modules. The black/blue lens parts on the modules is the actual sensor. Modules KY-033 or Tcrt5000 are suitable. Do not get the analog type sensor unless it also has digital output. Take note if it outputs high or low for detecting white objects. If white objects are low, you will need the following `pull_up=True`.
- Large-format paper sheets—A2 is good.
- A black marker pen.

The code for this chapter is at `https://github.com/PacktPublishing/Learn-Robotics-Fundamentals-of-Robotics-Programming/chapter8`.

Check out the following video to see the Code in Action:

`http://bit.ly/2zvYNce`

Attaching line sensors to the robot and Raspberry Pi

In this section, we will get to know the parts we are about to use and then mount them on the robot, wiring up to the Pi.

What are optical line sensors?

There are a few types of sensor that can be used. One type is known as **hall sensors**, which can detect magnetic strips or current carrying cables. The other type are **optical sensors**. Basic optical line sensing bounces infrared light off of whatever is below the robot. It then detects the intensity of the reflected light.

These send a data value depending on this. The sensor we will use turns this intensity into a binary, 1 or 0, value by seeing if the detected light passes a threshold. The following photo shows the sensors:

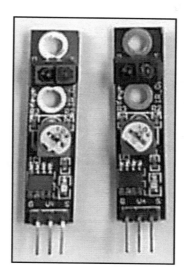

A pair of line sensors

The previous photo shows a typical pair of inexpensive optical line sensors. Between the two mounting holes, you can see there are black and blue lenses. These are the optical element. This element should be as close as it can be to the surface we are sensing, without causing the robot to drag.

Below the optical element (and a mounting hole) is an adjustment element. This adjustment sets the threshold that the sensors go from 0 to 1, based on the reflected light. One of the steps we will take when they are turned on is to adjust these.

What other new parts will we use?

In this chapter, to wire and attach sensors to the robot, we are introducing two other robot parts. The following photo shows a bunch of jumper wires and a breadboard:

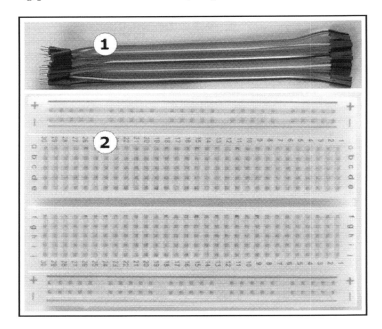

Some of the required tools

In the previous photo, there are jumper wires (1) and a breadboard (2). Jumper wires allow you to *jump* connections from one part to another, making connections between them. The breadboard lets you push wires and components into it, and also to make connections between them. The green lines illustrate the connections that are under the squares/holes you can see.

Construction plan

To attach the sensors, first we must create standoffs of the correct length. We then bolt the sensors to the bottom of the robot with them. After this, we stick the breadboard using a self adhesive strip to the USB battery. We then wire the sensors to the breadboard, and finally the Raspberry Pi to the right tie points on the breadboard.

Getting the correct length

For the sensors to work, they need to be as close to the ground as possible, without actually touching it. To get this length for your robot, you will need to combine a few of the 2.5 m standoffs to reach from the bottom of the chassis, so the bottom of the sensor ends up about 5 mm from the floor (the bottom of the wheels). We are going to build the assembly shown in the following diagram:

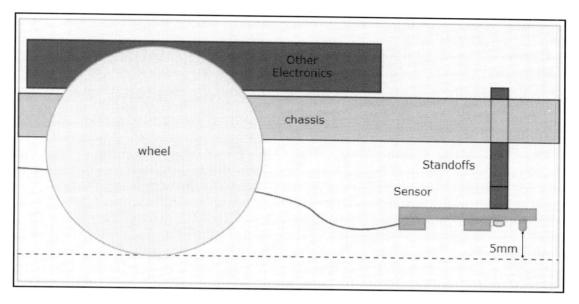

How the sensors should end up

Mounting sensor modules

The following photo provides details on actually mounting the modules onto the underside of the robot where they will be most effective:

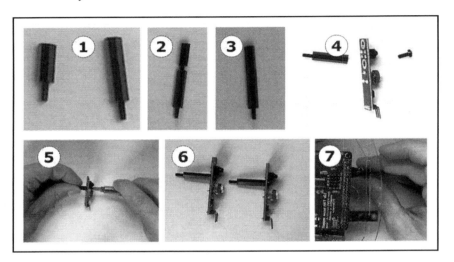

Attaching the sensors

You may need to try a few combinations, in my case, a 20 mm and 12 mm standoff together (giving 32 mm) worked. To attach the sensors to the robot with the standoffs, perform the following steps (each step corresponds to an image in the previous photo):

1. Bolt them together.
2. They should end up like this.
3. Take the combined standoff, a sensor, and the correct nylon screw for the standoff. The screw should be on the same side of the sensor board as the lumpy parts.
4. Bolt the sensor onto the standoff.
5. Repeat this—you should have two, with the same length.
6. Mount the two sensor modules under the robot. The sensor lenses should be facing forward, and the wiring points the back of the robot. This chassis has a handy slot here, allowing me to adjust how close together the two sensors are. Put them about 20 to 30 mm apart.

Wiring the sensor in

The next diagram shows how the connections (not wiring details) will look. Connections in red are new connections:

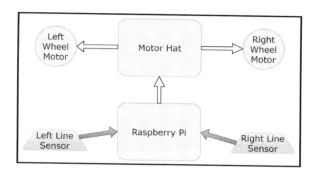

Diagram with line sensors added

First, we will need to place a breadboard onto the robot. A breadboard lets us poke wires and component leads into slots that are connected electrically to make connections without needing soldering that are easy to modify.

 Do not make connections to and from a breadboard on any circuit that is powered up! This may cause damage to the components, sensors, or controller boards. This is a very easy way to destroy a Raspberry Pi.

The following photo shows how to attach the breadboard:

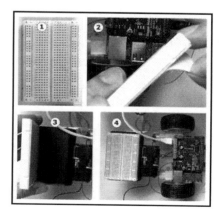

Attaching a breadboard

Perform the following steps:

1. This is the breadboard. On the back of it should be some backing to a self-adhesive strip.
2. Peel the backing from the strip.
3. Line the board up with the USB battery. Note that you should try to keep the battery level indicator, if your USB battery has one, clear. My indicator was on the underside of mine.
4. Stick the breadboard down firmly.

The next step is wiring the cables in. At this point, it is helpful to have the following Raspberry Pi GPIO diagram for reference:

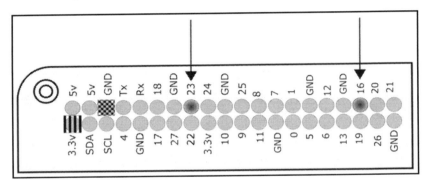

Raspberry Pi GPIO pins used for this sensor

In the previous diagram, I've changed my annotations to highlight the connections we will make. First, note that the bottom of the diagram would be the front of the robot, so the upper row would be the front row of GPIO pins. I've highlighted a **3.3v** pin and a **GND** pin. These will provide power to the sensor in the correct range for the Pi. I've also highlighted pins **23** and **16**. These will be the left and right sensor input pins respectively.

Next, we need to wire the sensor and bring the connections up to the top of the robot chassis. The following photo shows you the steps you'll need:

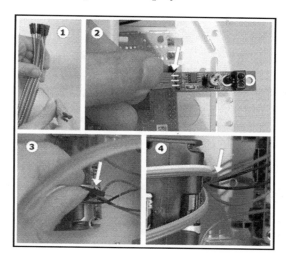

Sensor connections at the bottom of the robot

 Always use the darkest colored edge on grouped jumper wires for ground. If there are left and right groups, it can help to clearly mark one side, the left side, with a bit of insulation tape.

To wire the sensor, follow these steps using the preceding photo as a reference:

1. With the male-to-female jumper wire strip, make two strips of three. You can do this by taking three ends and gently pulling them apart from the others. Keeping the three attached will make it easier to work with than with three separate wires for each sensor.

2. For each cable, plug one end into a sensor. As a general guideline, if one side is a darker color, wire this one into ground, **G** or **GND** on the sensor. This pin may be marked "-" or "-ve" for negative too. This makes it easier to identify which way up it should be later. Take a note of the order of pins on the sensor—mine are "GVS": Ground, Voltage, and Signal.

3. Push the other end through a wider hole between the bottom of the chassis to the top. In my robot, this was the same hole I pushed the motor cables through. Repeat steps 2 and 3 for the other sensor.

4. At the top of the chassis, gently pull the cables through. You may knock the motor cables out doing this. I did have to reconnect a couple of my motor cables at this step. There should be plenty of cable for each sensor hanging over the breadboard:

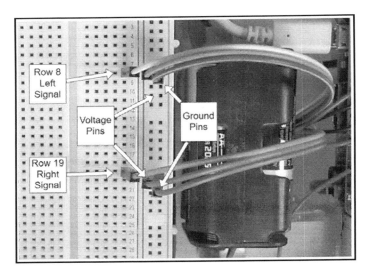

Connecting the sensors to the breadboard at the top of the robot

5. We can now take the wires we pulled through from underneath and wire them into the breadboard.

6. Connect the wires from the sensor so G/GND (this should be the darker colored wire) goes into the blue track on the breadboard, V/VCC (middle) goes to the red track, and S/OUT goes to a pin on the breadboard.

7. Keep the left sensor connections in a left-hand row (I went with row 8) and the right in a right hand row (row 19):

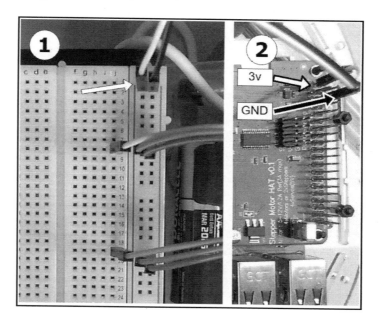

Connecting the power to the sensors from the Pi

Next, we need to make the power connections to the Pi as shown in the preceding photo. Peel off another strip of two cables—preferably with a black wire in them. These will be the power connections. Here is how to connect them:

1. At the leftmost row (1) of the breadboard, plug the black wire into the blue strip (ground) and the lighter color into the red strip (which will be 3.3v).

2. To plug these into the Raspberry Pi, reference the GPIO diagram in the photo, *Attaching a breadboard*; the black wire is GND, and should be on the top row, three pins in from the left. The lighter colored wire is 3.3v, and should be plugged into the the first pin from the left on the bottom row:

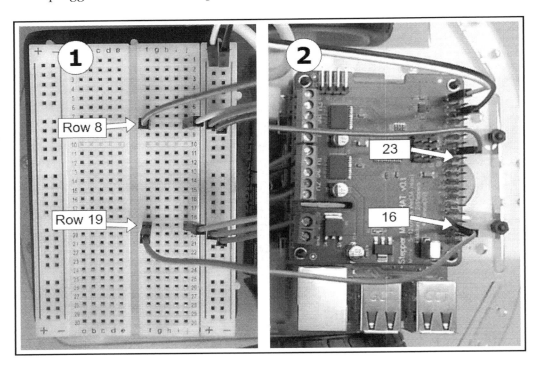

Wiring the breadboard sensor signals to the Pi

Now we need two individual wires; these carry the signal from the sensors to the Pi. Pull two individual ones from the strip. We will be using the breadboard rows we've plugged the sensor signal cables into. Holes in breadboard rows are connected horizontally up to the middle groove. I've added a green highlight to row 10 in the photo, *Connecting the power to the sensors from the Pi*, to show how that row's holes (also known as tie-points) are connected. The preceding photo shows how to wire the sensor signals from the breadboard to the Raspberry Pi. Refer to the following steps:

1. One cable should be plugged into the same breadboard row as the left sensor (row 8) and the other cable should be plugged into the same row as the right sensor (row 19).

2. We can wire these two sensor cables into the Pi. The left, from row 8, should be plugged into IO pin 23 on the Pi. The right, from row 19, goes into pin 16 on the Pi. Reference the GPIO diagram in the photo, *Attaching a breadboard*, to see where those pins are. Pin 23 is eight pins from the left on the top row. Pin 16 is three pins in from the right on the top row. Your sensor is now ready to test! The completed robot should look like this:

Completed line following robot on a test track

 Double check your wiring before applying power. Damage to the Raspberry Pi and sensors could occur if it's not wired correctly.

Painting the test track

To test our sensors and our code, you will need a test track. A test track for line-following needs to be a thick, continuous line, in a loop. It must not have any sharp turns and it's probably best it doesn't cross anywhere. Curving bends are good.

The thickness should be around 15 mm. The more consistent this is, the easier it will be for your robot—my own has a few curves that are too thick! Beware of this. This needs to be as close to a solid consistent black as you can manage. The contrast here is important. Any gaps may cause the robot to misbehave. The line should ideally be matte black, that is, not shiny as, if it's too shiny, it will still reflect enough light to be treated as white.

The next photo shows you how to draw or paint a test track:

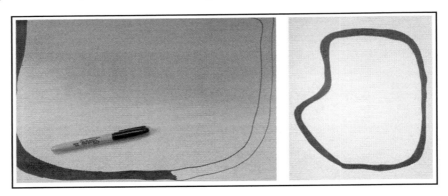

Drawing the test track

In the previous photo, I've started by making two outlines and shading between them. You may also find this easier with a thicker chisel-tip permanent marker than the type I used. A test track can also be printed if you have access to A3 or, better yet, A2 printing systems. It can be made from multiple sheets of A4 papers stitched together but try to ensure that these will not get separated by the robot rolling over them.

For a very large track, spray painting MDF boards white and using thick black tape is an option, but it is harder to get the curves with this. For larger tracks, I've taped paper sheets to MDF boards.

You'll note that the corners are all curves—none are sharp angles. This robot may drive right over an angle that is too tight for it; a robot with more sensors may be able to handle it. Some robots use arrays of sensors or downward-facing cameras for line following, with an increase in cost and complexity too. The angle I have drawn in the top left of my line is a bit tight, but the robot can be made to follow this by tweaking the sensor gap.

I also created a simple black bar, for calibration and a simple stop test. This can be in the middle of the same sheet of paper. This is shown in the following photo:

Drawing a calibration bar

Finally, when actually testing with this, you must ensure the test track is held down well. I placed coins or heavy flat objects in the corners, giving the robot some clearance or keeping them flat enough for the robot to drive over them. Without this, the track may slip under the robot and confuse the sensors.

Strong sunlight will be a problem as these sensors are based on infrared (IR) light—they are optical beams. We cannot see them, but it is the reflection of this beam that the sensor is looking for. Strong sunlight can flood the sensor with IR so it cannot see it's own beam any more and will not sense dark spots. Other IR beams can also interfere with it too, such as security systems and PIRs. Using the robot in an indoor setting is advisable. Having the sensor close to the ground will also help.

Writing the code – testing the sensors

We can now test the sensors out for real. Power up the Pi and motor board and log in.

First, we'll need another library—this time a more general library for talking to devices and sensors connected via the GPIO. Install this on the Pi:

```
pi@myrobot:~ $ pip install gpiozero
```

GPIO Zero is a library designed to make interaction with devices attached to the Pi GPIO very simple. It has lots of good examples and documentation on the internet. We will be using it where our hardware does not require more specialist libraries.

Calibrating the sensors

Now, if your sensor has an adjustment pot, you may need to calibrate the sensors a little. As mentioned, these sensors turn the amount of reflected light into a value and they then have a threshold that will output `true` or `false` for when the value crosses a threshold. The adjustment sets where this threshold is. The next photo shows how:

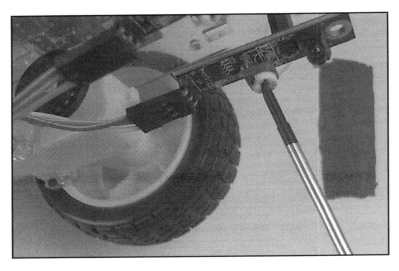

Calibrating the sensors

This means adjusting them to around the right value. On each of the sensors, there is an adjustable element—a **trimpot**, which you can put a screwdriver into. The light will be on; this means that the sensor is detecting white (ambient) light, "no line," and will be sending a low signal. Turn the adjustment slowly anticlockwise until the light just goes off. For the sensor I have, the light turning off means that the sensor is not detecting white, which would mean it has detected a line—the output would then be high:

- If the robot is close to a white reflective surface, such as paper, the light should be on. The output will be low as this is "no line."
- If the robot is not close to a white reflective surface, including a dark surface, the light will be off. The output will be high because this is "line detected."

If the light stays on, try this adjustment with the S (sense/signal) line disconnected and by making the same adjustment.

There are sensors that behave in the opposite way—their light goes on when over the black, and off when on the white. With them, the `pull_up` parameter should be removed.

Test code

Our test code is simple. We will drive the robot until we meet the line and then stop. I put this in a file called `stop_at_line.py`:

```
from robot import Robot
from time import sleep
from gpiozero import LineSensor

r = Robot()

lsensor = LineSensor(23, pull_up=True)
rsensor = LineSensor(16, pull_up=True)

lsensor.when_line = r.stop_motors
rsensor.when_line = r.stop_motors
r.set_left(60)
r.set_right(60)
while True:
    sleep(0.02)
```

You should be able to upload this to the robot, place the robot a few centimeters away from hitting a black line, then run it with `python stop_at_line.py`. The robot should drive to the line and then stop.

Let's examine how this works. The first three lines are imports:

```
from robot import Robot
from time import sleep
from gpiozero import LineSensor

r = Robot()
```

We import the `Robot` object from *Chapter 7, Drive and Turn - Moving Motors with Python*, so we can turn the wheels. `sleep` is imported so we can use time delays. From the `gpiozero` library, we can import a `LineSensor` object. This object does a bunch of handy things, as we'll find out. After the imports, we create our `Robot` object.

In two lines, we create objects to handle the sensors:

```
lsensor = LineSensor(23, pull_up=True)
rsensor = LineSensor(16, pull_up=True)
```

The `LineSensor` object is given the pin number it expects the input to be at. The `pull_up` parameter instructs the pin to enable a local pull up resistor, this stops the pin "floating" between high and low when the sensor is off, and will keep the signal on the pin at a logical high until something is detected, then the sensor will pull it low. There will be more detail on resistors later in this book. We call them `lsensor` and `rsensor` for left and right respectively:

```
lsensor.when_line = r.stop_motors
rsensor.when_line = r.stop_motors
```

These two lines do something slightly new. In the sensor objects, we set a member called `when_line`. We store the `stop_motors` method from the robot object in them. What this means is that either sensor then detects a transition from white to black, that it has crossed onto a black line, the `stop_motors` method will be called. A number of the sensors in the GPIO Zero library work this way, triggering code when something happens. This is known as event driven programming, where what the code does depends on things being triggered. The function that gets called (in this case `stop_motors`) is known as a **handler**.

In the following two lines, we start the motors moving forward:

```
r.set_left(60)
r.set_right(60)
```

They will now do this until the code stops (the `atexit` code we had before) or `stop_motors` is triggered by the sensors.

Finally, we go into a loop. The loop here just passes the time, since the triggers are now doing the actual work:

```
while True:
    sleep(0.02)
```

The sleep here is so the loop doesn't spin very fast—without that, the Pi could become unresponsive. Always have a small `sleep` (wait time) in a loop like this.

This code does not exit when it reaches the line so you will need to send a *Ctrl + C* sequence from PuTTY to stop it.

Troubleshooting

The following is a set of steps to troubleshoot when the robot does not drive and then stop at the line:

- If you see any errors, ensure you have installed the GPIO Zero library, and that you have the code from the last chapter working. Check your code for syntax errors or names typed differently.
- If the robot does not move at all, check that the motor wires are connected. They could have been dislodged while putting in the sensors.
- If the robot does not stop, do the following:
    - Check that the sensor wiring for both is complete and correct: going via the breadboard to the correct pins on the Raspberry Pi. Make sure the wires are firmly pushed in.
    - Ensure the sensors are lit over the white and off over the dark. If they stay lit, turn them gently anticlockwise until the light goes off.
    - If they will not light over the white, the sensors may be too far from the floor, so use different standoffs to get them closer. If they are as close as they can be to the white, they may need to be adjusted slightly clockwise.
    - Check that the contrast between the light and dark parts of your test track is strong and the track isn't too shiny.
    - It may not work in strong sunlight or if there are other IR sources nearby.
    - If it lights, the stop bar may be too narrow and the robot driven over it before it could be detected; try making the bar thicker.
    - Some sensors work the other way up, so you may need to remove `pull_up=True` from the parameters for the sensor in the code.

Writing the line-following behavior

Now we are ready to build a more interesting behavior. However, for the same reasons covered in Chapter 7, *Drive and Turn - Moving Motors with Python*, we now want to add our sensors into the robot object. This means that, on a different robot with sensor on different pins, or regardless of the pull up configuration, the behavior written on top of the robot layer will still work. We will add the sensors to this, then create the line-following behavior.

Adding the sensors to the Robot object

Open up `robot.py` from the last chapter. In the imports section, we will want the `LineSensor` object from GPIO Zero:

```
from gpiozero import LineSensor
```

In the constructor, the `__init__` method for the robot object, we can set up our line sensors. While the names `lsensor` and `rsensor` are fine for the test code, in the `robot` object, we will have other sensors later, also on the left and right. So it's better to be explicit in naming these. We'll call them `left_line_sensor` and `right_line_sensor`. The following is that section of the code, with the new code in **bold**:

```
def __init__(self, motorhat_addr=0x6f):
    # Setup the motorhat with the passed in address
    self._mh = Raspi_MotorHAT(addr=motorhat_addr)

    # get local variable for each motor
    self.left_motor = self._mh.getMotor(1)
    self.right_motor = self._mh.getMotor(2)

    # ensure the motors get stopped when the code exits
    atexit.register(self.stop_motors)

    # Setup the line sensors
    self.left_line_sensor = LineSensor(23, pull_up=True)
    self.right_line_sensor = LineSensor(16, pull_up=True)
```

 If your sensors did not need `pull_up`, you should remove that from this set up also.

As we saw in the test, we register handlers for the state of the sensor changing. We need to be aware that when the code is stopped, `atexit` stops the motors, but if the `LineSensor` handlers fire and start a motor just after, a motor could be turning left.

When working with code that calls back in this way, this kind of bug is called a **race condition**. This means we need a more sophisticated exit. This should ensure all those handlers are set to `None` when we exit the code. We also may just want to clear the sensor handlers anyway in a more sophisticated behavior.

So we'll create a `stop_all` method to do this, and make this our new `atexit` handler. Note that the handlers are cleared *before* we stop the motors—this is so the motors cannot be started between us stopping them and clearing the handlers. The modified code is in **bold**:

```
def __init__(self, motorhat_addr=0x6f):
    # Setup the motorhat with the passed in address
    self._mh = Raspi_MotorHAT(addr=motorhat_addr)

    # get local variable for each motor
    self.left_motor = self._mh.getMotor(1)
    self.right_motor = self._mh.getMotor(2)

    # ensure the motors get stopped when the code exits
    atexit.register(self.stop_all)

    # Setup the line sensors
    self.left_line_sensor = LineSensor(23, pull_up=True)
    self.right_line_sensor = LineSensor(16, pull_up=True)

def stop_all(self):
    self.stop_motors()

    # Clear any sensor handlers
    self.left_line_sensor.when_line = None
    self.left_line_sensor.when_no_line = None
    self.right_line_sensor.when_line = None
    self.right_line_sensor.when_no_line = None
...
```

The complete `robot.py` for my robot is in `https://github.com/PacktPublishing/Learn-Robotics-Fundamentals-of-Robotics-Programming/blob/master/chapter8/robot.py`, just note that yours may be slightly different if your sensor did not need the pull up settings.

Creating the line-following behavior code

This behavior will track the line we drew, driving around it and following its curves. Our line-following behavior can be described with a few simple sentences and then we can build it. Let's assume this code starts with the sensor either side of the line; when it crosses into the line, the robot needs to pull to the side to get that sensor back off it. The next diagram shows the behavior visually:

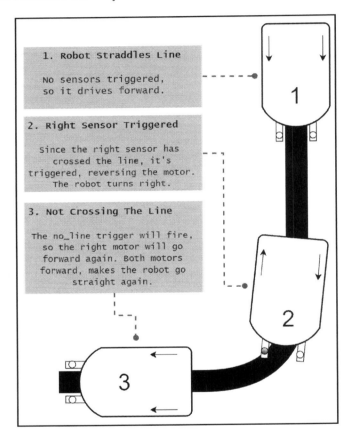

Robot line-following behavior

The same behavior can be described as follows:

- The robot starts driving
- When a sensor detects it is on the line, the same wheel will slow down or go backwards, turning the robot to put the sensor just outside the track, which will turn the robot back onto the line
- When the a sensor detects it is off the line, the wheel will go up to full speed, going forward in a straight line.

The last two points actually describe four events, two for each sensor.

It will need a little bit of fine-tuning and state. We will put the behavior code into an object so it can contain its tuning parameters and the handlers we will register. A good name for this is `line_following_behavior.py`.

We will start by importing the `Robot` object and `time.sleep`:

```
from robot import Robot
from time import sleep
```

Next, we will create our `LineFollowingBehavior` class. This will set up and manage the behavior. This has two variables that we can tune with our behavior. Variables intended to be tuned this way have a nickname, **fiddle factors**, as they are likely to need tweaking for the robot to work correctly. Depending on other factors, you may increase the speeds here, but 30% is a good starting point:

```
class LineFollowerBehavior:
    def __init__(self, the_robot, forward_speed=30, cornering=-30):
        self.robot = the_robot
        self.forward_speed = forward_speed
        self.cornering = cornering
```

The `__init__` method or constructor here takes one mandatory parameter, `the_robot`(plus `self`), and two optional ones. The first is the robot object it will use. `forward_speed` is the speed the robot will drive at when going forward on the line—too fast, and it is likely to overshoot a lot before reacting to line changes. You can tune this to be faster. The `cornering` member sets the speed of a motor when the robot is reacting to detecting a line. This may be a lower speed than `forward_speed` for longer turning circles or a negative speed for it to turn tighter circles or on the spot.

Let's create the first handler:

```
def when_left_crosses_line(self):
    self.robot.set_left(self.cornering)
```

This says when the left sensor crosses the line, we will set the left motor speed to the `cornering` speed. At -30, this will turn on the spot to the left. We'll do the same for the right one too:

```python
def when_right_crosses_line(self):
    self.robot.set_right(self.cornering)
```

Next, we need to straighten up when the robot has come off the line:

```python
def when_left_off_line(self):
    self.robot.set_left(self.forward_speed)

def when_right_off_line(self):
    self.robot.set_right(self.forward_speed)
```

This is simple—we set the motors to turn back to the `forward_speed` setting.

Next, we need a `run` method, to set everything up and start the robot moving. This `run` method connects the handlers to the sensors. It tells both motors to go to forward speed. Then, like the previous test code, it sits in a loop while the events take care of the rest of the behavior:

```python
def run(self):
    # Setup conditions
    self.robot.left_line_sensor.when_line = self.when_left_crosses_line
    self.robot.left_line_sensor.when_no_line = self.when_left_off_line
    self.robot.right_line_sensor.when_line =
self.when_right_crosses_line
    self.robot.right_line_sensor.when_no_line =
self.when_right_off_line
    # Start driving
    self.robot.set_left(self.forward_speed)
    self.robot.set_right(self.forward_speed)
    while True:
        sleep(0.02)


bot = Robot()
behavior = LineFollowerBehavior(bot)
behavior.run()
...
```

These last three lines will create a robot object, then create the behavior using this robot object and finally tell the behavior to run. This will be handy when we want ways to have more than one behavior.

The full code for this file is in `https://github.com/PacktPublishing/`
`Learn-Robotics-Fundamentals-of-Robotics-Programming/blob/master/`
`chapter8/line_following_behavior.py`.

More troubleshooting

Here is what to do if this does not result in the robot following the line at all:

- First, verify that you can still run the previous test code; if not, follow the troubleshooting there and come back when that works.
- Check for errors: Check that your file is like this code, that there are no syntax mistakes, and that you have typed the same names for things. Libraries should be present from the previous tests.
- Maybe the robot drives straight over the line, jitters, drives for a while following the line, then gets stuck somewhere, or misses a turn. This is where lots of fiddling and fine tuning comes in:
  - Check that you have not swapped the left and right sensor connections.
  - Reduce the speed.
  - The line may need to be thicker.
  - The line may have turns that are too tight.
  - Other markings on the sheet may be interfering.
  - The line darkness/contrast with the white may need to be stronger.
  - The line may be too shiny. Some line follower test tracks were unreliable because of this.
  - Beware of strong light or direct sunlight; it can play havoc by flooding out the sensor light.
  - Ensure that, for the whole of the line, the sensors are far apart enough to be either side of it. The red lights should be on when they are over the white on either side of the line when you start the robot; they should be far enough apart that both red lights can be lit.
  - You can alter `forward_speed` to be slower, or `corner_speed` to corner faster or slower depending on which way it jitters and veers.

- If it is turning a little too late, you can get the readings faster with a tweak in `robot.py`. Normally, the `LineSensor` object will queue around five values, at a rate of 100 per second; it will then start to base activation on the average of these. This means it could be around 30/40 milliseconds before it flips. Reducing the queue length for this will make the robot respond faster, but may make it more jittery:

```
        self.left_line_sensor = LineSensor(23, queue_len=3,
pull_up=True)
        self.right_line_sensor = LineSensor(16, queue_len=3,
pull_up=True)
```

Hopefully, by this point, you have a robot that can mostly follow lines. It does take lots of tuning to get this good and to make smooth turns.

Extra ideas

You can make a test track that crosses; this needs to work a little like train crossings—in that there are white lines cutting through the black lines for the two sensors either side to pass through.

Adding an LED facing down in the robot to control the light under may make the sensors more stable, although they do have their own IR LEDs too.

Using magnetic hall effect sensors and a wire, there are ways to make a hidden track under a floor or an MDF board, for example. The wire needs some electricity passing through. The full details are outside the scope of this book, but this is a fun idea.

You could also paint an inverted track, with a black background and a white line then modify the code to deal with that. Pi Wars supplies an autonomous event test track with a line painted this way.

Summary

In this chapter, you have learned how to connect your first sensor, a line sensor, to the robot. You've used a breadboard and wired the sensor into the Raspberry Pi.

You've added the sensor into the robot object, so it can be used in behaviors and so the behavior can be used with robots using sensors such as these on different pins. You have a test track to be able to test and demonstrate the line-following behavior and, if you are feeling excited, you know how to draw more of them. Finally, you've built a behavior for line tracking and seen it work—a simple bit of code but a behavior that starts to feel a little smart.

In the next chapter, we will make our robot both easier to debug and a little more visually engaging by using a multi-color LED strip with it.

Questions

1. What can happen if the test track is too shiny or not dark enough?
2. What are the other names for the GND or G pin?
3. Why would strong sunlight interfere with the sensor?
4. In event-driven programming, like we've used in this chapter, what do you call the section of code that will be called when an event is triggered?

Further reading

- If you found the pin numbering confusing, please read the notes on GPIO Zero and Raspberry Pi pin numbering at `https://gpiozero.readthedocs.io/en/stable/recipes.html#pin-numbering`.
- Additional troubleshooting and help on event handlers not firing from GPIO Zero: `https://gpiozero.readthedocs.io/en/stable/faq.html#my-event-handler-isn-t-being-called`.

Programming RGB Strips in Python

9

LED lights can be used with a robot to debug and give it feedback, so the code running on the robot can show its state. Colored RGB LEDs let you mix the red, green, and blue components of light to make many colors, adding brightness and color to a robot. We've not paid much attention to making it look fun, so this time we can add some of that.

In this chapter we will learn the following:

- How to choose and buy LED technologies that will work with the Raspberry Pi and look good on our robot
- How to attach them to the robot
- How to write lighting code to create dynamic displays
- How to integrate them with a behavior and display a rainbow

Technical requirements

- A computer with internet access and Wi-Fi
- The robot, a Raspberry Pi, and code from the previous chapter
- An APA102 or SK9822 LED arrangement
- A logic level converter (also known as a shifter) with at least two channels
- Some double-sided sticky tape
- Precut jumper wires for breadboard connections
- Optional: If the level converter or LED stick comes with separate headers, you will need the following:
  - A soldering iron and stand
  - Soldering iron tip cleaning coils

- Some solder
- Safety glasses
- Fume extractor
- A well-lit stable desk to solder at
- A second breadboard (to use to hold the headers in when soldering)

The code for this chapter can be found on GitHub at `https://github.com/PacktPublishing/Learn-Robotics-Fundamentals-of-Robotics-Programming/tree/master/chapter9`.

Check out the following video to see the Code in Action:

`http://bit.ly/2AsosCv`

Comparing light strip technologies

There are many competing technologies for light strips. We will limit it to LED types, as incandescent and fluorescent lighting tends to require far more power and are less suitable for these small robots.

The simplest are a set of lights that simply turn on when power is applied. These are of one color only and would not make for great information displays. If you want other colors, you would need to buy another color and attach it to a different output.

A improvement on these are strips that can have a color chosen, but this applies to the whole strip. You could change the color of a whole strip to display information. These require three IO pins per strip. If you wanted more than one color at a time, you would need many pins.

The most useful kind in our case, which we will work with in this chapter, are addressable RGB LEDs. Addressable means that each individual LED in the strip can be set, allowing a sequence of colors along the strip. As we have a limitation on the number of IO pins we can use, we will use the types with built-in controllers that allow us to use only a few pins. However, there are pitfalls in buying these to be aware of.

These LED controllers all take a stream of data. They take the red, green, and blue components that they need; then pass the remaining data to the next LED. This means that they can be arranged in strips, rings, or square matrices. The strips can be rigid sticks of eight or flexible strips meters long.

There are also some completely alternate technologies such as the LED Shim from Pimoroni and LED Matrices in color using shift registers. The LED Shim is one of the best and easiest to use of these technologies but, at the time of writing, is hard to find. We won't be using it in our examples; however, its electronics setup is a matter of sliding it over the GPIO pins. Code for the Pimoroni LED Shim will be included in the GitHub repository accompanying this chapter, but a stick of eight will be used for examples.

The other two major groups are synchronous (four-pin) and asynchronous (three-pin) LED strips. Both can be used with the Raspberry Pi, but the three-pin type have finer timing requirements, that do not play well with motor control and other sensors or devices. Because of this, I strongly suggest avoiding those types and using the four-pin types. They all have quirks, but are mostly compatible.

Here are the recommended types:

- APA102C Dotstar
- SK9822

If you intend to use other types, they are not guaranteed to be compatible, and you will have to alter the LED code.

Four-pin devices have a line for a clock and a line for data. The clock line is controlled by the Pi and the data output to the LED is synchronized to this. It means that the Pi does not need to have split precision timing as the LED device will only register data when the clock line changes. The following screenshot shows the clock versus a single data line for these LED types:

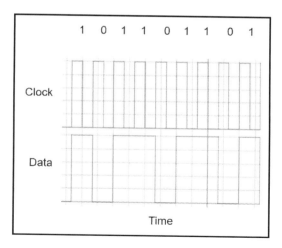

LED data with a clock

For our robot, we need eight or more LEDs ideally. There are a few products that provide this— Pimoroni's Blinkt, Sparkfun Lumenati 8-Stick, RasPiO Inspiring stick, and ChipperNut's StarChip16. Some will require soldering headers but work in a very similar way. If the rigid sticks of eight cannot be found, a higher density strip will do; however, you may want to cut and attach eight of them to a rigid backing.

The following photo shows some of the types of addressable RGB LED configurations I have experimented with:

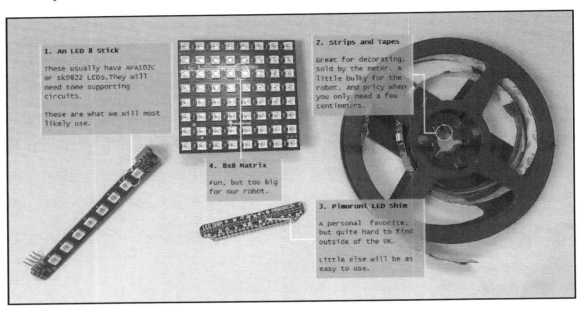

1. An LED 8 Stick

These usually have APA102C or sk9822 LEDs.They will need some supporting circuits.

These are what we will most likely use.

2. Strips and Tapes

Great for decorating, sold by the meter. A little bulky for the robot, and pricy when you only need a few centimeters.

4. 8x8 Matrix

Fun, but too big for our robot.

3. Pimoroni LED Shim

A personal favorite, but quite hard to find outside of the UK.

Little else will be as easy to use.

Types of addressable RGB LEDs

Other types that are not the SK9822/APA102C may not be compatible and may require changes to the code or electronics to adapt them.

These may need to be bought from specialist electronics or hobbyist stores local to your region. The best method is to look for resellers of Sparkfun, Pimoroni, or RasPiO parts on their own sites. The strips can be found on Alibaba.

RGB values

If you are not familiar with RGB values, the red, green, and blue light colors can be mixed to make any color combination. This is the same principle used by most, if not all, color display screens you have seen. TVs, mobile phones, and computer screens all mostly use this. LEDs use the same principle to produce many colors.

The amounts of each to mix are usually specified as three-number components. In this case, they are numbers ranging from 0 for absolutely turned off, to 255 for full intensity, with values in between for many levels of intensity. The colors are mixed simply by adding, so adding all of them at full brightness will make white.

Although this theoretically gives many colors, in practice, the differences between an intensity of 250 and 255 will not really be discernible on most RGB LEDs.

Attaching the light strip to the Raspberry Pi

Before we can write code to display color sequences on our LEDs, we need to wire them to our Raspberry Pi and attach them to our robot. After we have finished this section, the robot block diagram will look like the following:

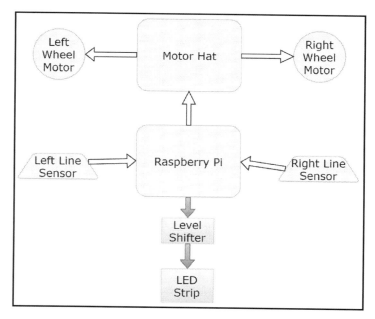

The robot block diagram with the LED strip

Logic levels

To attach an RGB LED strip to the Pi, we need to be aware that the Raspberry Pi GPIO pins operate at 3.3V, and the majority of these lights operate with logic at 5V. This logic level voltage applies to the high digital level. If we try to drive these directly from the Pi, at too low a voltage, the results may be inconsistent at best. If we are signalling back to the Pi, too high a voltage will damage it! This is a process we will need to get familiar with, as the next few sensors will also require this.

The simple answer to this is to use a logic level converter; the following photo shows two types of these:

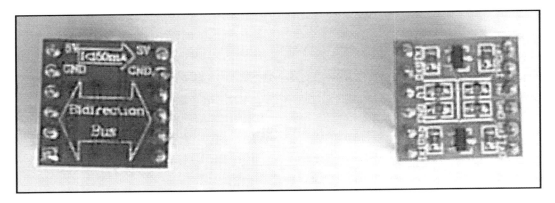

Logic level converters

Four channel bidirectional converters are relatively common online in packs of three to five, and I would suggest buying at least three as further sensors will also need these. Try to get the kind pictured previously in blue. It's worth noting that the generic type are similar to mine, but there are Adafruit and Sparkfun models with different wiring, so if you buy one of them, you will need to carefully look at the wiring labels and wire it differently to those connections.

Let's take a closer look at the logic level converter I am using in the following photo:

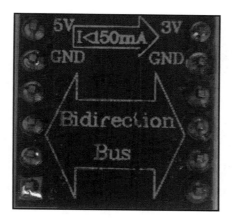

A close look at the logic converter

Level converters have a low side, marked 3V here, also known as **low voltage**, and a high side, marked 5V here, known as **high voltage**. There are ground connections on both sides, which are connected through to each other. There is then the section marked here as the **Bidirectional Bus**. This is a set of channels (four in this case), where logic levels presented at a pin on the 3V side of the channel will be output on the other side of the channel at 5V, and the reverse, with logic levels presented at the 5V side of the channel being output on the 3V side of the channel.

We will connect each GPIO pin for the LEDs to a level converter low side channel, and then the high side for each of those channels will go to the data and clock pins on our LED strip.

They usually come with separate headers to solder on, so we'll need to examine how to do so.

Soldering headers on

It is likely that two of the parts you have bought this time have come with headers in a bag that you can solder onto them. This means that you are going to need a small bit of tuition in soldering on these headers.

First, as mentioned in the requirements, as well as a soldering iron and solder, you should also have safety goggles, an extractor or well-ventilated space, an additional breadboard, and a well-lit work space.

You may be wondering why an extra breadboard. Since we are soldering headers on, one of the easiest ways to hold them is to place the long side of the headers into the breadboard, then place our device on top, as shown in following photo.

You should be wearing your safety goggles at this point. Warm up the soldering iron; depending on the iron you are using, this will take a few minutes. If you have a tip thinner or cleaner, I recommend using that both to get a good clean tip and to check that the iron is hot enough. Pull out a bit of solder ready to use too. The next photo shows how to make your first solder joint:

Making a solder joint

When soldering these, it is helpful usually to solder two opposite corners, so I started with the bottom left. Take a look at the previous photo. To actually make the joint, first heat the pin from the header and the pad (the ring that the pin goes through) on the board with the iron. Gently feed solder in to the other side of the cable—not too much. When it is hot enough, the solder will melt, and flow over the pad, making a rounded tent-like shape, which is just enough solder. You can then pull away the solder and the iron. Be sure to heat both the pad and the lead, otherwise you may end up with a **dry** joint, where the solder does not flow properly over the pad. After soldering the first pin, make sure that the board is level and the leg soldered right into it, heating it to make any adjustments. I recommend then soldering the pin at the diagonally opposite corner next to keep it straight. You can then solder the remaining pins.

For more detail on learning to solder, see the *Further reading* section for more detailed soldering instructions. When you have done this for your level converter board and the LED strip, they are ready to use.

Attaching the LED strip to the robot

Finding a place to put the LED strip can be tricky. Our robot is busy. Wire lengths to the board matter. The front of our robot will have many more sensors very shortly. We also want to see our lights from above instead of from the front. I chose to put the LEDs on top of the batteries, where there may be a little wiring over them, but they won't be competing for space with the sensors. It means I can see them from the top, which makes sense for a floor-driving robot. The following photo shows you how:

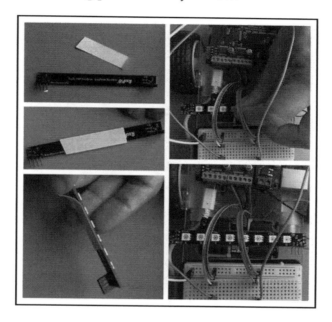

Fitting the LEDs

We will use double-sided sticky tape to fit these, as shown in the previous photo. You may also use Velcro strips for this. First, cut off a length to fit under the LED strip. Stick it to the the strip and pull off the backing. Then, as the previous photo shows, stick this down onto the 4xAA battery box. I suggest holding it in place for a short while for it to stick well.

Wiring the LED strip

First, we need to carefully wire the logic level converter into place. There are a number of configurations for wiring these, so the PIN labels are extremely important. The level converter should be placed over the notch on the breadboard, and then connections made to the rows it occupies. Importantly, the low voltage side of the logic converter should be facing the front of the robot (which I'll call the bottom of the breadboard). Have a look at the next photo to see how:

Logic level converter on the breadboard

Now we will arrange our circuit around this. The following Raspberry Pi connections diagram will help to see what we will connect:

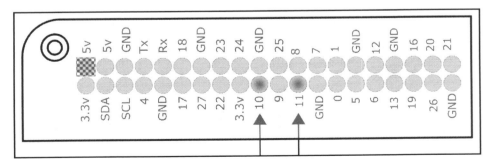

The Raspberry Pi connections to the LED strip

The Raspberry Pi connections show pins 10 and 11, which are the data SPI (MOSI) and clock SPI output from the Raspberry Pi. We will connect these to the logic level converter. The following screenshot shows the new wiring:

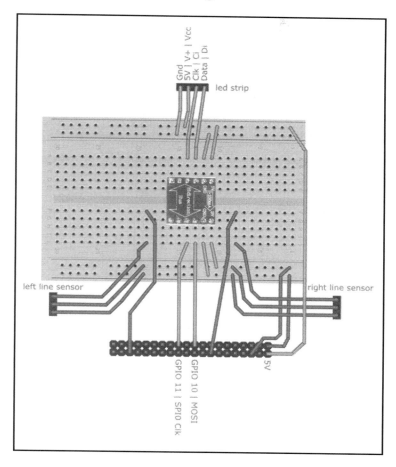

Recommended breadboard layout for the level converter and RGB LEDs

The connections in the brighter color are the new ones we will make now and the darker ones show connections you have made in previous chapters. We connect GPIO 10 and 11 to the low side of the channels on the level converter. We connect the low side of the level converter's power and ground connections. There is then a wire from a 5V pin on the Raspberry Pi to the red power strip at the top of the breadboard. We connect the high side logic converter power up to this 5V strip, and the ground from the high side to the blue ground line on the top power strip.

We then connect the LED strip using male to female jumper wires. The LED 5V should go to the top red power line on the breadboard, and the LED G or GND to the blue ground line at the top of the strip. The clock should go to the high side of the channel that GPIO 11 went into, and the data pin to the high side of the channel that GPIO 10 went to. You have now fully wired the LED strip. The robot will look like the next photo:

Fully connected and lit LEDs

Yours will not yet be lit. In the next section, we will get them lit too. What I hadn't noticed in this photo and, you should check for, is that one of the motor connections has come loose. Be sure to check that you've not knocked these loose while connecting the LEDs.

Double-check the connections; it is most important that the ground and voltage connections to the LEDs or logic level converters are not swapped. Ensure that the Pi GPIO pins 10 and 11 are connected to the low side of the logic converter only. The Raspberry Pi, LED, battery, and logic level converter can be damaged by wiring mistakes here. I personally have destroyed controllers by not being careful with wiring!

Adding a power switch

You'll note in the bottom of the breadboard in preceding photo that I've added a breadboard-friendly switch so I don't have to keep screwing that black cable into the robot for power, with a breadboard jumper going back to the robot. I suggest doing the same, but it's not essential. The next diagram shows this optional (but useful) addition to the breadboard:

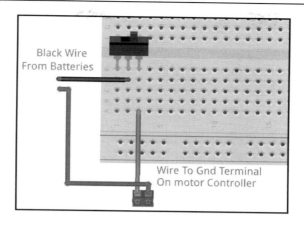

Black Wire
From Batteries

Wire To Gnd Terminal
On motor Controller

Adding a power switch

To do this, first find a breadboard-friendly slider switch. Unscrew the black cable between the motor batteries and motor controller, then push it into the breadboard location shown here—note that it's a bit thinner than normal breadboard jumpers, so it may not be the best connection. You then need a wire from the other terminal of the switch to the screw terminal on the motor controller. Note this is only for the motor power and will not switch off the Pi.

Making a robot display code object

As discussed previously, although we are building around an APA102C-based stick, there is more than one type of RGB LED system. We could choose something with any number of implementations. The best way to deal with this, as we saw in the chapter on motors, is to abstract it that is, to put the code into an object with an interface we've designed so that the small differences in interfaces between real hardware and their libraries is hidden from the behaviors.

So, what interface would we want for the LEDs? First, we'd want them to be available on the robot as methods in `robot.leds`. We will want to clear the LEDs (turn them all off), set an individual LED to an individual color, or set a bunch/range of LEDs to a list of colors.

We also want the robot code to tell us how many LEDs we have, so if the number changes, some of the animations or displays will still make some sense.

For colors, we will use three values (`r`, `g` and `b`) as tuples or small three-item lists when passed in. In Python, a **tuple** is a small number of items grouped together. When I say `color` as a parameter, this is a tuple of (`r`, `g`, `b`).

So, as a structure, we will use the following:

- robot.leds: This is an LEDs class, which we would put as a child of the existing robot class as a member leds. These are the members we would have in it:
  - set_one(led_number, color): This sets one LED at led_number to the specified color.
  - set_range(a_range, color): This sets a range of LEDs using an a_range Python range to color. Python ranges can be defined with a list of LED numbers or by using the range function, for example, range(2,8) will create the list [2, 3, 4, 5, 6, 7].
  - set_all(color): This sets all of the LEDs to the color specified.
  - clear(): This clears all of the LEDs to black, turning them all off.
  - show(): All of the other methods buffer a state, allowing individual LEDs to be set. This actually writes the LED states out to the device. The LEDs will not change or update until this is called. With the way most of these devices operate, they expect all the LEDs to be set in one stream of data.
  - count: This holds the number of LEDs in the strip.

So, let's write this code for the APA102C types (which should also be compatible with the SK9822). In the GitHub repository will be code for the LED Shim, too. First, we will need the spidev package to talk to SPI devices. So, on the Raspberry Pi, type the following:

```
pi@myrobot:~ $ pip install spidev
```

Our code must start by importing this and setting up the device. Put the following code in leds_8_apa102c.py (named after the device type and the number of LEDs in it):

```
import spidev

class Leds(object):
    def __init__(self):
        # MOSI - default output, (Master Out, Slave in) is 10. Clock is 11.
        self.device = spidev.SpiDev()
        self.device.open(0, 0)
        self.device.max_speed_hz = 15000
```

We create the default SpiDev connection self.device and open bus 0 and device 0 on it. Note I've left a comment in here about the pin numbers to keep this information handy. Bus 0 is always pins 9, 10, and 11. There is another SPI bus (number 1) on pins 19, 20, and 21 . It is also possible to "bit-bang" (using code to emulate dedicated bus functions) talking at much slower rates to some devices on any pins, but that may be too slow for these LEDs.

We must set `max_speed_hz` for the clock speed of our SPI bus, otherwise we have not defined the speed we expect it to work at, which may lead to the LEDs not getting correct data. We set this to 15 kHz, that is, 15,000 data items per second. You can increase this but this may reduce reliability.

We have set up a property for the number of LEDs in our LED class, called `count`. This property can be read like a variable, but is defined in a way that is read only and won't be accidentally overwritten.

We also set up a place to store the LED colors as `colors` we want to show until we are ready to display them. We set it up with all zeros—this is off. We make an array with a single color of `(0,0,0)` in it and then multiply it by `count` to give us an array with that many colors:

```
self.colors = [(0,0,0)] * self.count

@property
def count(self):
    return 8
```

Now, we create the methods to interact with the strip. Setting a single LED is fairly straightforward:

```
def set_one(self, led_number, color):
    self.colors[led_number] = color
```

This code will raise `KeyError` if the user attempts to set an LED out of range.

Setting a bunch of LEDs using a range means looping over the range:

```
def set_range(self, a_range, color):
    for led_number in a_range:
        self.colors[led_number] = color
```

Now, we get to setting all of the LEDs and clearing them. These are basically the same operation:

```
def set_all(self, color):
    self.colors = [color] * self.count

def clear(self):
    self.set_all((0, 0, 0))
```

In `set_all`, we use the same trick, multiplying an array of one color by the number of LEDs. The clear method just uses the `(0, 0, 0)` off color with `set_all`.

Finally, we need the show code, to actually send the colors we've configured to the LEDs. All of these LED strips require you to set them all at one time, so storing them in a buffer and then sending it allows us to compose displays with different colors. The APA102C has a particular way of sending data on the SPI bus, defined in the datasheet links in the *Further reading* section. We compose this using **bytes**, data components holding 8 binary bits, giving a numeric range of 0-255 when used alone:

Data purpose	Data format
Header—wake up LEDs	4 bytes of 0 or [0, 0, 0, 0]
First color brightness	1 byte - 224 (hex 0xe0) and a brightness from 0-31. I use 0xe1—low brightness in hex
First color components	3 bytes–the red, green, and blue components of the color
nth color brightness	1 byte—a prefix of 111 then 5 bits for brightness
nth color components	3 bytes—the red, green and blue components of the color
End of data	4 bytes of padding are recommended, a set of 0s again [0, 0, 0, 0]

You can see that our code will need to construct this dataset from our colors buffer and then send it to the device:

```python
def show(self):
    # Create the wake up header
    data = [0] * 4
    for color in self.colors:
        data.append(0xe1)
        data.extend(color)
    data.extend([0]* 4)
    # send it
    self.device.xfer(data)
```

This starts by setting a data variable to a list of four 0s. Then, for each LED, I first add the brightness byte, then extend the list with the color. In Python, a list has the append method, which will append a single item onto the end of a list. It also has the extend method, which treats the color as a list and places all of the values from the color list on to the data list.

We extend the list with four more 0s as an *end of data* section. We send it to led_device using the SPI xfer method, shorthand for *transfer*, which will transfer over all the bytes in data.

Other LED implementations would be more or less the same, although there are some, such as the Pimoroni LED Shim, which have a library that can be wrapped by this very easily.

Adding LEDs to the robot object

Next, we should update our robot.py file to deal with an LED system. This is clearly optional, but if we want to use it then we should set one up. We will start by adding it to the constructor (init) method for Robot (the new code is in bold):

```python
from Raspi_MotorHAT import Raspi_MotorHAT
from gpiozero import LineSensor
import atexit
import leds_8_apa102c

class Robot(object):
    def __init__(self, motorhat_addr=0x6f):
        # Setup the motorhat with the passed in address
        self._mh = Raspi_MotorHAT(addr=motorhat_addr)

        # get local variable for each motor
        self.left_motor = self._mh.getMotor(1)
        self.right_motor = self._mh.getMotor(2)

        # ensure the motors get stopped when the code exits
        atexit.register(self.stop_all)

        # Setup the line sensors
        self.left_line_sensor = LineSensor(23, queue_len=3, pull_up=True)
        self.right_line_sensor = LineSensor(16, queue_len=3, pull_up=True)

        # Setup the Leds
        self.leds = leds_8_apa102c.Leds()
```

We also want to ensure that when we stop our robot, the LEDs are turned off too:

```python
    def stop_all(self):
        self.stop_motors()

        # Clear any sensor handlers
        self.left_line_sensor.when_line = None
        self.left_line_sensor.when_no_line = None
        self.right_line_sensor.when_line = None
        self.right_line_sensor.when_no_line = None
```

```
# Clear the display
self.leds.clear()
self.leds.show()
```

The complete code can be found at `https://github.com/PacktPublishing/Learn-Robotics-Fundamentals-of-Robotics-Programming/blob/master/chapter9/`.

Testing the LEDs

Now, we can create code to test our LEDs and troubleshoot. We'll make something that simply flashes a couple of different colors on the LEDs. Create a file called `leds_test.py`.

First, we need to import our robot. We import `time` since this will be animated:

```
from robot import Robot
from time import sleep
```

Now, let's set up our bot along with a couple of named colors:

```
bot = Robot()
red = (255, 0, 0)
blue = (0, 0, 255)
```

The next part is a loop to alternate between the two colors as a test:

```
while True:
    print("red")
    bot.leds.set_all(red)
    bot.leds.show()
    sleep(0.5)
    print("blue")
    bot.leds.set_all(blue)
    bot.leds.show()
    sleep(0.5)
```

The prints are there for our benefit, so we can see when the system will be sending the data to the LEDs. We use the `set_all` method to prepare all the LEDs to show the red color, then call the `show` method to actually send it to the device. The code will `sleep` for half a second, making it reasonable time for a human to see the colors. It then does the same again with the `blue` color. The complete code is at: `https://github.com/PacktPublishing/Learn-Robotics-Fundamentals-of-Robotics-Programming/blob/master/chapter9/leds_test.py`.

When these files have been uploaded to the Raspberry Pi, typing the following should show the red/blue alternating LED display:

```
pi@myrobot:~ $ python leds_test.py
```

Troubleshooting

If you encounter problems trying to light the LEDs, please try these tips:

- For Pi booting issues, turn it off *immediately* then do the following:
    - Check your wiring. Ensure the level converters are the correct way around. There should be **no heat**.
    - The previous diagram shows the power from the LEDs coming from the 5V line on the Pi. The power supply may not be able to power the LEDs and the Pi. In this case, take a *female-female* jump cable, and wire the 5V for the light strip only to the *V* line on row 15 of the PWM/Servo connectors on the motor controller.
- If errors are shown, do the following:
    - Check you have enabled SPI (as shown in Chapter 7, *Drive and Turn - Moving Motors with Python*). On the Pi, the file /dev/spidev0.0 should exist:

        ```
        pi@myrobot:~ $ ls /dev/spidev0.*
        /dev/spidev0.0 /dev/spidev0.1
        ```

    - Check you have installed the SPIDev Python package.
    - Carefully check the code for mistakes and errors. If it's the code from GitHub, create an issue!
- The LEDs do not light at all:
    - Check your wiring. First ensure that power and ground are the right way around and fully connected. There should be **no heat**.
    - Ensure that the clock and signal lines are the right way around. After checking power, I usually swap these and test them.
    - Ensure that the wiring to the logic level converter is correct—nothing is missing or connected to the wrong side.
- The wrong colors are showing (or no light at all):
    - Try reducing the speed in self.device.max_speed_hz; if the cables are longer, or the logic converter is different then logic transitions may be lost.

- Carefully check the show code, it should be sending the correct number of colors for the light and the brightness code. If the lights are not based on the APA102c, check the datasheet for differences.
- This can happen if you skip the logic level converter or leave a signal cable disconnected, so check your wiring.

Using the light strip for debugging the line follower robot

Now we get to use these for some fun. We have our line follower robot kind of working, and it does have the LEDs underneath on the sensors, but we are now able to modify the line follower code to light up red when it it crosses the line and blue when it goes off the line.

Line follower basic LEDs

First open up the `line_following_behavior.py` code from the last chapter. After the imports, add the following new code (in bold):

```
from robot import Robot
from time import sleep

cross_line_color = (255, 0, 0)
off_line_color = (0, 0, 255)
...
```

We've added a couple of preset colors. Note I've not used the color names here, but names for their purpose. I can then tune the RGB values for purple/green, yellow/orange, or any other combination without changing any other code.

When making our LED class, we had a method for setting a range of LEDs, `set_range`. We are going to use this to create a left range and a right range. We are going to base these ranges on the number of LEDs so, if we drop in a different LED class, this design will respond to it and use a different number of left or right LEDs. We will divide the line into quarters, so the leftmost quarter is for `left_indicator` and the rightmost for `right_indicator`. We'll leave the middle two quarters blank for now. The changes for this are in bold code:

```
class LineFollowingBehavior:
    # Note - this is the robot ON the line.
    def __init__(self, the_robot, forward_speed=30, cornering=-30):
        self.robot = the_robot
        self.forward_speed = forward_speed
        self.cornering = cornering

        led_qtr = int(self.robot.leds.count/4)
        self.right_indicator = range(0, led_qtr)
        self.left_indicator = range(self.robot.leds.count - led_qtr,
self.robot.leds.count)
    ...
```

The calculations there mean that if we use a different number of LEDs, our indications still make sense. Note, these sides may be reversed on your strip, in which case, swap the left_indicator and right_indicator settings here.

We now modify the event handlers to set ranges of LEDs to different colors depending on the state of the sensors. We make sure the LEDs get shown:

```
def when_left_crosses_line(self):
    self.robot.set_left(self.cornering)
    self.robot.leds.set_range(self.left_indicator, cross_line_color)
    self.robot.leds.show()

def when_right_crosses_line(self):
    self.robot.set_right(self.cornering)
    self.robot.leds.set_range(self.right_indicator, cross_line_color)
    self.robot.leds.show()

def when_left_off_line(self):
    self.robot.set_left(self.forward_speed)
    self.robot.leds.set_range(self.left_indicator, off_line_color)
    self.robot.leds.show()

def when_right_off_line(self):
    self.robot.set_right(self.forward_speed)
    self.robot.leds.set_range(self.right_indicator, off_line_color)
    self.robot.leds.show()
```

Upload the replacement line_following_behavior.py and test it on the line track again, and you will see the colors blinking as the robot drives.

What if we wanted to have a rainbow for our robot?

Color systems

RGB is able to express colors in a method that is close to the way the hardware works, but it is less convenient for expressing intermediate colors or creating gradients between them. Colors that appear close to the eye can be a little far apart when in RGB. Because of this, there are other color systems. We will be using them in this chapter to make rainbow type displays and we will use them when visual processing to assist our code in detecting objects.

The other color system we will use is HSV—Hue, Saturation, and Value.

Hue

Imagine taking the colors of the spectrum and placing them on a circle, blending through red to orange, orange to yellow, yellow to green, green to blue, blue to purple and back round to red. The **hue** expresses a point around this circle. It does not say the brightness of the color or how vivid it is. The following diagram shows how these points can be represented on a color wheel:

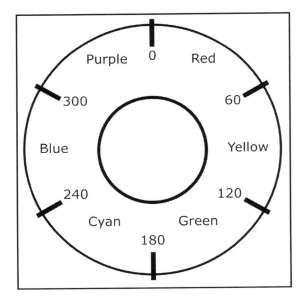

A color wheel of hues

In the previous diagram, the circle shows that between 0 and 60 degrees, a red hue is seen. As you look at the compass points around the circle, the colors they will show should be clear. Colors are blended as you move around from one hue to another. You may have seen something like this in a color wheel gadget on a painting or drawing computer program. A continuous wheel setup like this is what lets us make a rainbow.

Saturation

If you take a color such as red, it can be a grayish/dull red or a vivid strong red. **Saturation** is an expression of the vividness of the color. As you go towards a zero, only shades of gray will be seen. As saturation is increased, color begins to emerge—first in pastel tones, through to poster colors, and then to strong hazard sign or pure colors at the high end of the saturation scale. Setting saturation to 0 would make only shades of black, white, and gray.

Value

The **value** of the color is its brightness ranges from black at 0, through to a very dark version of the color, to a very bright color. Note that this does not approach white (in other words, pink colors), but a very bright red. To approach white, the saturation would need to be reduced too. Other color systems (such as HSL) specify a *light* component that would make things white this way.

Converting these

We will not need to deal with formulas to convert HSV into RGB, as Python, our chosen programming language, has a `colorsys` library to deal with these conversions. The only thing to note is that this library works in normalized values from 0 to 1, where fractions between express the full range. So, for the input, we'd have to turn our position around a circle into a 0-1 value and for the RGB output, we will need to turn the 0-1 values into 0-255 values. I'll show you how we do this in the code.

Adding a rainbow

We will set the middle LEDs to our rainbow, that is, from the first quarter of LEDs, to the whole set of LEDs minus a quarter. Looking at the hue wheel, a rainbow could be made by going around the hue wheel. We will, as mentioned, be working in values of 0.0 to 1.0 for the hue, so we'll divide this by the number of middle LEDs we use.

We want vivid colors, so set the saturation to 1.0 (fully colored). These LEDs can be intensely bright, so I tune this down by using a brightness of 0.6. You can tune this to taste.

For this, we will need to update the code in `line_following_behaviour.py` again. Let's start in the imports by getting the `colorsys` library to convert between hue and RGB values:

```python
from robot import Robot
from time import sleep
import colorsys
```

Now we can add the code to set the middle rainbow to our setup for the line-following behavior:

```python
def __init__(self, the_robot, forward_speed=30, cornering=-30):
    self.robot = the_robot
    self.forward_speed = forward_speed
    self.cornering = cornering

    led_qtr = int(self.robot.leds.leds_count/4)
    self.right_indicator = range(0, led_qtr)
    self.left_indicator = range(self.robot.leds.count - led_qtr,
self.robot.leds.count)

    led_half = int(self.robot.leds.count/2)
    hue_step = 1.0 / led_half

    for n in range(led_half):
        led_index = led_qtr + n
        hue = hue_step * n
        rgb = colorsys.hsv_to_rgb(hue, 1.0, 0.6)
        rgb = [int(c*255) for c in rgb]
        self.robot.leds.set_one(led_index, rgb)
    self.robot.leds.show()
    ...
```

The `led_half` variable is used to create our loop over the middle set of LEDs. `hue_step` is set up to 0.8 divided by the number of LED's in the middle bar, so we can use this in a loop to get the color.

We then loop from 0 to `led_half`, storing the index in n. We create `led_index` by adding the current index to `led_qtr`, giving the middle set of LEDs.

The `hue` value is calculated using `hue_step` times the current index. It is this hue value sweep that gives us the rainbow.

On the next line, the code uses the `colorsys.hsv_to_rgb` method to create an RGB color from our hue value, with full intensity and slightly lowered brightness, and to store it in a variable, `rgb`. This will still be in terms of 0.0 to 1.0, so we need to multiply all the components by 255 and make them integers again. We store this back in `rgb`.

We then call `self.robot.leds.set_one` to actually set the LED at `led_index` to the color stored in `rgb`.

After the loop, we call `self.robot.leds.show()` so we can see our rainbow.

Upload this and run it, and a rainbow should appear between the two indicator bars of your robot.

Summary

In this chapter, you have learned how to interact with and use RGB LEDs, how to choose and buy RGB LED strips that will work with the Raspberry Pi. We then understood the Logic-level conversion for interfacing with devices that do not run at the Raspberry Pi's 3.3V. Further we studied soldering basics and how to put headers on devices that arrive needing them. Finally we learnt how to wire in the LED's and stick them onto your robot, writing code to make them light, bringing LED code in with other robot behaviors and how the HSV color system works and can be used to generate rainbows

In the next chapter, we will look at servo motors, and build a pan and tilt mechanism for moving sensors.

Questions

1. When soldering, do you heat the pad, the pin, or the solder?
2. Why do you not connect the LED strip directly to the Raspberry Pi?
3. Why are we using fractions of the number of LED's in the LED class for our ranges?
4. What is the difference between a HSV color with a saturation of 0 and a saturation at the full range?

Further reading

Free detailed guides to soldering can be found at the following sites:

- Sparkfun: `https://learn.sparkfun.com/tutorials/how-to-solder-through-hole-soldering/`—a well illustrated first users guide to soldering
- Adafruit: `https://learn.adafruit.com/adafruit-guide-excellent-soldering`—as the title suggests, this guide shows how to do excellent soldering
- *The Basic Soldering Guide* by Alan Winstanley is an ideal place to learn more about how to solder and extend the skill you've started to pick up in this chapter. This goes into great depth about the tools and types of solder.
- *Make Electronics: Learning by Discovery* by Charles Platt: I've started to cover some basic electronics, such as shifting logic levels and timing diagrams. To get a real feel for electronics, *Make Electronics* is a superb introduction.
- *Practical Electronics for Inventors, Fourth Edition* by Paul Scherz and Simon Monk: This gives practical building blocks electronics that can be used to interface a robot controller with almost anything or build new sensors.

The datasheets for the LED types in use give you more detailed technical information about their operation and electrical characteristics: `APA102C Datasheet` and `SK9822 Datasheet`.

The `colorsys` library, like most Python core libraries, has a great reference: `https://docs.python.org/2/library/colorsys.html`.

Using Python to Control Servo Motors **10**

Servo motors can be used to make precise and quite repeatable motions. They can be controlled with the Raspberry Pi or add-on boards. We will be using them to build a pan and tilt mechanism—a **head** to position a sensor.

In this chapter, we will cover the following topics:

- What servo motors are and where you might see them in use
- How servo motors are positioned and how to position them with the Raspberry Pi
- What a pan and tilt mechanism is and how to build one with servo motors
- How to add this pan and tilt service to the robot object and test it

Technical requirements

For this chapter, you will require the following:

- The robot with the Raspberry Pi built in the previous chapters
- Screwdrivers—small pozi
- Small pliers or a set of miniature spanners
- Nylon bolts and standoffs kit—2.5 mm
- A two-axis mini pan-tilt micro servos kit

- Two micro SG90/9g servo motors if the kit does not include them, with their hardware and servo horns
- Cutting pliers or side cutters
- Safety goggles

Check out the following video to see the Code in Action:

```
http://bit.ly/2P4RqO1
```

What are servo motors?

Servo motors, or **servomechanism motors**, are used to position robotic appendages such as arms, grippers, and sensor mounts or to create other movements where position is the important factor. Unlike the wheel motors (DC motors), where speed is the factor, these motors are used where (to some level of accuracy) a position of 90 degrees or 110 degrees might be required. Code can be used to control these precise positioning movements or a sequence of them. The following photo shows a small selection of servo motors:

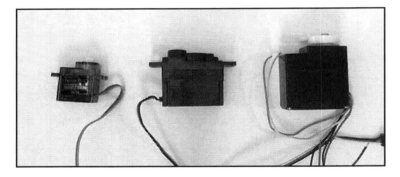

A small selection of servo motors

These come in many sizes, from the very small at around 20-30 mm (shown in my photo) to those large enough to move heavy machinery. The next photo shows some of these servos in use for a small variety of my robots:

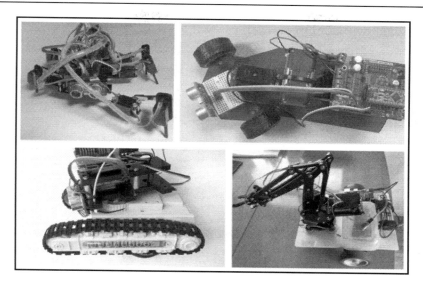

A small selection of servo motors in robots

SpiderBot uses 18 servo motors to precisely position and control legs. The slightly simpler UnoTron robot uses a single servo motor to steer the pair of wheels and sensor at the front. TankBot uses a single servo motor to position the turret on the robot, with the sensors and a Raspberry Pi mounted inside the turret. ArmBot has six servo motors of different sizes; they are used to position the arm and its gripper.

What is in a servo?

The compact form of a servo motor hides a controller, a gearbox, and sensors. These motors work by having a built-in feedback system. The feedback system requires some explanation. A servo motor takes input from a controller, which specifies a position for the motor to go to. The servo has its own controller and an internal sensor of the motor's current position. It will compare the current motor position with the position that has been requested, and will generate an error—a difference. Based on this difference, the servo will drive its motor to try and reduce that error to zero.

The following diagram shows this feedback loop:

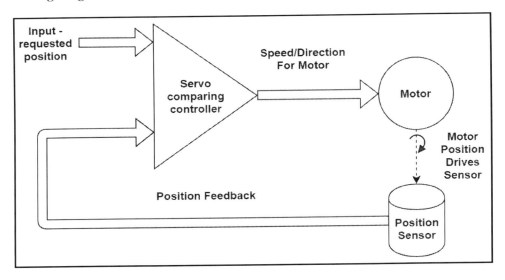

The servo motor control loop

Some special servo motors, such as those used in the aforementioned Armbot, have an additional output, allowing you to read the state of the position sensor in your own code too.

Sending input positions to a servo motor

Signals are sent to servo motors using **Pulse Width Modulation** (PWM). This a system also used to drive DC motors, and our robot has been generating these already. PWM is a square wave, that is, a wave of two states, **on** or **off** only. It is the timing of the signal that is interesting. You generate pulses, and the length in time of the pulse encodes the information. So, a shorter pulse is a lower value, and a longer pulse is a higher value. In some systems, the period must be the same, and it is the duty cycle (on time to off time ratio) that changes. Servo motors are less fussy, and the pulse length is the only important feature.

Refer to the following diagram for an example:

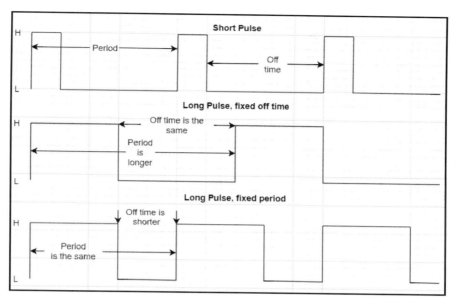

Pulse width modulation for servo motors

In the previous diagram, each graph has time as the **X** axis. The **Y** axis for each of the stacked graphs has **L** for a logic low and **H** for a logic high. The top graph shows short pulses being sent. The latter graphs at the bottom show where the pulse time has been increased; however, they vary in an important aspect. In the middle graph, the off time has been kept the same, but the period (how often the cycle repeats) has been changed.

In the bottom graph, the period has stayed the same, but the off time has been shortened. Current servos will respond to either type of timing, as long as the cycle frequency is at around 50 or 60 hertz (hz)—that is, it cycles 50 or 60 times a second. A **hertz** is a cycle per second.

Currently, in our robot, we already have a chip in the motor controller that is able to perform the fixed period PWM style (incidentally designed to control LEDs; see the *Additional reading* section at the end of this chapter). We can send when the off time and the on times should start in a fixed period, which means it will behave like the bottom graph for longer pulse widths. This leads us nicely into the next chapter, where we will make our robot do this.

Positioning a servo

To position a servo, we need to set up a servo **horn** so we can see it move, and then plug it into the motor controller board. A servo horn is a small collar with one or more arms, usually used to connect the servo spindle/axle to a mechanism they will move. Your servo motors will come with small bags of hardware, which will contain a few different horn types and screws to attach them both to the servo and the parts you want them to move. The following photo shows the bag and how to attach a horn to a servo:

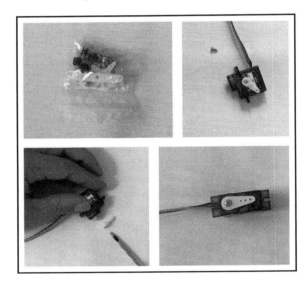

Fitting a servo horn

Screw a one arm horn together with the servo, as shown. Use the very short small screws for this as the longer screws will break the servo. Note that the long collar of the horn fits over the servo's output spindle. Try to line up the arm of the horn in the middle. Importantly, in the last image, don't over-tighten the collar screw though as, once the servo is powered up, you may need to loosen it and set the middle again. The following photo shows how to connect the servo to the full function motor hat board on the robot. Make sure the robot is fully powered down before connecting this:

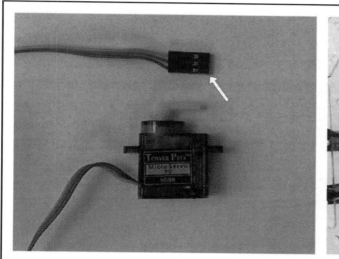

Plugging a servo into the control board

In the previous photo, the servo connector is indicated. There are three slots on the connector: brown is ground (**G**), red is voltage (**V**), and yellow/orange is signal (**S**). Looking at the motor hat, there is a 4 x 3 block of connectors. These are marked **PWM/Servo**. The columns are marked by a channel number (**0**, **1**, **14**, and **15**), and the rows are marked with a pin label (**GVS**).

This servo will go into channel 0. **GVS** refers to **ground**, **voltage**, and **signal**—so line up the yellow from the servo connector with row S and the brown with G. This should put the red in the middle. The connector from the servo should slot right in. This will be similar on controllers, such as the PiConZero, but may require some soldering work on the Adafruit motor hat.

Code for turning a servo

We'll write some test code that lets the user type a value in degrees and make the servo move to it. The library we are already using for the robot has a PWM module. We start our test code by importing the PWM module and creating the object to work with it. Note we must specify the address here—it's the same I2C device as we are using for the motors, and has the same address. This code is located in the `servo_type_position.py` file:

```
from Raspi_MotorHAT.Raspi_PWM_Servo_Driver import PWM
import atexit

pwm = PWM(0x6f)
# This sets the timebase for it all
pwm_frequency = 60
pwm.setPWMFreq(pwm_frequency)
```

Observe that we have `atexit` again, so we can ensure the controller stops signalling the motor. The servo works in cycles at 50 Hz or 60 Hz. We set up the PWM frequency, and keep this value for later use in calculations.

Next, let's set up the math needed to move the servo. On some controllers, you will not need this but, on this board, we need to set this up ourselves.

 When setting out calculations in code, use nice descriptive variable names and comments. This will aid you in understanding your code and thinking if the math makes sense. You will read code many times after writing it, so this principle applies well to any variable or function names —one that tells you what it means or what it does costs little to nothing.

To move a servo motor, you need to send pulses. For most servos, turning the motor to -90 degrees from the center requires a pulse of 1 ms, keeping at the center requires a pulse of 1.5 ms, and turning it to 90 degrees requires a pulse of 2 ms. We need to find the period at 1 divided by the frequency.

The chip we are using specifies its pulses in terms of a time, per cycle; it turns the pulse on and, per cycle, it turns the pulse off. These pulse times are in steps of 0 to 4095 (12 bit) where 4095 is the end of the period. So we need to calculate our servo's movement. Let's define a `convert_degrees_to_pwm` function to do all this math as it's nice to let the computer do it. Some calculations only need to be made once, so we can pull them above the function definition. Note I'm using descriptive variable names for this.

An *s* or *p* would mean far less than `steps_per_ms`—steps per millisecond. The .0 values ensure the calculations keep their decimals, otherwise Python will truncate them all to integers too early. We use the term *deflect* to mean how far from the center (to either side) the servo turns:

```
# Frequency is 1/period, but working ms, we can use 1000
period_in_ms = 1000 / pwm_frequency
# The chip has 4096 steps in each period.
pulse_steps = 4096.0
# Mid point of the servo pulse length in milliseconds.
servo_mid_point_ms = 1.5
# What a deflection of 90 degrees is in pulse length in milliseconds
deflect_90_in_ms = 0.5
# Steps for every millisecond.
steps_per_ms = pulse_steps / period_in_ms
# Steps for a degree.
steps_per_degree = (deflect_90_in_ms * steps_per_ms) / 90.0
# Mid point of the servo in steps
servo_mid_point_steps = servo_mid_point_ms * steps_per_ms

def convert_degrees_to_pwm(position):
    return int(servo_mid_point_steps + (position * steps_per_degree))
```

We imported `atexit` so we could make sure the servo is stopped, that is, not trying to seek or hold position, when our code stops. Let's set that up now. `pwm.setPWM` sets when the start and the end of the pulse is. By setting the PWM to 4096, this sets an extra bit that sets the pin to fully off; no pulses means the servo will *relax*. We can register this with `atexit`:

```
def stop():
    # Set pin off flag
    pwm.setPWM(0, 0, 4096)

atexit.register(stop)
```

We can now create a loop to ask for user input, convert it to a value, and send that to the servo motor. The `raw_input` function in Python asks the user to type something and stores it in a variable. We convert it into an integer to use it, then convert that into an end step time:

```
while (True):
    position = int(raw_input("Type your position in degrees (90 to -90, 0
is middle): "))
    end_step = convert_degrees_to_pwm(position)
    pwm.setPWM(0, 0, end_step)
```

We call `pwm.setPWM` with 0 as the pulse start, and our calculated PWM end step as the pulse end.

You can now turn the robot on and send this code to it. Zero should be in the middle. Do not give it values outside of the range as you may damage the servo. We will add code later to protect against this damage.

Calibrating your servos

The servo horn allows you to see the servo motors movement. Zero should be close to the middle. First, use a screwdriver with the horn to line zero up with the middle.

If the servo motors motion is impeded, including an attempt to move it past its limits, it will pull higher currents to try and reach the position; however, this stalling can cause a lot of heat and damage to the stalled motor.

Now try entering 90 and -90. You may find the two sides are not actually reaching 90. Servo's can vary slightly. To adjust this outward, the `deflect_90_in_ms` value can be increased. Do so in small 0.1 increments, as going too far here may lead to servo damage.

When your servo has been calibrated, it is a good idea at this point to use this code with each servo to ask it to go to position 0 before going to the next step. You can do this by plugging the second servo into the 1 channel on the servo's connector, then swapping the first parameter of every `pwm.setPWM` from 0 to 1. You will have tested both servos and both channels.

Adding a pan and tilt mechanism

We are now going to build and add a pan and tilt servo mechanism to our robot. This will be like a head for our robot to mount sensors on it. A **pan and tilt mechanism** allows a sensor (or anything else) to be moved through two axes under servo motor control.

Pan is to turn left or right. Tilt is to tilt up or down. The following photo shows a pan and tilt mechanism:

A pan and tilt mechanism from a common kit

If you can, get a kit that looks like the previous photo, if not, you will have to look at the vendors details for instructions to build it—ensure it is the type that uses two servo motors. We will build the kit, mount it onto our robot, and plug it into the controller.

Our robot block diagram will look like the following:

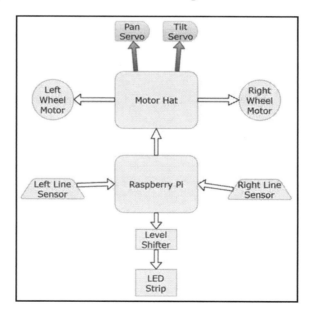

Block diagram of the robot with servo motors added

Building the kit

You will need your pan and tilt kit, a screw driver, and a cutter. The following photo shows the parts of the mechanism laid out:

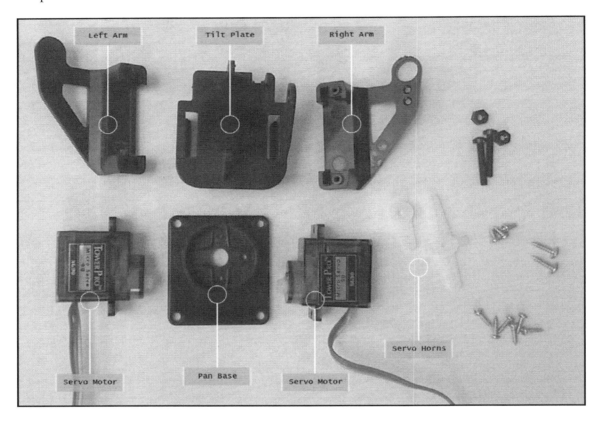

The parts of the pan tilt mechanism

In the parts shown in the photo, take note of the terms for the different plastic sections; I will be using those for the assembly. Next to these are the screws that would have come with the kit too.

First assemble the base as shown in the following photo:

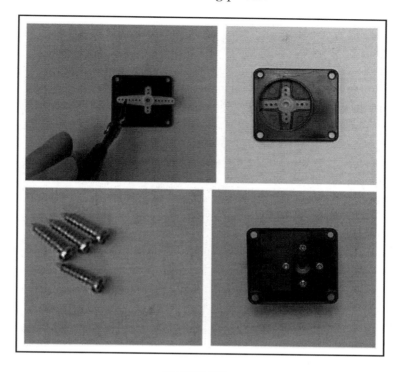

Preparing the pan base

 The plastic here will ping off, so don't do this without safety goggles. Be aware of other people in the room and tiny sharp plastic bits landing. Please wear safety goggles for this step!

Let's start building the kit by following the given steps:

1. Measure out and cut a cross-shaped servo horn to fit the base. There are ridges in the base it will need to fit into. You will need to shorten the long arms of the servo horn to just over three holes, and make them slightly thinner with the cutters. Line up the servo horn in the base, so the arms are in the recessed area, and the servo horn collar is facing away from the base.

2. Using the long tiny screws, screw them from the base into the tiny holes on the servo horn. Note that, with some servo horns, only the horizontal or the vertical screws may line up; two will suffice but four is more secure. The assembly continues in the following photo:

Assembling the left arm and tilt plate

3. To assemble the left arm, line up the stud with the hole on the tilt plate and push it in. Take one of the servo motors and the two screws with collars. The servo rests on the two brackets on the tilt plate, and when screwed in will hold the left arm in place. Ensure the servo's spindle aligns with the stud and hole before screwing it in. The next photo shows assembly of the right arm:

Assembling the right arm

4. To assemble the right arm, you will need another servo horn—this time the kind with just a collar and a single straight arm. You may need to cut it to fit the intended recess on the right arm. Use one of the tiny screws to bolt this onto the right arm of the mechanism. The servo horn you have attached will be at the front of the mechanism.

5. Slot another servo (this will be the pan servo) into the slots at the bottom lined up, as shown in the second panel of the photo, with the spindle facing the bottom of the photo, as shown in the third panel. This servo motor will face downward and be the pan servo. The next photo shows how to bring the left and right arm of the mechanism together:

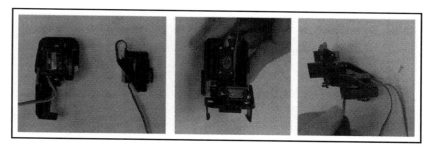

Combining the left arm and right arm

6. When combining the arms, note that there is a matching slot for the pan servo in the left arm assembly; mate this with the pan servo, and the collar of the right arm servo horn with the tilt servo you screwed onto the tilt plate.

7. Use one of the very short screws to attach the collar of the right arm to the tilt servo, keeping the tilt plate upright.

8. Use two of the small thin screws to screw the two arms together. The next photo shows how to attach the mechanism to its base:

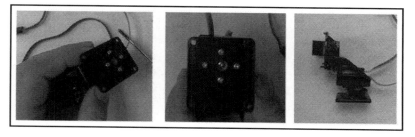

Combining the base with the mechanism

9. Push the collar from the servo horn screwed into the base, onto the pan servo spindle. Line it up so the long axis of the base is in line with the bottom of the mechanism. Use one of the very short screws to bolt the collar onto the servo. The final panel shows the fully assembled pan and tilt mechanism.

Attaching the pan and tilt to the robot

The next photo shows how to attach the pan and tilt mechanism to the robot:

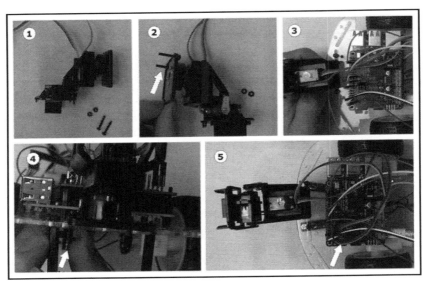

Attaching the pan and tilt to the robot

Follow these instructions along with the steps shown in the photo:

1. For this, you'll need two bolts, and two nuts to attach the pan and tilt to the robot.
2. Drop the screws into the short end of the pan and tilt base so they are pointing down.
3. The chassis I recommended has a slot across the front, which came in handy for the line sensor. This is perfect also for mounting this pan and tilt mechanism, with the screws through the slot.
4. Thread on the nuts and tighten from beneath the robot.
5. Wire in the servos. The tilt (up and down servo) should be plugged into servo channel 0 and pan (left and right) plugged into servo channel 1.

You are now ready to write code and try out the new head for your robot.

Creating pan and tilt code

For our pan and tilt code, we will again build this in layers. We will create a `servo` class and bury the previous calculations in it. We will then set up our robot class to have an instance of the `servo` class, and ways to access the servo setup to pan and the servo to tilt.

Making a servo object

In this object we will encapsulate (that is, create a module to hide the details of) converting an angle into a servo movement. We will make a `Servos` class in a `servos.py` file for this. The `servos.py` file starts off with only an import. So we'll go straight into the constructor (the `__init__` function).

This should look pretty familiar, we are taking the device address and the calibration parameter as the arguments, and then setting up all the calculations created in the last section within the `Servos` object. I've made that deflection/calibration parameter `deflect_90_in_ms` so that it can be overridden with the value obtained calibrating your servos:

```
from Raspi_MotorHAT.Raspi_PWM_Servo_Driver import PWM

class Servos(object):
    def __init__(self, addr=0x6f, deflect_90_in_ms = 0.6):
        """addr: The i2c address of the PWM chip.
        deflect_90_in_ms: set this to calibrate the servo motors.
                          it is what a deflection of 90 degrees is
                          in terms of a pulse length in milliseconds."""
        self._pwm = PWM(addr)
        # This sets the timebase for it all
        pwm_frequency = 60
        self._pwm.setPWMFreq(pwm_frequency)

        # Frequency is 1/period, but working ms, we can use 1000
        period_in_ms = 1000.0 / pwm_frequency
        # The chip has 4096 steps in each period.
        pulse_steps = 4096.0
        # Mid point of the servo pulse length in milliseconds.
        servo_mid_point_ms = 1.5
        # Steps for every millisecond.
        steps_per_ms = pulse_steps / period_in_ms
        # Steps for a degree
        self.steps_per_degree = (deflect_90_in_ms * steps_per_ms) / 90.0
        # Mid point of the servo in steps
        self.servo_mid_point_steps = servo_mid_point_ms * steps_per_ms
```

We are storing the PWM object in `self._pwm`. We only keep some of the variables for later, and the rest are intermediate calculations.

The triple-quoted string at the top of the constructor is known as `docstring` in Python. Any string declared at the top of a function, method, class, or file becomes a special kind of comment, which many editors can use to show you more help when using it. It's handy to use in any kind of library layer. This also complements all of the nice explanatory comments that we've carried in from the test code.

Next, we want a safety function in order, to turn all of the servo motors off. Sending no pulse at all will do that and relax the servos, protecting power and saving the motors from damage. As seen previously, setting a start time of 0 and 4096 for off flag will generate no pulse:

```python
def stop_all(self):
    # 0 in start is nothing, 4096 sets the OFF bit.
    self._pwm.setPWM(0, 0, 4096)
    self._pwm.setPWM(1, 0, 4096)
    self._pwm.setPWM(14, 0, 4096)
    self._pwm.setPWM(15, 0, 4096)
```

Now, we add our conversion function, much like we saw in the preceding but now localized to the class. This is only going to be used internally, so I've prefixed it with an underscore:

```python
def _convert_degrees_to_pwm(self, position):
    return int(self.servo_mid_point_steps + (position *
self.steps_per_degree))
```

Finally, in this class, we need a method to actually move the servo to a chosen angle:

```python
def set_servo_angle(self, channel, angle):
    """position: The position in degrees from the center. -90 to 90"""
    # Validate
    if angle > 90 or angle < -90:
        raise ValueError("Angle outside of range")
    # Then set the position
    off_step = self._convert_degrees_to_pwm(angle)
    self._pwm.setPWM(channel, 0, off_step)
```

I've used `docstring` again in this method to tell the user what it does and what the limits are. Next is a bit of validation. This adds a bit of limitation to protect the system from being sent an out of range value. It uses a Python exception and raises this. An exception pushes a problem like this up to calling systems until one of them handles it, killing the code if it wasn't handled. The full code can be found at `https://github.com/PacktPublishing/Learn-Robotics-Fundamentals-of-Robotics-Programming/blob/master/chapter10/servos.py`.

Adding the servo to the robot class

Next, we need to patch this into the `Robot` class in `robot.py`. First, let's import it. I have added it after our `leds_8_apa102c` import:

```
import leds_8_apa102c
from servos import Servos
. . .
```

This then needs to be set up in the constructor for `Robot`, passing along the address:

```
class Robot(object):
    def __init__(self, motorhat_addr=0x6f):
        # Setup the motorhat with the passed in address
        self._mh = Raspi_MotorHAT(addr=motorhat_addr)

        # get local variable for each motor
        self.left_motor = self._mh.getMotor(1)
        self.right_motor = self._mh.getMotor(2)

        # ensure the motors get stopped when the code exits
        atexit.register(self.stop_all)

        # Setup the line sensors
        self.left_line_sensor = LineSensor(23, queue_len=3, pull_up=True)
        self.right_line_sensor = LineSensor(16, queue_len=3, pull_up=True)

        # Setup the Leds
        self.leds = leds_8_apa102c.Leds()

        # Set up servo motors for pan and tilt.
        self.servos = Servos(addr=motorhat_addr)
    . . .
```

Now, we should make sure it is stopped when the robot is stopped, or the code breaks by adding it to the stop_all code:

```python
def stop_all(self):
    self.stop_motors()

    # Clear any sensor handlers
    self.left_line_sensor.when_line = None
    self.left_line_sensor.when_no_line = None
    self.right_line_sensor.when_line = None
    self.right_line_sensor.when_no_line = None

    # Clear the display
    self.leds.clear()
    self.leds.show()

    # Reset the servos
    self.servos.stop_all()
...
```

The last thing to do in the robot.py file is to map setting pan and tilt values to the actual servo motors:

```python
def set_pan(self, angle):
    self.servos.set_servo_angle(1, angle)
def set_tilt(self, angle):
    self.servos.set_servo_angle(0, angle)
```

I added these at the end of the file, although it doesn't matter, as long as it's in the class. I'd recommend making sure it is after the stop_all method.

Creating a behavior

We will make the pan and tilt head move in small circles of around 30 degrees. This behavior will demonstrate the mechanism and the parts of the code to talk to it. The code will create repeating animated kind of behavior. So, we will keep a time base—a current time. This allows us make our movement based on that. We will be using the time base to draw the circle.

Create a new file; I suggest the name circle_pan_tilt_behavior.py.

We will start with some imports; the `Robot` object, the `math` library, and some timing:

```
from time import sleep
import math

from robot import Robot
```

We prepare the `math` library as we are going to use sine and cosine to calculate that circle.

We'll make a `frames_per_circle` variable we can adjust to say how many steps it will go through.

The math functions work in radians, so we will take a full circle of radians, which is 2 * π and then divide that by `frames_per_circle`, this gives us a multiplier we'll call `radians_per_frame`. We can multiply this back out with the current frame to give us a radian angle for the place on the circle later. We work with radians and not degrees here because we'd end up with a constant multiplier taking the degrees into radians and dividing by frames per circle, so we'd end up back with `radians_per_frame` anyway:

```
class CirclePanTiltBehavior(object):
    def __init__(self, the_robot):
        self.robot = the_robot
        self.current_time = 0
        self.frames_per_circle = 50
        self.radians_per_frame = (2 * math.pi) / self.frames_per_circle
        self.radius = 30
```

When our behavior runs, we can then take `current_time`, and turn it into a frame by using the modulo (remainder) operation with `frames_per_circle`. This constrains the number between zero and the number of frames. This is all in a `while True` loop so it keeps running until the user stops it:

```
    def run(self):
        while True:
            frame = self.current_time % self.frames_per_circle
```

We then take this frame, and turn it back into radians, a position around the circle, by multiplying it back with `radians_per_frame`. This gives us a value we call `frame_in_radians`:

```
            frame_in_radians = frame * self.radians_per_frame
```

The formula for drawing a circle is to make one of the axes the cosine of the angle, times the radius, and the other the sine of the angle, times the radius. So, we calculate this and feed each axis to a servo motor:

```
self.robot.set_pan(self.radius * math.cos(frame_in_radians))
self.robot.set_tilt(self.radius * math.sin(frame_in_radians))
```

We do a small time sleep to give the motors time to reach their position, and then add one (increment) the current time:

```
sleep(0.05)
self.current_time += 1
```

That entire method together is as follows:

```
def run(self):
    while True:
        frame = self.current_time % self.frames_per_circle
        frame_in_radians = frame * self.radians_per_frame
        self.robot.set_pan(self.radius * math.cos(frame_in_radians))
        self.robot.set_tilt(self.radius * math.sin(frame_in_radians))
        sleep(0.05)
        self.current_time += 1
```

Finally, we just want to start up and run our behavior:

```
bot = Robot()
behavior = CirclePanTiltBehavior(bot)
behavior.run()
```

Running it

You will need to send `servos.py`, `robot.py` and `circle_pan_tilt_behavior.py` to the Raspberry Pi over SFTP, and then on the Pi, type `python circle_pan_tilt_behaviour.py` to see it. The head should now be making circles.

Troubleshooting

If you find problems getting this to run, try the following:

- Ensure that the servo motors are plugged into the correct ports and are the right way around. The "S" pin should go into a yellow cable on most servos.

- Lots of jittering can mean you have less than fresh batteries—please ensure they are nice and fresh.
- If you run DC motor behaviors from other chapters, you will note some odd behavior:
  - **First**: The servo may move and droop—this means you need fresh batteries or are not using Metal Hydride rechargeables.
  - **Second**: The drive motors may go very slowly, this is because you have set the PWM frequency lower to accommodate the servo's. You should increase the forward speed/cornering speed numbers—I doubled mine.

Summary

In this chapter, you have learned about Servo motors, how to control them with your motor controller, and how they work. You've built a pan and tilt mechanism with them, and added code to the `Robot` object to work with that mechanism. Finally, you've demonstrated all of the parts with the circling behavior.

In the next chapter, we will look at distance sensors and create behaviors for your robot to avoid objects.

Questions

1. What does the acronym PWM mean?
2. In terms of the servo motor's internal mechanism, from what components is the error calculated?
3. What is a servo horn?
4. What could result from a servo being impeded when trying to reach a requested position?

Further reading

- This servo motor control hat is based on the PCA9685 device. The PCA9685 product datasheet (`https://cdn-shop.adafruit.com/datasheets/PCA9685.pdf`) contains full information about operating this chip. I highly recommend referencing this.
- I also recommend looking at SG90 servo motor datasheet (`http://www.ee.ic.ac.uk/pcheung/teaching/DE1_EE/stores/sg90_datasheet.pdf`) for information about their operation.
- The AdaFruit guide to the pan and tilt (`https://learn.adafruit.com/mini-pan-tilt-kit-assembly`) mechanism has a set of assembly instructions. They are in a slightly different order from mine but may give a different perspective if this is proving to be tricky.

Programming Distance Sensors with Python

11

In this chapter, we will be taking a look at distance sensors and how to use them to avoid objects. We will look at the different types of sensors. We will then build a layer in our robot object to abstract away the hardware differences. By doing this, we can then create a behavior for object avoiding. We'll also take a slight diversion into menu modes for selecting them.

You will learn about the following topics in this chapter:

- What distance sensors are and how to choose them
- How to connect distance sensors to your robot and test them
- How to create a smart object avoidance behavior
- How to create a menu to select different robot behaviors

Technical requirements

You will require the following for this chapter:

- The Raspberry Pi Robot and the code from the previous chapters
- Two HC-SR04 ultrasonic sensors
- Male to female jumpers
- Breadboard pre-cut jumper wires kit
- Two additional bidirectional level shifters (I2C safe), soldered, as shown in `Chapter 9`, *Programming RGB Strips in Python*.
- Two brackets for the HC-SR04 sensor
- A crosshead screwdriver

- Miniature spanners or small pliers
- The code for this chapter will be available on `GitHub`

Check out the following video to see the Code in Action:

`http://bit.ly/2QjiLRg`

Choosing light versus ultrasonic sensors

The most common ways to sense distance are to use ultrasound or light. The principle of both types is to fire off a pulse and then sense its reflected return, using either its timing or angle to detect a distance. We will focus on the types of sensors that measure the time for a response, otherwise known as the **time of flight**. The following diagram shows how reflection time is used in these sensors:

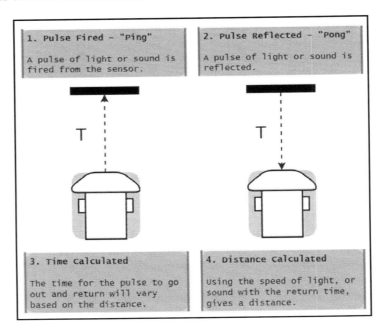

Reflections of a distance sensor

Optical sensors

Light-based sensors use infrared laser light that we cannot see. These devices can be very small, however they can suffer in strong sunlight and fluorescent light, making them misbehave. Some objects reflect light poorly or are transparent and are undetectable by these sensors. In competitions where course times are detected with infrared beams, the beams and these sensors can interfere with each other. However, unlike ultrasonic sensors, these are unlikely to cause false detections when placed on different sides of a robot. Optical distance sensors can have higher accuracy, but over a more limited range. They can be expensive, although there are cheaper fixed range types of light sensors out there. The following photo shows an optical-based sensor:

A VL530LOx on a carrier board

Ultrasonic sensors

Sound devices use ultrasonic sound with frequencies past human hearing limits, although they can annoy some animals, including dogs. Mobile phone microphones and some cameras pick up their pulses as clicks. Ultrasonic devices tend to be larger, but cheaper since sound travels fairly slowly with respect to light and is easier to measure. Soft objects that do not reflect sound, such as fabrics, can be harder for these to detect.

The following photo shows the HC-SR04, a very common and inexpensive sound-based distance sensor:

The HC-SR04

Regarding sound type devices, they are more expensive than I²C-based devices, but HC-SR04 are common and inexpensive. They have a range of up to 4 meters from a minimum of about 2 cm.

Why use two sensors?

Having two sensors allows a behavior to detect that side is closer, so the robot may be able to detect where openings are and make a move for where there is more space to drive. The following diagram shows how this works:

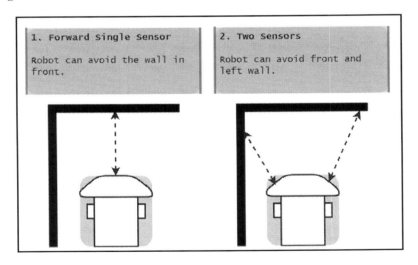

Using two sensors

Considering all of these options, we will use the HC-SR04 because it is cheap and because it is easy to add two or more of these sensors.

Attaching and reading an ultrasonic sensor

First, we should wire in and secure these sensors to the robot. We will talk about the requirements for wiring them and go a little further into the voltage levels that we touched upon in chapter 9 `Programming RGB Strips in Python`, explaining why we use them. We will then write some simple test code that we can use to base our behavior code on in the next section. After this selection, the robot block diagram will look like what's shown in the following diagram:

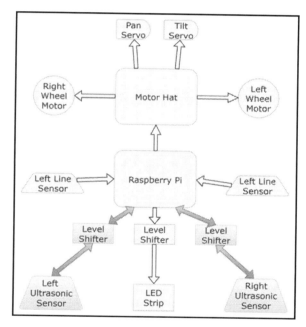

Robot block diagram with ultrasonic sensors

Securing the sensors to the robot

In the *Technical requirements* section, I added a HC-SR04 bracket. Although it is possible to make a custom bracket, without CAD and other making skills, it is more sensible to use one of the common market options. The following photo shows the bracket I'm using:

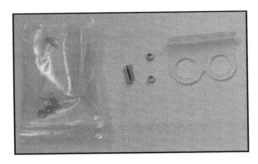

Ultrasonic HC-SR04 sensor brackets with the screws hardware

These are fairly easy to attach to your robot, assuming that your chassis is similar enough to mine, in that it has mounting holes or a slot to attach this bracket to:

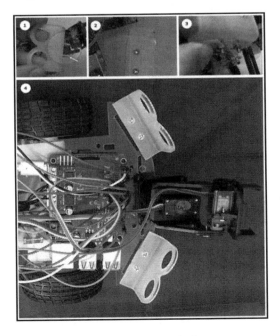

Steps for mounting the sensor bracket

To mount the sensor bracket while using the preceding photos as a guide, perform the following steps:

1. Push the two bolts into the holes on the bracket.
2. Push the bracket screws through the holes at the front of the robot.
3. Thread a nut from underneath the robot on each and tighten. Repeat this for the other side.
4. The robot should look like this, with the two brackets mounted.

The following photos show how to push the sensors into the brackets:

Pushing the sensors into the brackets

As shown in the preceding photos, the distance sensors can be simply pushed into the brackets, since they have a friction fit. The electrical connector for the sensor should be facing upward.

Wiring the distance sensors

Wiring these is a little tricky, and first needs a little more explanation on the use of voltage level shifters, which we saw in Chapter 9, *Programming RGB Strips in Python*. The sensors are 5V devices, and the Raspberry Pi GPIO pins operate at 3.3V. Therefore, we need more level shifting.

Voltages and level shifting

I want to take a closer look at level shifting and help you have more of an idea of voltages and how logic levels interact.

Voltage is a measure of how much pushing energy there is on the electrical flow. Different electronics are built to tolerate or to respond to different voltage levels. Putting too high a voltage through a device can damage it. Putting too low a voltage and your sensors or outputs may simply not respond. The following graph shows the effects that different levels have:

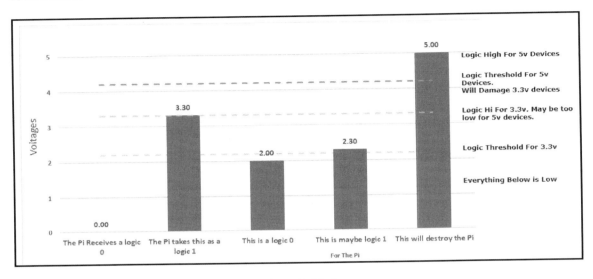

Voltages and logic levels

Although we are dealing with logic devices that output a true/false value, this is represented by a high or low voltage. These voltages must be above a threshold to be true, and below it to be false. We must be aware of these electrical properties, or we will destroy things or fail to get them to communicate.

Wiring the breadboard

Each ultrasonic sensor uses two wires, so a level shifter for the left-hand side and the right-hand side are needed. Ensure that the whole robot is switched off before proceeding any further.

The signal on one side is out and the other is in, so I²C safe bidirectional level shifters will leave the least room for problems. Here is a simplified view of the connections to illustrate how it works:

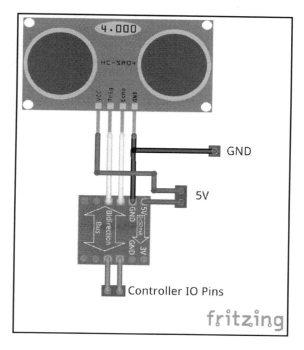

Simplified view of wiring distance sensors

In the simplified view, first note that the ground pins are connected. The 5V actually also supplies the 3V side, so you do not need to connect this to the Pi as an additional step. The wires above the bidirectional bus going to the HC-SR04 represent 5V logic level IO signal lines. The wires below represent 3.3V logic level IO signal lines going to the Raspberry Pi IO pins. We will need a circuit like this for each side. The reality is a bit messier as we now have a breadboard with other components to deal with.

The following diagram shows how this is really wired for the two sides, accommodating the breadboard with other sensors and outputs attached:

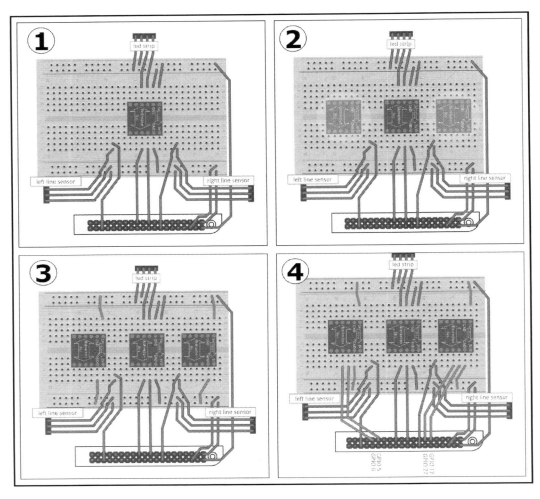

Wiring the level shifters for the HC-SR04 distance sensor

To wire the level shifters, use the preceding diagram as a guide, along with these steps:

1. The two marked wires must be moved to holes further from the middle notch to accommodate the level shifters.

2. Now, plug in two more level shifters. Ensure that they are the right way around, and that the Pi GPIO is only plugged into the 3.3V side.

3. The wires shown here are the power for the new level shifters. Use pre-cut jumper wires for this.

4. These wires from GPIO 5, 6, 17, and 27 will go via the level shifters to the ultrasonic sensor. Wire them, as shown here, to the 3.3V side of the level shifter bidrectional bus. Use male to female jump wires for this.

With the level shifters wired, the next step is to wire the breadboard over to the ultrasonic sensor. The following diagram shows how to do this:

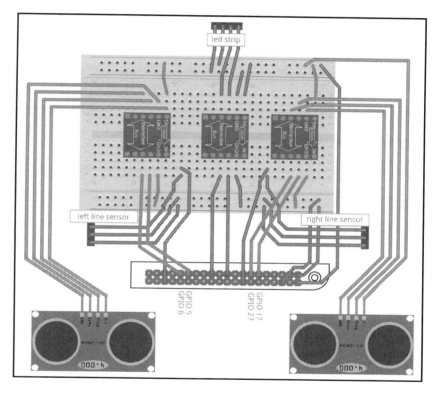

Wiring the HC-SR04 sensors into the level shifters

To wire the sensors into the breadboard, take a strip of 4 from the male to female jumper wires for each side. Then, wire them, as shown in the preceding diagram. Warning—depending on where your breadboard has been placed, the distance sensor wires may not reach. If this is the case, join two male to female wires, and use some electrical tape to bind them together.

As always, please double-check your connections before you continue.

Reading an ultrasonic distance sensor

To be able to write code for the distance sensor, we will need to look at a few areas of its operation. As suggested previously, this system works by bouncing sound pulses off of objects, and timing their travel time.

A pulse is used on the **trigger** pin to ask for a sound pulse and timing to be sent. 10 microseconds is this pulse length, that is, 0.00001 seconds:

$$10 \times 10^{-6} = 10^{-5} = 0.00001$$

The **echo** pin responds by returning a pulse with a length corresponding to the sound travel time. The following diagram shows the timing of these:

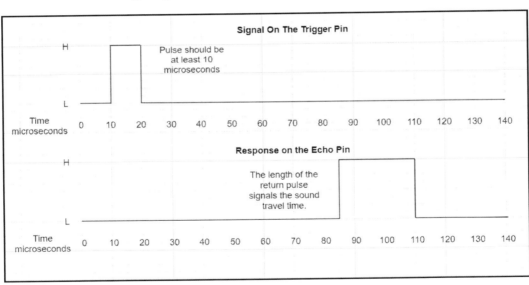

Timing of a pulse and the response for an HC-SR04 distance sensor

By measuring the time between the rising edge (when the pulse goes from low to high) and the falling edge (when a pulse goes down from high to low) of the response pulse, we can then multiply this by a factor to calculate the distance.

The distance factor depends on the speed of sound in air. We are looking to get a distance in centimeters. So, the right conversion would be to use centimeters per second. For the speed of sound in the air, it is around 34,300 cm/s (343 m/s). However, the time we have been given is the total time of the send and the return – which is twice the distance we want to measure—so we should divide that number by 2, giving a factor of 17,150. Therefore, we can multiply the return time in seconds by 17,150.

The speed of sound in centimeters per second is as follows:

$$343 \times 100 = 34300$$

The multiplication factor for distance is half this speed:

$$34300/2 = 17150$$

As we did with our servo motor control class previously, we should use comments and descriptive names to help us explain this part of the code. Let's write some code. This time, I'm going to let the comments in the code explain what it is doing. This is a good way to make code that remains maintainable. I've called this file test_hcsr04.py.

First, there are some imports:

```
import time
from gpiozero import DigitalInputDevice, DigitalOutputDevice
...
```

Then, we prepare the input and output pins for our sensors. Note that I'll be leaving in print statements to show what is going on when it is run:

```
...
# Setup devices, an input device and an output device, with pin numbers for
the sensors.
print "Prepare GPIO pins"

# Left sensor
left_trigger = DigitalOutputDevice(17)
left_echo = DigitalInputDevice(27)

left_trigger.value = False

# Right sensor
right_trigger = DigitalOutputDevice(5)
right_echo = DigitalInputDevice(6)

right_trigger.value = False
...
```

Now, the pin the sensors tied in may have been high, which may lead the sensor to produce an odd result, so we need it to settle. We only need to do this for the first time we use it:

```
. . .
# wait a little, to iron out spurious responses.
print "Warm up time"
time.sleep(0.5)
. . .
```

The `make_measurement` function that's shown in the following code actually gets the reading. It sets a timeout, so it won't wait forever for a reading. It signals the device with a pulse on the trigger pin for 10 microseconds. The device will emit an ultrasonic sound and wait for its return:

```
. . .
def make_measurement(trig_device, echo_device):
    """Function to get the distance measurement"""
    # Timeout - we'll use this to stop it getting stuck
    time_out = time.time() + 1

    # This off-on-off pulse tells the device to make a measurement
    trig_device.value = True
    time.sleep(0.00001) # This is the 10 microseconds
    trig_device.value = False
    . . .
```

Still in `make_measurement`, our code waits for the echo pin to rise, to go from low to high, and stores this as a pulse start time. Note that it will time out if we do not catch the pulse start:

```
    . . .
    # Here, we wait for the pin state to stop being 0, that is, to go from
low to high
    # When it rises, this is the real pulse start. Assign it once - it may
already have changed!
    pulse_start = time.time()
    while echo_device.pin.state == 0:
        pulse_start = time.time()
        # We ran out of time here.
        if pulse_start > time_out:
            print "timed out - missed pulse start"
            return 100
    . . .
```

Waiting for the echo pin to go low and storing that gives us a pulse end time. We will also watch out for a timeout here:

```
...
    # Now we wait for the echo_device pin to stop being 1, going from high,
to low, the end of the pulse.
    pulse_end = time.time()
    while echo_device.pin.state == 1:
        pulse_end = time.time()
        if pulse_end > time_out:
            print "timed out - pulse end too long"
            return 100
...
```

Subtracting the pulse start from the pulse end gives us a pulse duration, which, on this sensor, is exactly the flight time of the sound from pulse to echo. We multiply this by 17,150 to get a distance. I've heavily commented that multiplication:

```
...
    # The duration is the time between the start and end of pulse in
seconds.
    pulse_duration = pulse_end - pulse_start
    # This number is the speed of sound in centimeters per second - 34300
cm/s. However, the pulse has travelled TWICE
    # the distance, so we get half of this. (34300 / 2) = 17150.
    distance = pulse_duration * 17150
...
```

This distance will have lots of decimal places, but actually, two decimal places takes us to a 10th of a millimeter, which is more than enough, so we round up the distance. Now, make_measurement can return it:

```
...
    # Round it to 2 decimal places, any finer doesn't really make sense.
    distance = round(distance, 2)
    return distance
...
```

Now, we have a measurement function, and have done some setup—we can use a loop to read each sensor, print the output, and wait a little before measuring again:

```
...
while True:
    # Make our measurements and print them
    left_distance = make_measurement(left_trigger, left_echo)
    right_distance = make_measurement(right_trigger, right_echo)
    print "Left: ", left_distance, "cm", "Right:", right_distance
```

```
# Sleep a bit before making another.
time.sleep(0.5)
```

Now, you can turn on your Raspberry Pi and upload this code. Put an object anywhere between 4 centimeters and a meter away from the sensor and start the code on the Pi with `python test_hcsr04.py`. As you move around the object, your Pi should start outputting distances like the following:

```
pi@myrobot:~ $ python test_hcsr04.py
Prepare GPIO pins
Warm up time
Left:   7.63 cm Right: 32.87
Left:   8.47 cm Right: 32.18
Left:   6.88 cm Right: 32.24
Left:   8.45 cm Right: 30.87
Left:   8.47 cm Right: 31.66
Left:   8.5 cm Right: 31.37
Left:   7.73 cm Right: 34.08
Left:   7.7 cm Right: 32.45
Left:   8.08 cm Right: 33.68
Left:   12.39 cm Right: 5.81
Left:   10.22 cm Right: 6.19
Left:   10.37 cm Right: 6.09
Left:   18.62 cm Right: 6.21
Left:   10.51 cm Right: 77.04
Left:   11.47 cm Right: 63.1
^CTraceback (most recent call last):
   File "test_hcsr04.py", line 63, in <module>
      time.sleep(0.5)
KeyboardInterrupt
```

Testing our sensors

Because it is in a loop, you will need to press *Ctrl + C* to stop the program running.

Troubleshooting

The following points should be taken into consideration while troubleshooting:

- The most common problem is that the trigger and echo pins are swapped. I highly recommend swapping the trigger/echo pin numbers in the code and testing it again. **Don't** swap the cables on a live Pi!

- Next, ensure that the surface you are testing on is hard. Soft surfaces, such as clothes, curtains, or your hand will not respond as well as glass or plastic.
- Make sure that your surface is fairly big. Anything smaller than about 5 cm square may be harder to measure.
- Please check the code and indentation if you are getting invalid values.
- Did you double-check the wiring? Turn off the Pi and try this.
- As a last resort, it's possible that the device or the level shifter are faulty. This is rare, but not impossible. Try swapping the sensor out on the affected side first, and if that still doesn't work , then swap out the level shifter.

Avoiding walls – a script to avoid obstacles

Now that we have tested both sensors, it's time to integrate our new sensors with our robot class, and then create an obstacle avoidance behavior for them. We've seen how to write line sensor code that was event-based. For this sensor, we will use a different style, that is, polling. Our behavior loop will read the sensors, and then choose behavior accordingly. For the most part, the way the code will react to things does not change, and it is a decision about where to put the loop for checking sensor state—in the sensor object, or in your own code.

Making our distance sensor object

To integrate this into our robot, we will start by creating a `DistanceSensor` object. It will have a simple `get_distance` method. This is a simple interface which we could swap out for implementations of other distance sensors. We will construct it with the two pin numbers. This code will look quite familiar to the code we tested. Put this into `distance_sensor_hcsr04.py`.

Start again with some imports, and this time, a docstring for the module. Module docstrings usually state why a module exists or what it is for:

```
"""Object for the HC-SR04 distance sensor type."""
import time # import the whole thing, we need more than just sleep
from gpiozero import DigitalInputDevice, DigitalOutputDevice
...
```

As we saw in the testing, the system can time out when the reading is too close, or too far away. To avoid timeouts being as clumsy as 100 and making our robot behave badly, we can use an exception to show that the data wasn't good. An exception is a way of returning an error condition from functions, until something is able to handle it, and is used for when something invalid occurs. Our behavior can use this to detect that we are missed a reading and respond or ignore to the reading as needed. We can define our own exception, NoDistanceRead , to show this condition:

```
...
class NoDistanceRead(Exception):
    """The system was unable to make a measurement"""
    pass # We aren't doing anything special, but python syntax demands us
to be explicit about this.
...
```

Now, we can create our sensor class in such a way that we can make an instance of it for each distance sensor. The constructor will set up the pins:

```
...
class DistanceSensor(object):
    """Represents a distance sensor."""
    def __init__(self, trigger_pin, echo_pin):
        # Setup devices, an input device and an output device, with pin
numbers for the sensor.
        self._trigger = DigitalOutputDevice(trigger_pin)
        self._trigger.value = False
        self._echo = DigitalInputDevice(echo_pin)
    ...
```

The core of this class is a method to get the distance using the sensor on the pins we just set up. It should look familiar as it is the code we looked at previously. First, we set up timeouts, and then we send a pulse:

```
...
    def get_distance(self):
        """Method to get the distance measurement"""
        # Timeout - we'll use this to stop it getting stuck
        time_out = time.time() + 2

        # This off-on-off pulse tells the device to make a measurement
        self._trigger.value = True
        time.sleep(0.00001) # This is the 10 microseconds
        self._trigger.value = False
        ...
```

Now, we time the start of the pulse. Notice that this time, if it times out, we raise the
NoDistanceRead exception:

```
    . . .
    # Wait for the pin state to stop being 0, going from low to high
    # When it rises, this is the real pulse start. Assign it once - it
may already have changed!
    pulse_start = time.time()
    while self._echo.pin.state == 0:
        pulse_start = time.time()
        # We ran out of time
        if pulse_start > time_out:
            raise NoDistanceRead("Timed Out")
    . . .
```

And then we time the end of the pulse with the same exception if we fail to get it in good
time:

```
    . . .
    # Wait for the echo pin to stop being 1, going from high, to low,
the end of the pulse.
    pulse_end = time.time()
    while self._echo.pin.state == 1:
        pulse_end = time.time()
        # Pulse end not received
        if pulse_end > time_out:
            raise NoDistanceRead("Timed Out")
    . . .
```

And yet again, we get the pulse duration and turn it into a distance in centimeters, and then
round it up a bit:

```
    . . .
    # The duration is the time between the start and end of pulse in
seconds.
    pulse_duration = pulse_end - pulse_start
    # Speed of sound in centimeters per second - 34300 cm/s. However,
the pulse has travelled TWICE
    # the distance, so we get half of this. (34300 / 2) = 17150.
    distance = pulse_duration * 17150
    # Round it to 2 decimal places, any finer doesn't really make
sense.
    distance = round(distance, 2)
    return distance
```

Adding the sensor to the robot class

We will then create an instance of one of these `DistanceSensor` objects for each side in the robot class. First, regarding the imports in `robot.py`, we add the following to get us the class definition, as well as a convenient link to `NoDistanceRead` (the new code is in bold):

```
from Raspi_MotorHAT import Raspi_MotorHAT
from gpiozero import LineSensor
import RPi.GPIO as GPIO

import atexit

import leds_8_apa102c
from servos import Servos
from distance_sensor_hcsr04 import DistanceSensor, NoDistanceRead
...
```

Now, we need to set these up in the constructor for our robot:

```
class Robot(object):
    def __init__(self, motorhat_addr=0x6f):
        # Setup the motorhat with the passed in address
        self._mh = Raspi_MotorHAT(addr=motorhat_addr)

        # get local variable for each motor
        self.left_motor = self._mh.getMotor(1)
        self.right_motor = self._mh.getMotor(2)

        # ensure the motors get stopped when the code exits
        atexit.register(self.stop_all)

        # Setup the line sensors
        self.left_line_sensor = LineSensor(23, queue_len=3, pull_up=True)
        self.right_line_sensor = LineSensor(16, queue_len=3, pull_up=True)

        # Setup The Distance Sensors
        self.left_distance_sensor = DistanceSensor(17, 27)
        self.right_distance_sensor = DistanceSensor(5, 6)

        # Setup the Leds
        self.leds = leds_8_apa102c.Leds()

        # Set up servo motors for pan and tilt.
        self.servos = Servos(addr=motorhat_addr)
```

Notice how I've grouped them next to the line sensors here. We are not using handlers with these, so there is no particular cleanup needed, so we won't add anything to the robot's stop method. We are now ready to add a behavior.

Making the obstacle avoid behaviors

This chapter is all about getting a behavior; how can a robot drive and avoid (most) obstacles? It will of course be limited by the sensor's specifications, smaller objects, or objects with a soft/fuzzy shell such as upholstered items, which will not be detected. Let's start by drawing what we mean:

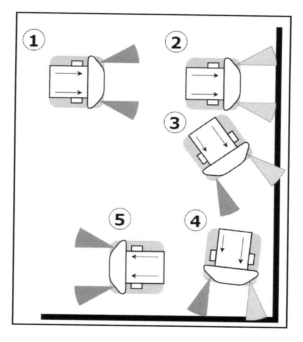

Obstacle avoidance basics

In the preceding example, a basic robot will detect a wall, turn away, keep driving until another wall is detected, and then turn away from that. We can use this to make our first attempt at a wall avoiding behavior.

First attempt at obstacle avoidance

Here, we will need a loop that does the following:

- Gets the distances from each sensor
- If a sensor reads less than 20 cm (a reasonable threshold), then set the opposite motor in reverse to turn the robot away from the obstacle
- Wait a small time and loop round again

We'll put this loop in a `run` method. There's a small bit of setup regarding this. We need to set the pan and tilt to 0 so that it won't obstruct the sensors. I've put this code in `simple_avoid_behavior.py`. Start with importing the robot, the exception, and the sleep for timing:

```
from robot import Robot, NoDistanceRead
from time import sleep
...
```

The following class will be the basis of our behavior:

```
...
class ObstacleAvoidingBehavior(object):
    """Simple obstacle avoiding"""
    def __init__(self, the_robot):
        self.robot = the_robot
        ...
```

In this behavior, we will use the LEDs on the robot to show a bar graph so that the closer a sensor detects an object, the more lights will be lit. These calculations in the constructor set up the display. `leds_per_distance` is a multiplier to turn on the right number of LEDs. The commented out print statement can be put in to check this value. We also define a color for this bar graph:

```
...
# Calculations for the LEDs
led_half = int(self.robot.leds.leds_count/2)
self.max_distance = 100
self.leds_per_distance = led_half / float(self.max_distance)
# print("Leds per distance", self.leds_per_distance)
self.sense_colour = (255, 0, 0)
...
```

Still thinking about the display, which will greatly aid in debugging, we will take a distance and make an LED count. First, we will use the `min` function—a Python that's built-in for getting the minimum of two values—and we limit to a max distance, then subtract this distance from our max distance, only allowing a minimum of 0, so that we light more LEDs when an object is closer. We multiply it by the `leds_per_distance` value, which is calculated in the constructor. This will give us a floating point number. We then round this up to an integer with `int(round())`, as we can only have a whole number of LEDs turned on. This means that after our division, if we end up with a value like 3.8, which we'll round up to 4.0, then convert into an integer to light four LEDs:

```
...
def distance_to_led_bar(self, distance):
    # Invert so closer means more LED's.
    inverted = self.max_distance - min(distance, self.max_distance)
    led_bar = int(round(inverted * self.leds_per_distance))
    return led_bar
...
```

Now, we have a way to get the number of LEDs from a distance, and we can create a `display` function to take a distance from each sensor and turn it into a display. It uses `distance_to_led_bar` for each side. Note that your LEDs may be the other way around, in which case swap the `left_distance` and `right_distance` in this `display` method:

```
...
def display_state(self, left_distance, right_distance):
    # Clear first
    self.robot.leds.clear()
    # Right side
    led_bar = self.distance_to_led_bar(right_distance)
    self.robot.leds.set_range(range(led_bar), self.sense_colour)
    # Left side
    led_bar = self.distance_to_led_bar(left_distance)
    # Bit trickier - must go from below the leds count, to the leds
count.
    start = self.robot.leds.leds_count - led_bar
    self.robot.leds.set_range(range(start, self.robot.leds.leds_count),
self.sense_colour)

    # Now show this display
    self.robot.leds.show()
...
```

The following method is how we'll choose a speed for each motor, depending on a distance sensor. A close sensor will go backward:

```
    ...
    def get_motor_speed(self, distance):
        """This method chooses a speed for a motor based on the distance
  from it's sensor"""
        if distance < 20:
            return -100
        else:
            return 100
    ...
```

The run method is the core, since it has the main loop. First, we should put the pan and tilt mechanism in the middle so that it doesn't obstruct the sensors:

```
    ...
    def run(self):
        self.robot.set_pan(0)
        self.robot.set_tilt(0)
```

Now, we will start the main loop:

```
        while True:
            # Get the sensor readings
            try:
                left_distance =
  self.robot.left_distance_sensor.get_distance()
            except NoDistanceRead:
                left_distance = 100
            try:
                right_distance =
  self.robot.right_distance_sensor.get_distance()
            except NoDistanceRead:
                right_distance = 100
            ...
```

We still chose to default to 100, but we could skip to the next loop instead. We will then display our readings by using the display_state method that we defined previously:

```
            ...
            # Display this
            self.display_state(left_distance, right_distance)
            ...
```

Now, we will use the distances with our `get_motor_speed` method and send this to each motor. We will print these values for debug aid, too:

```
...
# Get speeds for motors from distances
print("Distances: l", left_distance, "r", right_distance)
self.robot.set_left(self.get_motor_speed(left_distance))
self.robot.set_right(self.get_motor_speed(right_distance))
```

Since this is our main loop, we will wait a little before we loop again. Under this is the setup and starting behavior:

```
...
# Wait a little
sleep(0.1)

bot = Robot()
behavior = ObstacleAvoidingBehavior(bot)
behavior.run()
```

To test this, set up the test space to be a few square meters wide. Avoid obstacles that the sensor will miss, such as upholstered furniture or thin obstacles such as chair legs.

Send the code to the robot and try it out. It will start to drive until it encounters an obstacle. This kind of works; you can tweak the speeds and thresholds, but the behavior gets stuck in corners and gets confused quite a lot.

Perhaps it's time to consider a better strategy.

More sophisticated object avoidance

As we mentioned previously, the preceding behavior can leave the robot stuck. It will appear to be indecisive regarding some obstacles, and will occasionally end up ramming things. It may not stop in time, or turn into things. It's time to make a better one that will behave a bit more smoothly.

So, what is our strategy? Well, first, let's think in terms of the nearest sensor and the furthest. We can work off of the speeds of the motor nearest to it, the motor further from it, and a time delay. The reason for the time delay is so that we can do things such as turn right away from a wall, and not alternate between two states just in front of it. Let's build some code, similar to the last behavior, around this change.

First, copy the `simple_avoid_behavior.py` file into a new file called `avoid_behavior.py`.

We won't be needing `get_motor_speed`, so remove that; we will replace it with a function called `get_speeds`:

```
...
    def get_speeds(self, nearest_distance):
        if nearest_distance > 100:
            nearest_speed = 100
            furthest_speed = 100
            delay = 100
        elif nearest_distance > 50:
            nearest_speed = 100
            furthest_speed = 80
            delay = 100
        elif nearest_distance > 20:
            nearest_speed = 100
            furthest_speed = 60
            delay = 100
        elif nearest_distance > 10:
            nearest_speed = -40
            furthest_speed = -100
            delay = 100
        else:  # collison
            nearest_speed = -100
            furthest_speed = -100
            delay = 250
        return nearest_speed, furthest_speed, delay
...
```

These numbers are all for fine-tuning, but the important factor is that, depending on the distance, we slow down the motor further from the obstacle, and if we get too close, it will drive away. Since our only estimate of how far the robot drives is time, we have a delay, and we will increase this to ensure that we go far enough to not jitter. This is only a part of the whole behavior, but a vital part. Based on this, and knowing which motor is which, we can then drive our robot. Most of the remaining code will stay the same.

We then need to change our `run` function so that it can use the `get_speeds` method for the nearest sensor. The code remains the same for the setup, loop, reading sensors, and displaying state:

```
...
def run(self):
    # Drive forward
    self.robot.set_pan(0)
    self.robot.set_tilt(0)
    while True:
        # Get the sensor readings
        try:
```

```
                left_distance =
self.robot.left_distance_sensor.get_distance()
            except NoDistanceRead:
                left_distance = 100
            try:
                right_distance =
self.robot.right_distance_sensor.get_distance()
            except NoDistanceRead:
                right_distance = 100
            # Display this
            self.display_state(left_distance, right_distance)
            ...
```

Now, we use these to determine a nearest and furthest distance. Notice that we take the `min` or minimum of the two distances, which we will feed into the `get_speeds` method. We get back the speeds for both motors and a delay, then print out the variables so we can see whats going on:

```
            ...
            # Get speeds for motors from distances
            nearest_speed, furthest_speed, delay =
self.get_speeds(min(left_distance, right_distance))
            print("Distances: l", left_distance, "r", right_distance,
  "Speeds: n", nearest_speed, "f", furthest_speed,
            "Delays: l", delay)
            ...
```

Now, we need to check which side is actually nearer, left or right, and set up the correct motors:

```
            ...
            # Send this to the motors
            if left_distance < right_distance:
                self.robot.set_left(nearest_speed)
                self.robot.set_right(furthest_speed)
            else:
                self.robot.set_right(nearest_speed)
                self.robot.set_left(furthest_speed)
            ...
```

Instead of sleeping a fixed time, we sleep the delay time. The delay is in milliseconds, so we need to multiply it to get seconds:

```
            ...
            # Wait our delay time
            sleep(delay * 0.001)
    ...
```

The rest of the code will remain the same. The full code for this file can be found at `https:/` `/github.com/PacktPublishing/Learn-Robotics-Fundamentals-of-Robotics-` `Programming/blob/master/chapter11/avoid_behavior.py`.

When you run this code, you should see far smoother avoidance. You may need to tweak the timings and values. The bottom two conditions with reversing, and reverse turning, are the ones that may need to be tuned higher if the robot isn't quite pulling back enough.

There are still flaws in this behavior, though. It does not construct a map at all, and has no reverse sensors, so while avoiding objects in front, it can quite easily reverse into objects behind it. Adding more sensors could resolve some of these problems, but we cannot construct a map just yet as our robot does not have the sensors to accurately determine how far it has turned or traveled.

Menu modes – choosing your robot's behavior

We now have a collection of robot behaviors, and we will be growing a few more of them, but beside the behaviors, we are going to create a simple menu system to select them. A convenient and phone friendly way to do this is to serve it to a browser, so we will also take that approach with our robot. Using HTTP and HTML also means that we could later let other systems make requests to our robot too. HTTP sends requests in a URL—first, the `http://` protocol identifier, a server hostname, `myrobot.local`, a path, `/mode/foo`, and it may have additional parameters after that. We will be using the path of the URL to determine what our robot will do.

As we have done with other systems, we will create a few logical sections and blocks to handle different aspects of this:

- We will have code to manage the robot's modes, and start and stop known scripts. It can also give us a list of those known scripts.
- A web server will be used for the code to send pages to the user, and respond to requests.
- A template for the server to send to the user, with some placeholders replaced by code. The actual user interface is here.

An overview of how this will work is as follows:

1. The browser will ask our web server for a page to display
2. Our web server will ask our mode management for a list of scripts it can start
3. The web server will use this list to make a menu, using a template to render it into a page, and send that to the user
4. In the browser, when the menu item links are clicked, they will make requests to the web server
5. The web server will act on mode change requests by making calls to the mode system to act on the requests
6. The server will send statuses back to the browser after these requests

Managing robot modes

We can manage modes by starting and stopping our behavior scripts as subprocesses. The mode manager will have a configuration for our known modes.

Let's start a file called `robot_modes.py`. This will contain a class called `RobotModes` that will handle robot processes and return a list of known scripts. Let's start with some imports and the top of the class definition:

```
import subprocess


class RobotModes(object):
    """Our robot behaviors and tests as running modes"""
    ...
```

The first thing we will provide is a configuration. The configuration comes in two sections; one maps a mode name to a file—a Python file. Note that we are specifying a list of files, and not inferring it. Although we could take our mode/path section and add `.py` to get a file, this would be bad for two reasons:

- It would couple us directly to script names; it would be nice if we could change underlying scripts for the same mode name
- Although the robot is not a secure environment, allowing arbitrary subprocesses to run is very bad, so restricting it keeps the robot a little more secure

Here is the mode config, mapping a mode to a filename. The mode name is a short name, also known as a **slug**, a compromise between human readable and machine readable – they are usually restricted to lower case and underscore characters, and are shorter than a full English description. Our filenames are quite close to slug names already:

```
...
# Mode config goes from a "mode_name" to a script to run. Configured
for look up.
mode_config = {
    "avoid_behavior": "avoid_behavior.py",
    "circle_head": "circle_pan_tilt_behavior.py",
    "test_leds": "leds_test.py",
    "test_hcsr04": "test_hcsr04.py",
    "stop_at_line": "stop_at_line.py",
    "line_following": "line_following_behavior.py",
    "behavior_line": "behavior_line.py",
    "behavior_path": "behavior_path.py"
}
...
```

The next half of the configuration is a list, with a mode named slug and human intended text to show on a screen. We can use the order of this to configure our menu. If we want to add a behavior to the menu, we must add it to both lists:

```
...
# Menu config is a list of mode_names and text to display. Ordered as
we'd like our menu.
menu_config = [
    {"mode_name": "avoid_behavior", "text": "Avoid Behavior"},
    {"mode_name": "circle_head", "text": "Circle Head"},
    {"mode_name": "test_leds", "text": "Test LEDS"},
    {"mode_name": "test_hcsr04", "text": "Test HC-SR04"},
    {"mode_name": "stop_at_line", "text": "Stop At Line"},
    {"mode_name": "line_following", "text": "Line Following"},
    {"mode_name": "behavior_line", "text": "Drive In A Line"},
    {"mode_name": "behavior_path", "text": "Drive a Path"}
]
...
```

With the fixed configuration aside, this class is also managing processes. Therefore, we need to keep track of the current process and check whether it is running:

```
...
def __init__(self):
    self.current_process = None

def is_running(self):
```

```
        """Check if there is a process running. Returncode is only set when
a process finishes"""
        return self.current_process and self.current_process.returncode is
None
    ...
```

Note that we can check for both a process being set, and if it has a returncode. Python only sets the returncode for a process that has completed, so this can indicate that a process is still running.

Now, we need to look at how we can start a process from a mode name. Before we run it, we need to check that the previous behavior has stopped. Running two modes simultaneously could have quite strange consequences, so we should be careful not to let that happen.

This code then maps the mode_name to a process name, and starts it with Python. It returns True if a process was started:

```
    ...
    def run(self, mode_name):
        """Run the mode as a subprocess, but not if we still have one
running"""
        if not self.is_running():
            script = self.mode_config[mode_name]
            self.current_process = subprocess.Popen(["python", script])
            return True
        return False
    ...
```

Finally, the class needs a way to ask it to stop a process. Note that this will not try to stop a process when it is not running. When we stop the scripts, we will use Unix signals, which let us ask them to stop in a way that lets their atexit code run. You can send a signal via SIGINT, which is the equivalent of the *Ctrl + C* keyboard combination:

```
    ...
    def stop(self):
        """Stop a process"""
        if self.is_running():
            # Sending the signal sigint is (on Linux) similar to pressing
ctrl-c.
            # The behavior will do the same clean up.
            self.current_process.send_signal(subprocess.signal.SIGINT)
            self.current_process = None
```

An alternative implementation of this kind of menu would be to update all our behaviors in such a way that they could be imported, and making sure that their cleanup was a bit tighter than leaving it down to the `atexit` logic.

Currently, a user must ask for a process to stop before starting another process. This could be improved by signalling the old process to stop and waiting when a new behavior is requested. We would have to be careful not to make the menu block when this happens.

The web service

Python on Linux has many ways to make a simple web server, and many of these extend quite well to the Raspberry Pi. We will be using a popular framework for this known as **Flask** (see the *Further reading* section to find out more). Let's use it to run some code on your robot in response to a click on a web page. Flask lets us use a page layout that lets us replace parts of the page in our code, known as a template.

We will need to prepare our Raspberry Pi by installing flask via SSH:

```
$ sudo pip install flask
```

Flask lets us set up handlers for links to perform tasks. Let's make a script that acts as our menu webservice, which uses Flask and our RobotModes. Flask scripts are just Python; they consist of some setup, helper functions, and routes—functions that are associated with a path in the URL. I've called mine `menu_server.py`.

First comes the imports. We need the parts of Flask to make an app and render a template, as well as our robot modes:

```
from flask import Flask, render_template
from robot_modes import RobotModes
...
```

Now, we will create a Flask app to contain the routes, and an instance of our RobotModes class from before:

```
...
# A Flask App contains all its routes.
app = Flask(__name__)
# Prepare our robot modes for use
mode_manager = RobotModes()
...
```

Next, we need a helper function to render the menu. The menu will be a template called `menu.html` (which we'll define later), which takes a menu config and an optional status message to display. Most of our modes will need this:

```
...
def render_menu(message=None):
    """Render the menu screen, with an optional status message"""
    return render_template('menu.html', menu=mode_manager.menu_config,
message=message)
...
```

Flask works by decorating Python functions with routes, that is, how a URL typed at the web server can reach them. We only need three routes: the index at the top, running a behavior mode, and stopping the mode. Notice that for the run and stop, we set a message when rendering the menu:

```
...
@app.route("/")
def index():
    return render_menu()

@app.route("/run/<mode_name>")
def run(mode_name):
    # Use our robot app to run something with this mode_name
    mode_manager.run(mode_name)
    return render_menu(message="%s running" % mode_name)

@app.route("/stop")
def stop():
    # Tell our system to stop the mode it's in.
    mode_manager.stop()
    return render_menu(message='Stopped')
...
```

Finally, now that we have our routes, we can start the web app. Without specifying any other port, our server will run on port 5000. I've enabled debugging so that we can see any problems with this in our browser:

```
...
# Start the app running
app.run(host="0.0.0.0", debug=True)
```

However, before we can run it, we need to provide the template, `menu.html`.

The template

Our HTML template actually defines our display, and lets us separate the way the robot menu looks from how it is handled. This template combines HTML and the **Jinja2** template system. We need to make a templates folder and put this file in there. We could add further styling to this later, but here are some basics. Put this in a file called templates/menu.html.

Our template starts with a header that sets the page title and a heading, both saying My Robot Menu. Feel free to change these to your robot's name:

```
<html>
<head>
  <title>My Robot Menu</title>
</head>
<body>
  <h1>My Robot Menu</h1>
  ...
```

Next, we have an if statement. When we issue commands, we want the robot to be able to respond with a status. The double brackets {{ }} are used to surround a replacement; the content will have message in the paragraph:

```
  ...
  {% if message %}
    <p>{{ message }}</p>
  {% endif %}
  ...
```

The next section is a list, that is, the menu itself. We use the <ul> tag and then a for loop, which will create a list item with a link for each menu item. It will use .mode_name and .text to make that link, combining /run with the mode name:

```
  ...
  <ul>
    {% for item in menu %}
      <li><a href="/run/{{ item.mode_name }}">{{ item.text }}</a></li>
    {% endfor %}
    ...
```

Before closing our list, we need to add one more menu item—the Stop button:

```
    <li><a href="/stop">Stop</a></li>
  </ul>
</body>
</html>
```

The nice thing with a template like this is that you can preview this code as it is in a browser without the server and make some sense of what it should look like. The following screenshot shows it in preview mode:

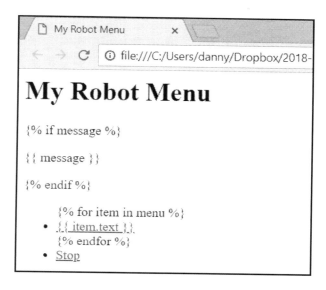

Previewing the template

You'll note that when you preview it, all of the template bits are showing as the browser doesn't know them. You'll need to run the app to see it properly rendered.

Running it

Upload the `robot_modes.py` and `menu_server.py` files to the robot, and then the `templates` folder. On the Raspberry Pi, via SSH, it can be started with the following code:

```
$ python menu_server.py
 * Serving Flask app "test_flask" (lazy loading)
 * Environment: production
   WARNING: Do not use the development server in a production environment.
   Use a production WSGI server instead.
 * Debug mode: on
 * Running on http://0.0.0.0:5000/ (Press CTRL+C to quit)
```

You can now point your browser at your robot (`http://myrobot.local:5000/`) to see the menu. You should be able to click a mode, and see the robot start that behavior. Clicking stop will do the equivalent of a *CTRL + C* to stop the behavior. The following screenshot shows how it should look (with a few menu items clicked):

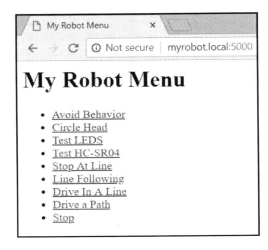

The My Robot Menu in a browser

When you click a behavior or stop, the output from this is shown in the message area:

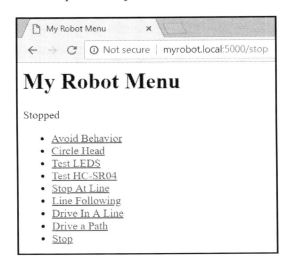

The stop button has been clicked – a Stopped message is shown

Notice that the behavior's outputs; it's `print` statements—are coming out in the web server console:

```
192.168.0.57 - - [03/Sep/2018 21:12:24] "GET / HTTP/1.1" 200 -
192.168.0.57 - - [03/Sep/2018 21:12:28] "GET /run/test_leds HTTP/1.1" 200 -
red
blue
red
blue
red
blue
Traceback (most recent call last):
  File "leds_test.py", line 16, in <module>
    sleep(0.5)
KeyboardInterrupt
192.168.0.57 - - [03/Sep/2018 21:12:32] "GET /stop HTTP/1.1" 200 -
```

You will need to press *CTRL + C* on the Pi to exit this menu server app. We have only scratched the surface of this, and this system is quite rudimentary. The menu system could be made far prettier with CSS and bootstrap. Tools like jQuery could be used so that a page isn't reloaded every time you click options, and there are ways to get the console output from a script onto the page. I recommend looking at the additional reading recommendations in the *Further reading* section for Flask.

 This tiny robot web app has no security mechanism, authentication, or passwords. It is beyond the scope of this book, but is a serious consideration worth further research if you plan to use this on shared Wi-Fi systems.

Summary

In this chapter, we have learned how to add distance sensing to our robots, along with the different kinds of sensors that are available. We've seen code to make it work. We then created behaviors to avoid walls, and looked at how a simplified, but flawed behavior could be made, and how a more sophisticated and smoother behavior would make for a better system.

At the end of this chapter, we added a small menu system to our robot to start different modes from a connected web browser.

In the next chapter, we will be looking again into driving predetermined paths and straight lines, but using an encoder to make sure that the robot moves far more accurately.

We will use an encoder to compare our motor's output with our expected goals and get more accurate turns.

Questions

1. What might interfere with a light-based distance sensor?
2. Why do we divide the speed of sound by two?
3. Why, in the more complicated behavior, has a variable delay been introduced?
4. Why could the robot still reverse into things?

Further reading

There are a number of other tutorials on these sensors on the internet worth reading for further knowledge and experimentation:

- First, I recommend looking at the datasheet for the sensor. You can search for the HC-SR04 datasheet. The Mouser link for it can be found at `https://www.mouser.com/ds/2/813/HCSR04-1022824.pdf`, but be warned that this may change.
- ModMyPi has a tutorial with an alternative way to wire these and level shift their IO: `https://www.modmypi.com/blog/hc-sr04-ultrasonic-range-sensor-on-the-raspberry-pi`.
- Raspberry Pi Tutorials also has a breadboard layout and Python script, using RPi.GPIO instead of gpiozero, at `https://tutorials-raspberrypi.com/raspberry-pi-ultrasonic-sensor-hc-sr04/`.
- GPIOZero has its own class for dealing with the distance sensor, but it is only suitable for longer distances: `https://gpiozero.readthedocs.io/en/stable/api_input.html#distance-sensor-hc-sr04`.

We've started to use many pins on the Raspberry Pi. When trying to find pins to use, I highly recommend visiting the Raspberry Pi GPIO at `https://pinout.xyz/`.

There are many scholarly articles on more interesting or sophisticated object behavior. I recommend reading *Simple, Real-Time Obstacle Avoidance Algorithm* (`https://pdfs.semanticscholar.org/519e/790c8477cfb1d1a176e220f010d5ec5b1481.pdf`) for Mobile Robots for a deeper look at these behaviors.

For getting to know Flask, the Flask website at `http://flask.pocoo.org` is highly recommended. I also recommend the book *Mastering Flask* (`https://www.packtpub.com/web-development/mastering-flask`), written by Jack Stouffer, published by Packt.

Jinja2, the Python template engine we used, is documented for reference at `http://jinja.pocoo.org/`.

The HTML used in this chapter is extremely simple. To get a deeper look into the ways you could enhance the simple menu system, I recommend the eLearning video guide *Beginning Responsive Web Development with HTML and CSS [eLearning]* (`https://www.packtpub.com/web-development/beginning-responsive-web-development-html-and-css-elearning-video`). Another good place to get to grips with HTML is `https://www.freecodecamp.org/`, which offers assessed online courses in coding web pages.

12
Programming Encoders with Python

It is useful in robotics to sense the movements of motors and wheels. We've driven a robot along a path, but it's unlikely that it has stayed on course. Detecting this and travelling a specific distance is useful in creating behaviors. In this chapter, we will investigate the sensors that can be used for this and then program the robot to move in a straight line, and for a specific distance. We will then look at how to make a specific turn. Please note that this chapter will contain math.

In this chapter, you will learn about the following topics:

- Distance and speed measuring sensors—encoders and odometry
- How to attach the sensors to your robot
- Creating code to work with these sensors and detect a basic distance (in ticks)
- Seeing how to correct for veer in a robot and actually drive in a straight line
- Calibrating the sensors to travel a specified distance
- Calibrating to make a known turn

Technical requirements

Refer to the following requirements for this chapter:

- The Raspberry Pi robot and the code from the previous chapters (you will require level shifters from Chapter 11, *Programming Distance Sensors with Python*, regarding the breadboard).
- Two slotted speed sensor encoders. Search for slotted speed sensor, Arduino speed sensor, LM393 speed sensor, or Photo Interrupter module. See the *The encoders we will be using* section for images of these.

- Long male-to-female jumper cables.
- A ruler to measure the size of the wheels on your robot, or better yet calipers, if you can use them.
- The code for this chapter is available in `GitHub`.

Check out the following video to see the Code in Action:

`http://bit.ly/2r4j5VK`

What are encoders?

Encoders are sensors that change value based on the movement of a part. They detect where the shaft is or how many times an axle has turned. These can be rotating, or sensing, along a straight line track.

Sensing how far something has traveled is also known as **odometry**, and the sensors can also be called **tachometers**, or **tachos** for short. The sensors suggested in the *Technical requirements* section may also show up as **Arduino tacho** in searches.

Use of encoders

Our robots use electronic sensors. Cars and large commercial vehicles use electronic or mechanical sensors for speedometers and tachos.

Encoders are used as an alternative to stepper motors in items such as printers and scanners. Sensing the amount turned is an essential component of servomechanisms, which we saw in `Chapter 10`, *Using Python to Control Servo Motors*. They are also used in control dials for high-end audio or electrical test/measurement systems. These are self-contained modules that look like volume knobs, but can be turned indefinitely.

Types of encoders

The following photo shows some ways that you can measure movement, along with an encoder wheel and strip:

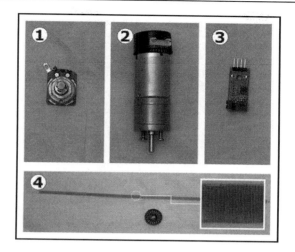

Encoder sensors

The sensors shown in the preceding picture fall into a few categories, and correspond to the points that follow:

1. This is a variable resistor. These analog devices can measure a turn, but don't tend to allow continuous rotation. They have mechanical wipers on a metal or resistant track, which can wear down. This is not strictly an encoder, but handy. On the Pi, they require analogue to digital conversion, so they aren't really suitable for this application. They are used inside servo motors.
2. This motor includes magnet sensing encoders, known as **hall-effect sensors**. Magnets on a wheel or strip pass next to the sensor, causing the sensor values to go high and low.
3. This is a common optical sensor. Using a slot with an IR beam passing through, they sense when the beam is interrupted. These are used in computer trackballs, printers, and robotics. These produce a chain of pulses. Due to the beam being interrupted, they are known as **photo-interrupters** or **opto-interrupters**. We will be using this kind.
4. Optical sensors usually use a slotted wheel, or a slotted strip for linear encoding, with transparent and opaque sections. A variation can be made by using a light sensor and light/dark sections, but these are less common.

Encoding direction and speed

Basic encoding measures how many wheel slots pass the sensor. This will give speed and distance. By using two sensors slightly apart, you can also encode the direction. The following diagram shows how this would work:

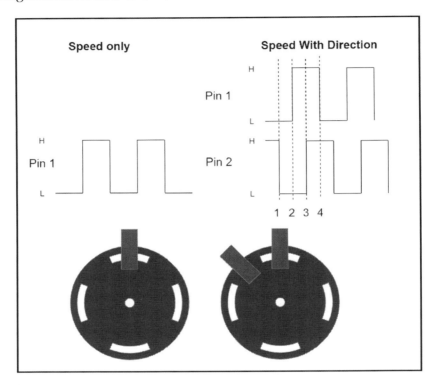

Encoding speed and direction with multiple sensors

The system on the left only encodes the speed. The wheel on the right encodes direction, with a sequence of 1, 2, 3, 4. The direction of the sequence indicates the direction of the wheel.

To build a robot with a **record and replay** type user interface, or a mouse/trackball, direction is important information, so the additional complexity and space needed to encode the directions is needed. We are using the cheaper option of speed only, so we will need to account for this in the code.

Each pulse has a **rising** edge, where it goes up, and a **falling** edge, where it goes down. To count the number of pulses, we can count one of these edge types, or both types for double the number of transitions.

The encoders we will be using

We will use slot encoders that fit right above the encoder wheels we added in Chapter 6, *Building Robot Basics - Wheels, Power, and Wiring*. These encoders have digital outputs, and we can count the pulses from them in Python to sense how far a wheel has turned. The following photo shows two types of sensor that I recommend:

The types of sensor we are using

On the left is the FC-03 photo interrupter module, and on the right is the Waveshare Photo interrupter module.

We are going to use encoder wheels that are attached to the motor shafts. These are in line with the wheels. If there are encoder wheels running at a different rate from the wheels, this will need to be accounted for. There are conditions they cannot account for such as slipping, and wheel and tire sizes. Encoders attached to separate idler wheels give better data, but they are trickier to attach to a robot and keep in contact with the floor.

The following diagram shows what the robot block diagram will look like after attaching the encoders:

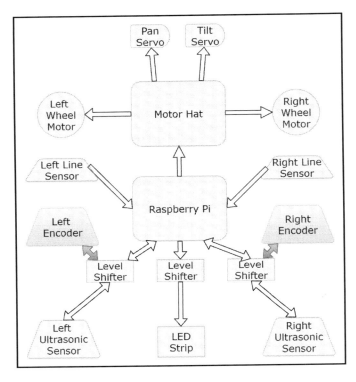

Robot block diagram with encoders

Attaching encoders to the robot

Our robot is now getting quite busy, and our Raspberry Pi is above the slots for the encoders. We may need taller Pi standoffs to accommodate the encoders. Due to them being under the Pi, we should wire them in a little before returning the Pi. After bolting in the Pi, we will wire them through the level shifters to the Pi, as well as the power and ground.

Before we start changing the robot and making it harder to see, we will need to know the number of slots in the encoder wheel for later, which is shown in the following photo:

Encoder wheel

My encoder wheels came out at having 20 slots. If the seller you bought the robot chassis from printed this, you would be able to check that your number is the same as theirs.

Lifting up the Raspberry Pi

These sensors will need to go underneath the Pi, so it will need to be gently lifted up (without disrupting wires) to accommodate them. The following sequence of photos shows how to lift it:

Unscrewing and lifting off the Pi

You will need to carefully unscrew the bolts holding the Pi to the chassis so that the Pi can gently lift away without disrupting the cables. Keep the screws for replacing the Pi on the robot, which we will do later. Do not reattach the Pi yet.

Preparing the encoders

Before we can use the encoder sensors, we need to prepare and fit them:

1. As the encoders will be going under the Raspberry Pi, we should attach the male to female jump wires to the sensors now. I also suggest covering the electrical contacts that will be sticking up under the Pi with a little insulation tape:

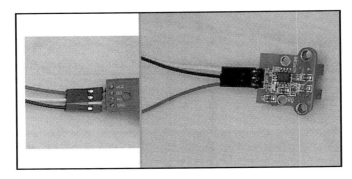

The sensors with cable connections

2. Importantly, the cables should be plugged into the ground (GND), voltage (5V or VCC), and digital output (D0/OUT). If it is present, the analog output (A0) pin should **not** be connected. If it is possible, the ground pin should have the darkest color, or the voltage should be the lightest color. To help keep this clear, I suggest wrapping a small stripe of insulation tape around the end of the signal line.

As these sensors' pin configurations can vary, get a reference photo of the sensor pin labels before putting it under the Pi.

3. Now that they are wired, you can fit them to the robot chassis. As a guide, the following picture shows a bare chassis with each of the sensor types fitted to show you where you would push them in:

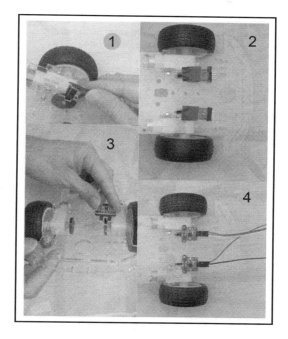

Fitting the encoder Sensors

4. The sensors should friction fit into the slots above the encoder wheels and stay in place.
5. Once these are in place, you can replace the screws to attach the Pi to the chassis.

 At this point, check that all your connections are back in place—I found that the motor connections in their terminals came loose and had to be reconnected at this point.

Wiring the encoders to Pi

The following diagram shows a simplified breadboard circuit for these sensors. Please note that some of these sensors work with 3.3V, in which case the level shifter can be skipped.

If you are not sure, leave the level shifter in:

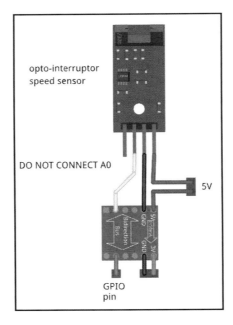

Simplified speed sensor connections

We will make this circuit in the context of a busy robot with other connections. If the cables from the sensors to the robot are not long enough, use a further set of male-to-female cables, as shown in the following photos:

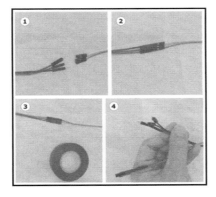

Joining the cables to extend them

1. Bring the male end of one, and join it to the female end of the other.
2. Use insulation tape to keep this joint from separating. If the extension colors are different, try tagging the signal (D0) line with some insulating tape at each end.

The following diagram shows the current robot wiring, which is for comparison with the new wiring for these sensors:

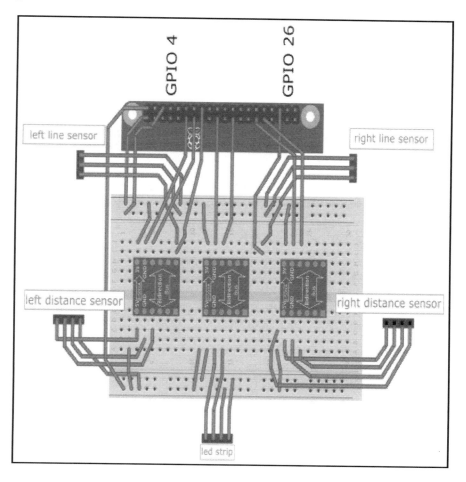

The current wiring of the robot

The following diagram shows the new connections for these sensors:

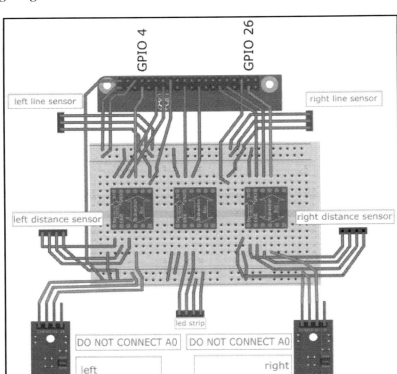

The steps for connecting the encoders to Raspberry Pi

Let's perform the following steps:

1. Connect the Raspberry Pi GPIO pins 4 and 26 to the free channels of the low voltage side of the level shifters.
2. Now, connect the sensor's D0 pins to the high side of the level shifter channels. Pay attention to the labels on the sensor – some have a different pin ordering. Use the photo reference suggested earlier if you need help with this.
3. Connect the sensor to the power connectors at the back of the breadboard.
4. The sensors are now ready for programming.

The number of wire-to-wire points on this robot will make it hard to add new connections or repair. Although beyond the scope of this book, making your own PCBs would make this thicket of cabling much neater. This would also be less fragile, and take up less space. It does, however, come with a cost to changing it.

Detecting the distance traveled in Python

Using these devices requires us to count pulses. In this section, we will create some code to turn on the motors, and count pulses for a while. This will validate that the sensors are connected correctly. We will then take this code and make it part of the robot class as a behavior.

Simple counting

This code will count the number of cycles up and down on the signal pin for each wheel, and print them as we go to test the sensors. We will run our motors for about 1 second.

The following code can be found in GitHub under Chapter 12 as test_encoders.py (https://github.com/PacktPublishing/Learn-Robotics-Fundamentals-of-Robotics-Programming/blob/master/chapter12/test_encoders.py).

Let's start with the usual robot class import and time:

```
from robot import Robot
import time
...
```

Next, we'll add an import for a GPIOZero input device. We can use the pin it sets up to count our pulses:

```
...
from gpiozero import DigitalInputDevice
...
```

The encoders generate pulses; we will want to count them and track their state. We will use more than one of them. Creating a class from the outset seems like the right strategy. From here, we can pass our pin number to the constructor. The first thing it needs to do is set up a pulse counter:

```
...
class EncoderCounter(object):
    def __init__(self, pin_number):
        self.pulse_count = 0
        ...
```

Still in the constructor, we need to set up the device and how we will count pulses with it. The device has a `.pin` object, which was set up from our pin number. The `.pin` has a `when_changed` event, which we can drop our own handler into so that it can be called every time the pin changes. The pin will change from up and then to down (rising and falling) for every slot:

```
        ...
        self.device = DigitalInputDevice(pin=pin_number)
        self.device.pin.when_changed = self.when_changed
    ...
```

We need to define `when_changed` for our class to add one to the `pulse_count`:

```
    ...
    def when_changed(self):
        self.pulse_count += 1
...
```

We can set up our `robot` object and create an `EncoderCounter` for each side's sensor. We connected our devices to pins 4 and 26:

```
...
bot = Robot()
left_encoder = EncoderCounter(4)
right_encoder = EncoderCounter(26)
...
```

To display values, instead of just using `sleep`, we will loop, checking against an end time. We will start the motors, and go into the main loop:

```
...
stop_at_time = time.time() + 1

bot.set_left(90)
bot.set_right(90)
```

```
while time.time() < stop_at_time:
    ...
```

In this loop, we print the readings on both sensors.

Since tight loops can cause things to break (especially with our sense threads), it should sleep a little, too:

```
    ...
    print "Left:", left_encoder.pulse_count, "Right:",
right_encoder.pulse_count
    time.sleep(0.05)
```

When the loop ends, the program will be done, so our robot will automatically stop. You can send this code to the robot and run it. You will now be able to see the robot veering through the encoder's values. The output will look a little like this:

```
pi@myrobot:~ $ python test_encoders.py
Left: 0 Right: 0
Left: 0 Right: 1
Left: 2 Right: 2
Left: 3 Right: 4
Left: 5 Right: 7
Left: 8 Right: 10
Left: 10 Right: 14
...
Left: 56 Right: 74
```

The encoders are counting, and it shows that the robot moved less on the left wheel, and more on the right wheel, and veered left. The distances are in encoder **ticks**, a tick being each counted event.

If the encoder values stay at zero, go back and check your wiring and pin number usage carefully. Note that if you do not use level shifters, a pull down or pull up resistor may be required.

Adding encoders to the Robot object

To use this sensor in other code or behaviors, we should move it into the Robot object. We can then import our code into the Robot object, and set up the two sides with the correct pins. The encoders need some cleanup code to be added to them.

Extracting the class

We'd already made a class, so this can be moved to the `encoder_counter.py` (`https://github.com/PacktPublishing/Learn-Robotics-Fundamentals-of-Robotics-Programming/blob/master/chapter12/encoder_counter.py`) file. This needs the import for the `DigitalInputDevice` and has the same constructor, which is also the case when changed. The `direction` member has been added to account for reversing:

```python
from gpiozero import DigitalInputDevice

class EncoderCounter(object):
    def __init__(self, pin_number):
        self.device = DigitalInputDevice(pin=pin_number)
        self.device.pin.when_changed = self.when_changed
        self.pulse_count = 0
        self.direction = 1
    ...
```

Our `when_changed` handler should use the direction, and we need a method to set this direction. We can use `assert` to validate our setting, which will throw an exception if it doesn't meet the condition with the given text. A cheap but brutal way of ensuring input values make sense:

```python
    ...
    def when_changed(self):
        self.pulse_count += self.direction

    def set_direction(self, direction):
        """This should be -1 or 1. """
        assert abs(direction)==1, "Direction %s should be 1 or -1" % direction
        self.direction = direction
    ...
```

For cleanup, add a reset and a way to stop the counters so that the handler isn't called again:

```python
    ...
    def reset(self):
        self.pulse_count = 0

    def stop(self):
        self.device.close()
```

Adding the device to the Robot object

We need to modify Chapter 11, `robot.py` (https://github.com/PacktPublishing/Learn-Robotics-Fundamentals-of-Robotics-Programming/blob/master/chapter11/robot.py) code to add the sensors. Start by importing `EncoderCounter`:

```
...
import leds_8_apa102c
from servos import Servos
from distance_sensor_hcsr04 import DistanceSensor, NoDistanceRead
from encoder_counter import EncoderCounter
...
```

In the `__init__` constructor method, we need to set up left and right encoders. I did this just after the distance sensors:

```
...
# Setup The Distance Sensors
self.left_distance_sensor = DistanceSensor(17, 27)
self.right_distance_sensor = DistanceSensor(5, 6)

# Setup the Encoders
self.left_encoder = EncoderCounter(4)
self.right_encoder = EncoderCounter(26)
...
```

To make sure that the encoders are cleaned up when our `Robot` object has stopped, we call the encoder's `stop` methods in the `stop_all` method:

```
...
# Clear any sensor handlers
self.left_line_sensor.when_line = None
self.left_line_sensor.when_no_line = None
self.right_line_sensor.when_line = None
self.right_line_sensor.when_no_line = None

self.left_encoder.stop()
self.right_encoder.stop()
...
```

The finished code for `robot.py` is on GitHub (https://github.com/PacktPublishing/Learn-Robotics-Fundamentals-of-Robotics-Programming/blob/master/chapter12/robot.py). As we made a behavior from this, we'll use it to measure distance in millimeters.

Turning ticks into millimeters

To calculate real distances, we need the sizes of the wheels. We cannot account for slipping, but we can know how much a wheel has turned, which is at the same rate as the encoders. Using the wheel's diameter, we can calculate how far it has turned. Using a ruler or calipers, measure the diameter across the wheel. The following photo shows you how you can do this:

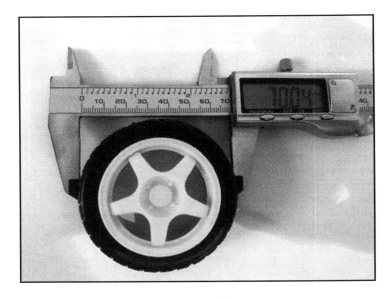

Measuring the wheel

My wheel came out at 70 mm to the nearest mm. Also measure the width from midpoint to midpoint of the two motor-driven wheels on the robot. We will need this information soon. Mine came out at about 130 mm.

We know how many slots are on the encoders, and we expect two ticks (the rising and falling) per slot, so we can take the number of slots * 2, which would be the number of ticks per whole turn of the wheel – in my case, this is 40.

Pi is the ratio of the diameter to the circumference of the wheel. To get the circumference, we multiply the diameter by Pi, giving us πD, where D is the diameter. We can divide Pi by the number of total edges per revolution, and then when we multiply this by the number of ticks T and then the diameter D, and we will get a number for the distance d that wheel has traveled:

$$d = \frac{\pi}{40} \times D \times T$$

So, how would we turn this into code? Refer to the following steps:

1. Make a new file called `test_distance_travelled.py`. First, at the top of the file, we will need to import `math` for the calculations, the `Robot` object, and time:

```
from robot import Robot
import time
import math
. . .
```

2. Next, we can define our constants—the wheel's diameter and the number of ticks per revolution. Please use the values you obtained, not the ones that I have shown here:

```
. . .
wheel_diameter_mm = 70.0
ticks_per_revolution = 40.0
. . .
```

3. Create a function to convert the ticks, counted into a distance. It's converted to integers, since fractions of a millimeter are just not appropriate for this measurement. Since part of the conversion doesn't change, we make that a constant, too:

```
. . .
ticks_to_mm_const = (math.pi / ticks_per_revolution) *
wheel_diameter_mm

def ticks_to_mm(ticks):
    return int(ticks_to_mm_const * ticks)
. . .
```

4. Next, we define our robot, set up a stop time, and start the motors:

```
. . .
bot = Robot()
stop_at_time = time.time() + 1

bot.set_left(90)
bot.set_right(90)
. . .
```

5. In the loop, we display the distance by calling `ticks_to_mm` on the pulse counts:

```
...
while time.time() < stop_at_time:
    print "Left:", ticks_to_mm(bot.left_encoder.pulse_count), \
        "Right:", ticks_to_mm(bot.right_encoder.pulse_count)
    time.sleep(0.05)
```

6. When uploaded to the robot and run, the output will look this:

```
pi@myrobot:~ $ python test_distance_travelled.py
Left: 0 Right: 0
Left: 5 Right: 0
Left: 16 Right: 10
Left: 32 Right: 21
...
...
Left: 368 Right: 384
Left: 395 Right: 417
```

Driving in a straight line

By now, you may have seen differences in the outputs, that is, a veer. In only 400 mm, my left side is around 20 mm behind the right, an error that is climbing. Depending on your motors, your robot may have some veer too. It is rare for a robot to have driven perfectly straight. We'll use the sensors to correct this.

Note that this is still dead reckoning; slipping on surfaces or incorrect measurements can still set this off course. This works better on wooden flooring or MDF boards, and poorly on carpet.

Concepts for correction

Driving in a straight line needs a closed feedback loop. The following diagram shows how this loop works:

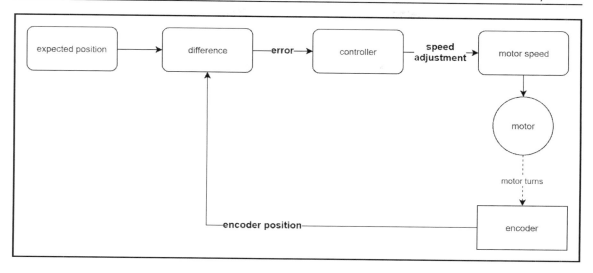

Closed loop control of a motor's speed

We take an **expected position** or **set point**. The **encoder position** (feedback data from the real world) is subtracted from the expected position to get an **error** value. This is fed into a **controller**, which generates **speed adjustment**. Apply that speed adjustment to the **motor speed** so that the motor turns more or less, changing the feedback received from the encoder.

To go straight, we pick the left motor as a primary and use its encoder as the **expected position**, then aim for the right encoder to keep up with it. Our **error** will therefore be the difference between the encoders. Set a constant speed for the left motor, and the right speed will come from the controller.

We will use a **PID** controller to adjust the speed of the right motor. This has three components:

- **P** -> **proportional**: The error value multiplied by a constant. This corrects for immediate errors.
- **I** -> **integral**: The sum of the error values so far, multiplied by a constant. This corrects for continuing errors.
- **D** -> **derivative**: This takes the difference between the last error value and now, also multiplied by a constant. This is to push back a little against sudden changes.

By manipulating the constants, we can **tune** the controller so that each factor will influence the final outcome more. For our behaviors, we won't be using the derivative component, which is equivalent of having its constant set to zero.

The integral can give the robot some self-tuning, but it needs to have a very small constant, as high values can make the robot start to wobble instead.

The right motor speed will be as follows:

```
...
integral_sum = integral_sum  + error
right_motor_speed = speed + (error * proportional_constant) + (integral_sum
* integral_constant)
...
```

We need unused motor speed capacity for our right motor to speed up or slow down to match the left. If the speed is too close to 100%, we will get clipping. An integral behavior with clipping here can make the robot behave quite strangely, so watch out for clipping at 100%! Use no more than 80% input speed.

Creating a Python PID Control object

We will use this in a few places, so let's make a PID Control object. I put this in a file named `pid_controller.py`. Note that this is really only a **PI** (**proportional integral**) controller. This needs no imports. Here is the class and its constructor:

```
class PIController(object):
    def __init__(self, proportional_constant=0, integral_constant=0):
        self.proportional_constant = proportional_constant
        self.integral_constant = integral_constant

        # Running sums
        self.integral_sum = 0
...
```

The constructor takes the constants; I've preloaded these with zero so the components can be isolated. The class stores these values. Then, we set up a variable to store the integral sum, which grows with time. It is not unusual to abbreviate the `proportional_constant` as pK and the `integral_constant` as iK. You may do so if you wish; I've used the longer names in the code examples to make it easier to read.

The following code handles the values for the two components. Handling the integral has the effect of increasing the integral sum:

```
...
    def handle_proportional(self, error):
        return self.proportional_constant * error

    def handle_integral(self, error):
        self.integral_sum += error
        return self.integral_constant * self.integral_sum
...
```

The following bit of code handles the error to generate the adjustment:

```
...
    def get_value(self, error):
        p = self.handle_proportional(error)
        i = self.handle_integral(error)
        return p + i
```

I've left the proportional and integral parts available here as `p` and `i`; the reader may want to print them to debug and tune their controller.

Straight line code

I called this `straight_line_drive.py` (https://github.com/PacktPublishing/Learn-Robotics-Fundamentals-of-Robotics-Programming/blob/master/chapter12/straight_line_drive.py). Let's import the `Robot` object, time, and our new PI Controller. Set up the `Robot` object too, and set up a slightly longer `stop_at_time` value so that our robot drives a bit further:

```
from robot import Robot
from pid_controller import PIController
import time

bot = Robot()
stop_at_time = time.time() + 60
...
```

Instead of setting each motor to a speed, start with a master speed value of 80, and set both motors to this:

```
...
speed = 80
bot.set_left(speed)
bot.set_right(speed)
...
```

Before going into our main loop, set up the controller. You may need to tune these constants. Note how small the integral constant is:

```
...
pid = PIController(proportional_constant=4, integral_constant=0.2)
...
```

In the loop, start by sleeping so that our encoders have something to measure. Get the encoder values, and compute the error:

```
...
while time.time() < stop_at_time:
    time.sleep(0.02)
    # Calculate the error
    left = bot.left_encoder.pulse_count
    right = bot.right_encoder.pulse_count
    error = left - right
    ...
```

That error needs to be handled by the controller, and used to make the `right_speed`. We print debug information here:

```
...
# Get the speed
adjustment = pid.get_value(error)
right_speed = int(speed + adjustment)
print "left", left, \
    "right", right, \
    "right_speed:", right_speed, \
    "error:", error, \
    "adjustment: %.2f" % adjustment
...
```

We then set the right motor speed to the newly adjusted value, and the loop is done:

```
...
bot.set_right(right_speed)
```

When we run this, the robot should be following a fairly straight course. It may start off unstable, but should hone in on a constant adjustment:

```
pi@myrobot:~ $ python straight_line_drive.py
left 0 right 0 right_speed: 80 error: 0 adjustment: 0.00
left 0 right 0 right_speed: 80 error: 0 adjustment: 0.00
left 0 right 0 right_speed: 80 error: 0 adjustment: 0.00
left 0 right 1 right_speed: 75 error: -1 adjustment: -4.20
left 1 right 2 right_speed: 75 error: -1 adjustment: -4.40
left 2 right 2 right_speed: 79 error: 0 adjustment: -0.40
left 2 right 4 right_speed: 71 error: -2 adjustment: -8.80
left 3 right 5 right_speed: 70 error: -2 adjustment: -9.20
left 4 right 6 right_speed: 70 error: -2 adjustment: -9.60
left 5 right 7 right_speed: 70 error: -2 adjustment: -10.00
left 6 right 8 right_speed: 69 error: -2 adjustment: -10.40
...
left 32 right 34 right_speed: 58 error: -2 adjustment: -22.00
...
left 109 right 108 right_speed: 74 error: 1 adjustment: -5.20
left 110 right 110 right_speed: 70 error: 0 adjustment: -9.20
left 112 right 112 right_speed: 70 error: 0 adjustment: -9.20
left 114 right 114 right_speed: 70 error: 0 adjustment: -9.20
left 116 right 116 right_speed: 70 error: 0 adjustment: -9.20
left 117 right 117 right_speed: 70 error: 0 adjustment: -9.20
```

The robot starts off with no error as the motors engage, but the right engages faster. At 32 ticks, the integral pulls the adjustment pretty high. By around the 100's, the integral caused a small overshoot, but it settles in for this -9.20 adjustment, which keeps both motors driving at the same speed, and the robot straight. Tuning of the P and I constants, as well as the loop timing, may result in earlier corrections—the initial encoder values are too small to be useful.

Troubleshooting this behavior

Here are a few steps to take if the robot is wobbling, or doesn't manage to travel in a straight line:

- **The robot takes too long to compensate:** Increase the proportional component.
- **The robot overshoots massively (that is, it swerves one way, then the other):** Reduce the height of both components.
- **The robot is making increasing wobbles:** The integral is too high, and that right speed may be going above 100. Bring down the integral component, and perhaps the requested speed.

Driving a specific distance

For this behavior, we'll use the PI Controller again, and incorporate the distance measurements into our encoder object. We will calculate how many ticks we want the left wheel to have turned for a given distance, and then use this instead of a timeout component.

Refactoring unit conversions into the EncoderCounter class

We'll want the conversions for our encoders in the the EncoderCounter class so that we can use them in these behaviors. Open up your encoder_counter.py class. First, we need the math import:

```
from gpiozero import DigitalInputDevice
import math
...
```

At the top of the class, add ticks_to_mm_const as a class variable (not an instance variable) so that we can use it without any instances of the class. Set this to none initially so that we can calculate it:

```
...
class EncoderCounter(object):
    ticks_to_mm_const = None # you must set this up before using distance
methods
    ...
```

In our class, we want to be able to retrieve the distance the wheel has traveled directly from the encoder, in mm. Add this at the end of the file:

```
...
def distance_in_mm(self):
    return int(self.pulse_count * EncoderCounter.ticks_to_mm_const)
...
```

Notice that ticks_to_mm_const is pulled from the class, and not self (the instance). We want to calculate the opposite, that is, the number of ticks from a distance in mm. To do that, divide the distance in mm by the same constant we multiplied by. This is a staticmethod, so that it does not require an instance to be used:

```
...
@staticmethod
def mm_to_ticks(mm):
    return mm / EncoderCounter.ticks_to_mm_const
...
```

Add a way to set the constants in the file (for different robot configurations):

```
...
@staticmethod
def set_constants(wheel_diameter_mm, ticks_per_revolution):
    EncoderCounter.ticks_to_mm_const = (math.pi / ticks_per_revolution) *
wheel_diameter_mm
...
```

Save this file.

Setting the constants

So far, we can use our robot metrics in our behaviors. Now, we want the Robot object to store our measurements, and register them with the encoders. In robot.py, just before the constructor, specify some of these numbers:

```
...
class Robot(object):
    wheel_diameter_mm = 69.0
    ticks_per_revolution = 40.0
    wheel_distance_mm = 140.0
    def __init__(self, motorhat_addr=0x6f, drive_enabled=True):
        ...
```

Register these with the encoders:

```
...
# Setup the Encoders
EncoderCounter.set_constants(self.wheel_diameter_mm,
self.ticks_per_revolution)
    self.left_encoder = EncoderCounter(4)
    self.right_encoder = EncoderCounter(26)
    .....
```

Creating the combined behavior

I'll put this code into `drive_distance_behavior.py`. The starting point is a few imports and creating the robot instance. Import the `EncoderCounter` to use its metrics, the `PIController`, and the robot object:

```
from robot import Robot, EncoderCounter
from pid_controller import PIController
import time
...
```

Define the `drive_distance` function, which will take a robot instance, a distance in ticks, and an optional speed defaulting to 80. We'll start by making a primary and secondary motor and controller decision:

```
...
def drive_distance(bot, distance, speed=80):
    # Use left as "primary" motor, the right is keeping up
    set_primary = bot.set_left
    primary_encoder = bot.left_encoder
    set_secondary = bot.set_right
    secondary_encoder = bot.right_encoder
    ...
```

Note that we store the `set_left` and `set_right` functions in variables—we can just call the variables like functions. We now have a well-defined primary and secondary motor. Set up the `PIController`, and start the two motors:

```
...
    controller = PIController(proportional_constant=5,
integral_constant=0.2)

    # start the motors, and start the loop
    set_primary(speed)
    set_secondary(speed)
    ...
```

Now, we are in the driving distance loop. We should continue the loop until both encoders reach the right distance. We need to sleep before the rest of the loop so that we have some data for our calculations:

```
...
    while primary_encoder.pulse_count < distance or
secondary_encoder.pulse_count < distance:
        # Sleep a bit before calculating
        time.sleep(0.05)
        ...
```

Get the error, and feed it into the controller:

```
. . .
# How far off are we?
error = primary_encoder.pulse_count - secondary_encoder.pulse_count
adjustment = controller.get_value(error)
. . .
```

We can send this to the secondary motor, and debug the data too. Because the adjustment is non-integer, we allow two decimal places by using `{:.2f}`:

```
. . .
# How fast should the motor move to get there?
set_secondary(int(speed + adjustment))
# Some debug
print("Primary c:{} ({} mm)\tSecondary c:{} ({} mm) e:{}
adjustment: {:.2f}".format(
        primary_encoder.pulse_count, primary_encoder.distance_in_mm(),
        secondary_encoder.pulse_count,
secondary_encoder.distance_in_mm(),
        error,
        adjustment
    ))
. . .
```

Set up the robot, calculate how far you want it to go, and get it moving:

```
. . .
bot = Robot()
distance_to_drive = 1000 # in mm - this is a meter
distance_in_ticks = EncoderCounter.mm_to_ticks(distance_to_drive)
drive_distance(bot, distance_in_ticks)
```

We will use the robot cleanup (`atexit`) to stop the motors. When this is run, the robot drives for around a meter and stops. My robot, when stopping, looked like this:

```
. . .
left 986 right 986 right_speed: 64 error: 0 p 0 i -15.20
left 997 right 991 right_speed: 70 error: 1 p 5 i -15.00
```

There is a 6 mm discrepancy between the motors. 3 mm may have been lost in rounding values to integers – we can't really make partial ticks.

There are a few ways this could be improved. Applying a **PID** controller to the distance moved by the primary could make it close in more precisely on the exact distance to travel. Detecting no movement in either encoder could be used to make the code stop after a timeout so that it doesn't drive off without stopping.

Making a specific turn

The next task we can use our encoders for is to make a specific turn. When turning a robot, each wheel is going through an arc. The following diagram illustrates this:

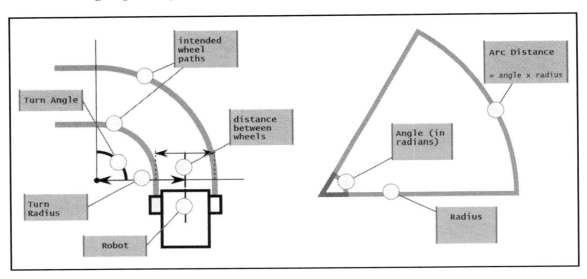

Illustrating wheel movement when turning through an arc

The inner wheel clearly drives a smaller distance than the outer wheel, and from the basics of differential steering, this is how we make the turn. To make an exact turn, we need to calculate these two distances, or the ratio between them. The following diagram shows how the wheels and the turn relate to each other:

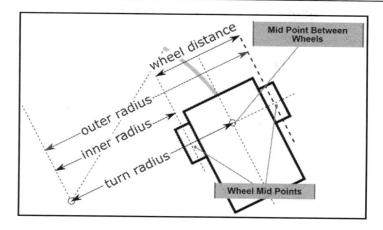

Relating wheels to turn radiuses

If we consider the turn radius as setting where the middle of the robot would be, an inner wheels turn radius will be the **difference** between the turn radius and half the distance between the wheels. The outer wheel's turn radius would be the turn radius **added** to half the distance.

We convert our angle to turn into **radians**, and we can then multiply this angle by each wheel radius to get the distances that each wheel needs to move through. Python has math functions to convert degrees to radians.

Start with a copy of `drive_distance_behavior.py` and call it `drive_square_behavior.py`. Add the math import, like so:

```
from robot import Robot, EncoderCounter
from pid_controller import PIController
import time
import math
...
```

At the end of this file, let's modify it to do what we want it to do. It can be helpful to state what functions you would like to have, and then implement them to fit. We'll make it a bit smaller than a meter, too. For a radius to test with, I've added 100 mm to the robot's wheel distance. Anything less than the wheel distance, and the center of the turn will be between the wheels instead of outside of them:

```
...
bot = Robot()

distance_to_drive = 300 # in mm
distance_in_ticks = EncoderCounter.mm_to_ticks(distance_to_drive)
```

```
radius = bot.wheel_distance_mm + 100 # in mm
radius_in_ticks = EncoderCounter.mm_to_ticks(radius)

for n in range(4):
    drive_distances(bot, distance_in_ticks, distance_in_ticks)
    drive_arc(bot, 90, radius_in_ticks, speed=50)
```

Since we are driving in a square, we want to drive four times. For straight lines, drive each wheel the same distance, then make 90 degree arcs of our radius. I've reduced the speed for the arc so that there is less of a slipping problem.

Go back up in the file to upgrade our method for driving a distance to one to drive two distances, one for each wheel. I've renamed the `drive_distance` function to `drive_distances`:

```
...
def drive_distances(bot, left_distance, right_distance, speed=80):
    ...
```

Depending on the angle we want to turn, either motor could be the outer motor, and driving a longer distance. Since there is an upper limit in speed, we choose our primary and secondary motors based on which is the longer distance. Swap the code that set up the primary/secondary for this:

```
    ...
    # We always want the "primary" to be the longest distance, therefore
the faster motor
    if abs(left_distance) >= abs(right_distance):
        print("Left is primary")
        set_primary = bot.set_left
        primary_encoder = bot.left_encoder
        set_secondary = bot.set_right
        secondary_encoder = bot.right_encoder
        primary_distance = left_distance
        secondary_distance = right_distance
    else:
        print("right is primary")
        set_primary = bot.set_right
        primary_encoder = bot.right_encoder
        set_secondary = bot.set_left
        secondary_encoder = bot.left_encoder
        primary_distance = right_distance
        secondary_distance = left_distance
    primary_to_secondary_ratio = secondary_distance / (primary_distance *
1.0)
    secondary_speed = speed * primary_to_secondary_ratio
    print("Targets - primary: %d, secondary: %d, ratio: %.2f" %
```

```
(primary_distance, secondary_distance, primary_to_secondary_ratio))
    ...
```

The encoders and motors are as they were in the preceding code. However, the decision is made using abs, the absolute value, because a longer distance in reverse should **still** be the primary motor. So, to determine how far the secondary wheel should go, we compute a ratio—to multiply with the speed now, and later the primary encoder output.

Since we are using this method more than once, reset the encoder counts. I put this in before setting up the PIController:

```
    ...
    primary_encoder.reset()
    secondary_encoder.reset()
    controller = PIController(proportional_constant=5,
integral_constant=0.2)
    ...
```

Since we can be going in either direction, set the encoder direction. Python has a copysign method to determine the sign of a value. Then, start the motors:

```
    ...
    # Ensure that the encoder knows which way it is going
    primary_encoder.set_direction(math.copysign(1, speed))
    secondary_encoder.set_direction(math.copysign(1, secondary_speed))

    # start the motors, and start the loop
    set_primary(speed)
    set_secondary(int(secondary_speed))
    ...
```

When we start this loop, we again need to be aware that one or both motors could be going backwards:

```
    ...
    while abs(primary_encoder.pulse_count) < abs(primary_distance) or
abs(secondary_encoder.pulse_count) < abs(secondary_distance):
        # And sleep a bit before calculating
        time.sleep(0.05)
    ...
```

Calculating the error for the secondary depends on the ratio between the two distances:

```
    ...
        # How far off are we?
        secondary_target = primary_encoder.pulse_count *
primary_to_secondary_ratio
```

```
error = secondary_target - secondary_encoder.pulse_count
...
```

This will still go into the same adjustment calculation through the `pid`, however, this adjustment may also cause a change in direction here:

```
...
set_secondary(int(secondary_speed + adjustment))
secondary_encoder.set_direction(math.copysign(1,
secondary_speed+adjustment))
...
```

The reader may also want to expand the debug that we had to take into account for the secondary speed and targets. Now, because we are trying for precision, the primary motor may reach its goal before the secondary, and isn't set up to reverse. So, stop this motor when it reaches its goal, and set the base speed of the secondary to zero, which will mean only adjustments will apply, if any. Note that we still use the absolute values here:

```
...
# Stop the primary if we need to
if abs(primary_encoder.pulse_count) >= abs(primary_distance):
    print "primary stop"
    set_primary(0)
    secondary_speed = 0
...
```

And we are done with the drive distances function.

The drive_arc function

Here is where we convert to radians, determine the inner radius, and set up the distances for each wheel to drive. This code is to be added in `drive_square_behaviour.py`, after the `drive_distances` function.

Start with a function definition, and a helpful docstring:

```
...
def drive_arc(bot, turn_in_degrees, radius, speed=80):
    """ Turn is based on change in heading. """
    ...
```

We turn the robot's width into ticks, the internal measurement of distance, and use half of that to get the wheel radiuses. We also determine which is the inner wheel:

```
. . .
# Get the bot width in ticks
half_width_ticks =
EncoderCounter.mm_to_ticks(bot.wheel_distance_mm/2.0)
if turn_in_degrees < 0:
    left_radius = radius - half_width_ticks
    right_radius = radius + half_width_ticks
else:
    left_radius = radius + half_width_ticks
    right_radius = radius - half_width_ticks
print "Arc left radius {:.2f}, right_radius {:.2f}".format(left_radius,
right_radius)
. . .
```

We display the debug on what the radii are. Combine this with the turn in radians to get distances. We convert the absolute value of the turn in degrees. We don't want to reverse into a turn, but to turn the other way:

```
. . .
radians = math.radians(abs(turn_in_degrees))
left_distance = int(left_radius * radians)
right_distance = int(right_radius * radians)
print "Arc left distance {}, right_distance {}".format(left_distance,
right_distance)
. . .
```

Finally, feed these distances into the `drive_distances` function:

```
. . .
drive_distances(bot, left_distance, right_distance, speed=speed)
. . .
```

The robot should be able to drive in a square shape. It can still miss due to slipping, or inaccuracies in the measurements. Tuning of the proportional and integral control values will be required.

Examining the full code for `drive_distances` and `drive_arc`, it may become apparent that there is some repetition in determining the inner/outer and the primary/secondary parts. This may also not behave correctly if reversing through a corner.

Further ideas

You could now use this code to make further geometric shapes, or to follow paths without a line. By combining the sensors here with distance sensors, it may be possible to start memorizing distances between walls. High level left turn/right turn 90 degree functions could be added as building blocks for right-angled path construction.

Summary

In this chapter, we have seen how to incorporate wheel encoder sensors into our robot, and used them to determine how far each wheel has turned. We've seen how to use this to get the robot onto a straighter path using a reduced PID Controller and then used this to drive a specific distance. We then took the calculations further to calculate turning a corner in terms of wheel movements, and drive the robot in a square.

In the next couple of chapters, we will be exploring giving our robot even more interactive and intelligent behaviors, with chapters on visual processing using a Raspberry Pi Camera, speech processing on a handset with MyCroft, and adding a gamepad to the handset to remotely drive or select modes on the robot.

Questions

1. What are the edge types we are counting with our encoder code?
2. Why should we not drive motors at 100% for these control systems?
3. What are some factors that encoders on the wheels/motors like this cannot account for?

Further reading

PID Control is a deep subject. It is a key area in self-balancing robots, drones, and other autonomous control systems. Here is a great video series so that you can explore these further:

- Youtube: Brian Douglas - PID Control - A brief introduction

I've greatly simplified some of the corner turning algorithms. A very in-depth article on how this was used for a competition winning Lego Mindstorms robot holds a more detailed method:

- G W Lucas - Using a PID-based Technique For Competitive Odometry and Dead-Reckoning
- http://www.seattlerobotics.org/encoder/200108/using_a_pid.html

13
Robot Vision - Using a Pi Camera and OpenCV

Giving a robot the ability to see things allows it to behave in ways to which humans relate well. Computer vision is an area that much research is currently devoted to, but some of the basics are already available for use in our own code, with the Pi Camera and a little bit of work. In this chapter, we will use the robot and camera to drive to objects, and follow faces with our pan-and-tilt mechanism. I'll also give you a way to see what your robot is seeing. In this chapter, you will learn the following:

- Setting up a Raspberry Pi Camera on your robot, in terms of both software and hardware
- Revisiting Flask, the web server from Chapter 11, *Programming Distance Sensors with Python*, to see what the robot sees on your phone or laptop
- Revisiting color models, covered in Chapter 9, *Programming RGB Strips in Python*, and learning how to mask images with them.
- Using contours to detect the largest blob of color in an image and pointing the robot at it
- Using Haar cascades to detect faces, and pointing the pan-and-tilt mechanism at them

Technical requirements

For this chapter, you will need the following items:

- The robot with the pan-and-tilt mechanism from `Chapter 12`, *Programming Encoders with Python.*
- The Python code for the robot up to `Chapter 12`, *Programming Encoders with Python,* which can be downloaded from the GitHub at `https://github.com/PacktPublishing/Learn-Robotics-Fundamentals-of-Robotics-Programming/tree/master/chapter12`. We will be extending and modifying this for new functionality.
- The Raspberry Pi Camera v2.
- A 300 mm-long Pi Camera cable. This is because the cable included with the camera is too short. Be sure this is a Raspberry Pi 3 cable, and not a Pi Zero cable.
- 2 M2 bolts and M2 nuts.
- A small square of thin cardboard—a cereal box will do.
- A small jeweler's screwdriver.
- A kids' bowling set—the type with differently colored pins (plain, with no pictures).
- A well lit space for the robot to drive in.
- You will also require internet access while working on this project.

The code for this chapter is on GitHub, available at `https://github.com/PacktPublishing/Learn-Robotics-Fundamentals-of-Robotics-Programming/tree/master/chapter13`.

Check out the following video to see the Code in Action:

`http://bit.ly/2KCklbE`

Setting up the Raspberry Pi Camera

We will first attach the camera to the pan-and-tilt assembly. We can then use a longer cable to wire the camera into the Pi.

When we have completed this installation, our robot block diagram will look like the following:

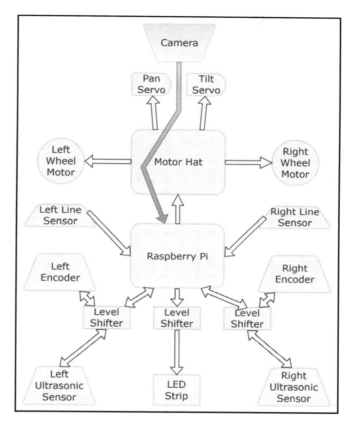

Our robot block diagram with the camera added

Attaching the camera to the pan and tilt mechanism

In `Chapter 10`, *Using Python to Control Servo Motors,* you added a pan-and-tilt mechanism to your robot. The camera will be mounted onto the front plate of this mechanism. There are brackets and kits, but they are not universally available. Feel free to use one of these if you can adapt it to the pan-and-tilt mechanism; if not, I have a few plans.

Building a robot requires creative thinking and being adaptable, as well as the necessary technical skills. I frequently look through the materials I have for possible solutions before I go and buy something. Sometimes, the first thing you attempt will not work, and you'll need a plan B. My plan A was to use a hook-and-loop fastener (like Velcro), stuck directly to the camera, but it does not adhere well to the back of the camera. So I had to adapt my plan: plan B was to use a square of cardboard and make holes for 2 mm screws in it, bolt the camera to the cardboard, and then use the hook-and-loop fastener to attach this to the Pi.

The following photo shows the parts needed for this:

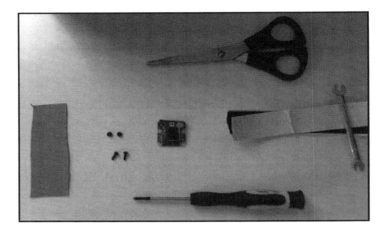

The parts needed for our plan to fit the camera module

In the preceding photo, we have some thin card, 2 mm bolts and screws, the Pi Camera module, some scissors, a small spanner (or pliers), some hook-and-loop tape, and a small screwdriver.

The following photos show the steps to mount the camera. Work carefully through each numbered step in the following list:

1. First, cut a small amount for one side of the hook-and-loop fastener, and adhere it to the pan and tilt mechanism:

Some hook-and-loop tape on the pan and tilt mechanism

2. Cut out a small square of cardboard the right size to fit the camera, then use a pencil to poke through the camera screw holes to mark a dot. Then take a pointed tool, and, on a firm surface, punch a hole where you made the pencil mark:

Using a pen to mark screw positions

3. Use a couple of M2 bolts and nuts to fasten the camera onto the cardboard carrier. Note that the bolt-facing side is at the back—this is so any protruding thread won't interfere with the hook and loop:

Bolting the camera to the cardboard

4. Now cut a small amount of the hook-and-loop fabric, to which the fabric on the pan and tilt mechanism will fasten, and stick it to the back of the cardboard:

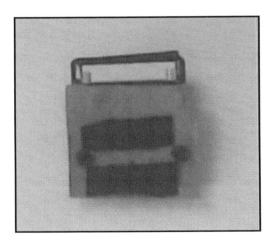

The back of the cardboard/camera assembly with our hook-and-loop fastener

Don't attach the camera yet, as we need to change the cable first. Note that the camera may have film covering the lens—this should be removed.

Wiring in the camera

The next sequence of images shown how we will wire the camera into the Raspberry Pi:

The camera connector slot and the motor board

Please follow these steps:

1. The Raspberry Pi has a slot specifically for the camera—the camera cable fits into this. We will be wiring our camera into this slot, but on our robot, this is currently covered by the motor board.
2. To get around this, we will need to lift this board gently off the Pi. If the cables for the motors are tight, disconnect them for these steps.
3. When you connect the camera to the Pi, the long cable will need to pass through this board. Keep this in mind as you perform the next step.

Now, I recommend following this guide on *How To Connect The Raspberry Pi Camera Module* (https://www.techcoil.com/blog/connect-raspberry-pi-camera-module-raspberry-pi-2-raspberry-pi-3/) using the long 300 mm cable. After following the guide, you should have the cable installed the correct way around in the camera, then going through the slot in the motor board, and into the port the right way around on the Raspberry Pi. Double-checking that your connections are the right way around before replacing the motor board will save you a lot of time. The next photo shows the steps to complete this assembly:

Completing the camera interface

Follow these steps, using the preceding as a reference:

1. Gently replace the motor board, pushing it down onto the Pi and the spacers. Reconnect the motor cables if needed.
2. Push the camera onto the hook-and-loop attachment on the pan-and-tilt head, with the cable facing upwards.

This camera is now wired and ready to use.

Setting up OpenCV

In this section, we will set up the camera, activating it in Raspbian and getting a test picture. Then we will add the libraries to start interacting with the camera for visual processing.

We will then build our first app with the tool, to demonstrate that the parts are in place and give us a starting point for the behaviors.

Setting up the Pi Camera software

Power up the Pi on external power (that is, plugged into a USB wall adapter) for this operation, leaving the motors powered down for now, and log in via PuTTY. At the Terminal, type the following:

```
pi@myrobot:~ $ sudo raspi-config
```

In `raspi-config`, select the **5 Interfacing Options** option by selecting it, then pressing *Enter*, and then selecting **P1 Camera**. You will then be asked if you would like the camera interface to be enabled. Select **Yes** and **Ok**, then **Finish**. If you are asked to reboot at this point, answer **Yes**.

Getting a picture from the Pi

The first thing we need to do, to confirm that our setup was successful, is to ask the Pi camera to take a picture for us. This will check whether all the connections are good or not. If there are problems detecting the camera, please go back and check that the cable connection is correct, that you have installed picamera, and that you have enabled the Raspberry Pi camera in raspi-config.

Reconnect to the Raspberry Pi with PuTTY, and type the following to get a picture:

```
pi@myrobot:~ $ raspistill -o test.jpg
```

`raspistill` takes a still image, and the `-o` parameter tells it to store that image in `test.jpg`. You can then use your SFTP client (which we set up in the headless chapter) to download this image and verify it on your computer. You will notice that the picture is upside down, due to how the camera is mounted. Don't worry—we will correct this with our software.

Installing libraries

OpenCV is a library with a collection of tools for manipulating pictures and extracting information from them. The name is an abbreviation of *Open Computer Vision*. The tools are strung together to make useful behaviors and pipelines for processing images. To be able to run our code on the Raspberry Pi, we will need to install the Python OpenCV library there.

We will also install **NumPy**, the numeric python library. This lets us to do manipulations of large blocks of numbers. An image stored on a computer is essentially a large block of numbers, with each tiny dot having similar content to the three-color numbers we sent to the LEDs in Chapter 9, *Programming RGB Strips in Python*.

Also, at a Terminal, install the following before rebooting. This may take five minutes or so to complete:

```
pi@myrobot:~ $ sudo apt install python-opencv opencv-data
.
.
.
pi@myrobot:~ $ sudo pip install picamera[array] numpy
pi@myrobot:~ $ sudo reboot
```

After a reboot, the system will be ready to use with the camera. We will continue testing on external power for the next few operations. At the time of writing, this installation will give you OpenCV 2.4.9—the code will have to be adapted for later versions. The later OpenCV versions are still quite complicated to install.

Building our first app with these tools

Downloading one picture at a time is fine, but we actually need to be able to do things with those pictures on the robot. We also need a handy way to see what the robot is doing with the camera data. For that, we will reach back into our toolkit, and use a Flask web server to serve up our pictures. We can use the core of this app to make a few different behaviors. We'll keep the base app around for them.

OpenCV camera server app overview

The following diagram shows a pipeline, with our image data going from the camera, through the pipeline, and out to our web browser. The **process image** step can be anything we require; for this example, we'll apply a color mask, which we explore in more depth in the next section:

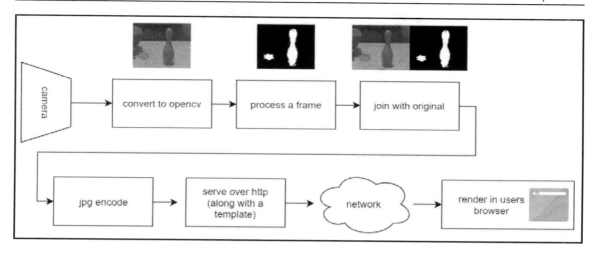

The image server app

It's time to start building the code to do this. Because this is fairly complex, we'll break it down into two major parts: first, a `CameraStream` object, which will send our frames to an `image_server.py` script, the second part of our code project.

The CameraStream object

This will act as a helper library, to set up the camera, and get data streams from it. I suggest putting it in `pi_camera_stream.py`:

```
from picamera.array import PiRGBArray
from picamera import PiCamera
import numpy as np
import cv2
...
```

These imports give us the `PiCamera` code needed to access our camera. `cv2` is OpenCV, the computer vision libraries used to process the images. Here, NumPy is *aliased*, or nicknamed, `np`. The next few lines set up a few reusable parameters:

```
...
size = (320, 240)
encode_param = [int(cv2.IMWRITE_JPEG_QUALITY), 90]
...
```

We will keep the images we capture at a small resolution of 320 by 240—this means we are sending less data, so we will process less too, which will keep the system reasonably quick. Also, higher resolutions may lead to more noise and edge defects, which would require further filters to compensate for. The encode parameter will be used when we convert the images to send to the browser. This function will set up the camera:

```
...
def setup_camera():
    camera = PiCamera()
    camera.resolution = size
    camera.rotation = 180
    return camera
...
```

After initializing the camera, we set its resolution to the size. I mentioned that the camera is the wrong way up, so we set its rotation to 180 degrees to turn it round. We will need a function to start capturing a stream of images (a video, but at our own rate of control):

```
...
def start_stream(camera):
    image_storage = PiRGBArray(camera, size=size)

    cam_stream = camera.capture_continuous(image_storage, format="bgr",
use_video_port=True)
    for raw_frame in cam_stream:
        yield raw_frame.array
        image_storage.truncate(0)
...
```

For storing our image, we need to set up the `PiRGBArray`, which is designed for storing RGB images. We then set up the stream of data with `capture_continuous`. This is a `picamera` method setup to repeatedly take photos. We give it the image store and tell it to format the output data as `bgr`, which is the way OpenCV stores color data. The last parameter to this is `use_video_port`, which, when set to true, results in a reduction in image quality in exchange for faster production of frames.

The `cam_stream` it returns can be looped through for frames, until we choose to stop. Python has a concept of **iterators**—data structures that can be looped through, such as lists and generators. Generators are like lists, but instead of holding all of the content, they produce the next bit of data just in time for when it's needed.

This loop is actually a generator itself. The line after `for` gets the raw `.array` from the frame that was captured. It then uses `yield`. What this means is that the output of this function can also be looped over as a generator, so when called, its return value can be looped over, and the code in this `for` loop will execute just enough to produce one raw frame, then the next, and so on. Python generators are a way to construct processing pipelines.

The last line of the loop calls `truncate` on the output array. This resets it, ready to hold the next image. The PiRGBArray can be configured to store many images in sequence, but we only operate on one at a time, so we must truncate it.

The final thing we can place in our `pi_camera_stream.py` script is a function to encode an image with OpenCV, as shown here:

```
...
def get_encoded_bytes_for_frame(frame):
    result, encoded_image = cv2.imencode('.jpg', frame, encode_param)
    return encoded_image.tostring()
```

We will be using this `pi_camera_stream` utility for a few of our behaviors.

Building a template

Just like the Flask app we built previously, this one will require an HTML template to render. Create a file in the `templates` folder named `image_server.html`.

First, our video server sets up an HTML document, with a title and a level 1 heading:

```
<html>
    <head>
        <title>Robot Image Server</title>
    </head>
    <body>
        <h1>Robot Image Server</h1>
...
```

Now, we add the image link that will display the output of our server:

```
...
        <img src="{{ url_for('display') }}">
...
```

Note the `url_for` here. This is asking the Flask renderer (via Jinja2) to insert the URL for a route in flask. This will make more sense with the following Flask code. Finally, we just close the tags in the template:

```
...
    </body>
</html>
```

The image server main app

This part of the app will set up Flask, start our camera stream, and link them together. We will put this in our `image_server.py` script. First, we need to import all of these components and set up a Flask app, as follows:

```
from flask import Flask, render_template, Response
import pi_camera_stream
import time

app = Flask(__name__)
...
```

The first route is one we've seen before, an index page, using the preceding template:

```
...
@app.route('/')
def index():
    return render_template('image_server.html')
...
```

Now we get to the tricky bit, the video feed. Although some of the encoding is done in the preceding section, we need to turn this into an HTTP stream of data; that is, data that your browser expects to be continuous:

```
...
def frame_generator():
    """This is our main video feed"""
    camera = pi_camera_stream.setup_camera()

    # allow the camera to warmup
    time.sleep(0.1)
...
```

We will need to let the camera warm up. I've put this in the app, and not in the camera setup, as if it's combined with other setup activities (like servo movements), the `time.sleep` could account for both:

```
. . .
    for frame in pi_camera_stream.start_stream(camera):
        encoded_bytes = pi_camera_stream.get_encoded_bytes_for_frame(frame)
        # Need to turn this into http multipart data.
        yield (b'--frame\r\n'
               b'Content-Type: image/jpeg\r\n\r\n' + encoded_bytes +
b'\r\n')
. . .
```

This function is actually another Python generator. It loops over every frame coming from `start_stream`. It then gets the JPG-encoded bytes for each of those frames. The line at the end surrounds the data with HTTP content declarations, and gives it to `yield`. We place `b` in front of this string to tell Python to treat this as raw bytes, and not perform further encoding on the information. The `\r` and `\n` items are raw line-ending characters.

This function will then generate a loopable stream of those HTTP content frames:

```
. . .
@app.route('/display')
def display():
    return Response(frame_generator(),
        mimetype='multipart/x-mixed-replace; boundary=frame')
. . .
```

This Flask `display` route generates a response with our preceding `frame_generator` function. If that is a generator, then Flask will keep consuming items from that generator, and sending those parts to the browser. It also specifies a content type. Note the boundary we called `frame`. We could call it anything, as long as both this part and the `--frame` in the preceding data stream agree on what to call it. Frame just seems sensible.

Now we can just add the code to start Flask. I've put this app on port 5001, so it can be started from the menu server in Chapter 12, *Programming Encoders with Python*. They could possibly be integrated, but this may make setup/tear down complicated:

```
. . .
app.run(host="0.0.0.0", debug=True, port=5001)
```

Now we can upload all three of these parts, ensuring that the template is uploaded into the `templates` directory on the Pi. Start the app with `python image_server.py`.

Point your browser at the app by going to `http://myrobot.local:5001` (or your robot's address), and you should see a video served there like the following:

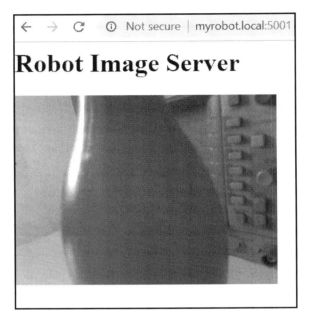

Screen capture of the robot image server

If you see errors while running this, please check that you are able to capture an image with `raspistill`, then check your code for errors.

Visual processing with behaviors

Our image service works, but has a major flaw. If we want our robot to be doing something, even when the network is not perfect, we need to be able to run a behavior in parallel with this. That behavior needs access to the image data, as well as the server too.

We will approach this by making the Flask web app a secondary process, with the behavior as the primary process for the robot when it is running. Python has a handy tool for exactly this kind of structure, called multiprocessing. Find out more at `https://docs.python.org/2/library/multiprocessing.html`.

Communicating between multiple processes is tricky. If two processes try to access (read or write) the same data at the same time, the results can be unpredictable and cause strange behavior. So, to save them trying to access data at the same time, we will use the multiprocessing queue object. These are set up so processes can safely put copies of items into the queue for the other to take off. We will use one queue to send images to the server, and another to get control data from user interactions in the browser.

The following diagram shows the way data will flow through behaviors such as these:

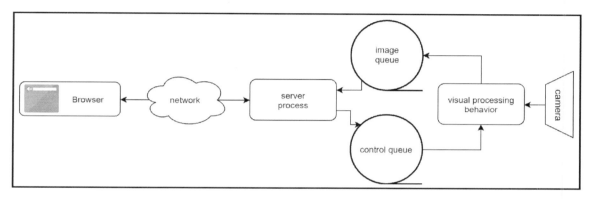

Data flow between a browser, server process, and robot behavior

There are a few caveats: we will only place images in the image queue when it's empty, so it will only ever contain one image. However, this prevents the visual processing behavior trying to overwrite an image in shared memory when a server is trying to output it. The control queue has no such restriction; we'll just expect that users interactions will not produce control messages faster than the behavior loop will consume them.

We will separate out the web app as a core and then write a behavior based on it. We can use this multiple times.

Web app core

In this design, the web app core will handle setting up the queues, running the server process, and the Flask-based routing. It will be written in Flask style, which tends to consist of plain Python functions in a module. We'll put this code in `image_app_core.py`.

As an interface to this, our other behaviors will be able to do the following:

- `start_server_process(template_name)` will start the web app server, with a template name passed in.
- `put_output_image(encoded_bytes)` can be used to put images into the display queue.
- `get_control_instruction()` is used to check and return instructions from the control queue. It has no opinion about what is in them; plain text seems good.

Let's start off with some documentation and imports:

```
"""The flask/webserver part is slightly independent of the behavior,
allowing the user to "tune in" to see, but should not stop the
robot running"""
import time
from multiprocessing import Process, Queue

from flask import Flask, render_template, Response
...
```

We import `Queue` and `Process` to create the process and communicate with it. We then use the same imports for Flask that we used previously. Note—we are *not* importing any of the camera parts in this module.

Next, we define our Flask app and the queues. We will also define a global `display_template` here, in which we'll store the main app template. When we use this app core, we'll set this with it. We only really want 1 frame queued, but we put in 2 in case of hiccups while transmitting—although we can check if a `Queue` is empty, this is not 100% reliable, and we don't really want one part of the app waiting for the other:

```
...
app = Flask(__name__)
control_queue = Queue()
display_queue = Queue(maxsize=2)
display_template = 'image_server.html'
...
```

Now we have our routes. The index route is only different in that it uses the `display_template`:

```
...
@app.route('/')
def index():
    return render_template(display_template)
...
```

Next, we will create the loop for getting frames: a new version of `frame_generator` that gets frames from the `display_queue` (we'll put frames into the queue later). So that it doesn't **spin** (that is, run very quickly in a tight loop), we put in a sleep that limits the frame rate to 20 frames per second. This loop also turns our data into multi-part data:

```
...
def frame_generator():
    """This is our main video feed"""
    while True:
        # at most 20 fps
        time.sleep(0.05)
        # Get (wait until we have data)
        encoded_bytes = display_queue.get()
        # Need to turn this into http multipart data.
        yield (b'--frame\r\n'
                b'Content-Type: image/jpeg\r\n\r\n' + encoded_bytes +
b'\r\n')

@app.route('/display')
def display():
    return Response(frame_generator(),
        mimetype='multipart/x-mixed-replace; boundary=frame')
...
```

The display route is exactly as in the preceding snippet. The next route allows us to put messages in the control queue for the robot behavior:

```
...
@app.route('/control/<control_name>')
def control(control_name):
    control_queue.put(control_name)
    return Response('queued')
...
```

That gives us all the internals of the core, but now we need the interface for the behaviors to use. We'll start with `start_app_process`:

```
...
def start_server_process(template_name):
    """Start the process, call .terminate to close it"""
    global display_template
    display_template = template_name
    server = Process(target=app.run, kwargs={"host": "0.0.0.0", "port":
5001})
    server.start()
    return server
...
```

This takes a `template_name` and stores it in the global `display_template`, used in the `index` route in the preceding code block. Instead of calling `app.run`, we create a `Process` object. This takes a function to run (`app.run`), and some parameters need to be given to it (the host and port settings). We then start this process, and return it so it can be stopped later.

The next interface task is putting an image into the queue. We only want to do this if there isn't an image there, so we don't run up a big buffer. It means if nothing is connected, the first frame will be stale, but another one will be along so quickly that it won't affect the user:

```
...
def put_output_image(encoded_bytes):
    """Queue an output image"""
    if display_queue.empty():
        display_queue.put(encoded_bytes)
...
```

Finally, for this interface, we need the function to get the control messages out. Here, we also check if the queue is empty, and return `None` for *no message* if there is nothing. If we have a message, we get it from the queue:

```
...
def get_control_instruction():
    """Get control instructions from the web app, if any"""
    if control_queue.empty():
        # nothing
        return None
    else:
        return control_queue.get()
```

Controllable behaviors

We can try out our core with a behavior that senses images to the web service, and accepts a simple *exit* control message.

This can be put in the `control_image_behavior.py` file. The imports will be the `image_app_core` interface, and the `pi_camera_stream`:

```
import time

from image_app_core import start_server_process, get_control_instruction,
put_output_image
import pi_camera_stream
...
```

We then add a function that runs our simple behavior with a main loop. It sets up the camera and waits. The waiting is outside the `setup_camera`, so other activities, such as servo motor movement, can be added:

```
...
def controlled_image_server_behavior():
    # Setup the camera
    camera = pi_camera_stream.setup_camera()
    # allow the camera to warmup
    time.sleep(0.1)
    ...
```

And then, still in this function, we get frames from a camera stream:

```
...
# Send frames from camera to server
for frame in pi_camera_stream.start_stream(camera):
    encoded_bytes = pi_camera_stream.get_encoded_bytes_for_frame(frame)
    put_output_image(encoded_bytes)
    ...
```

In that `for` loop, which will consume all the frames, it gets each one, then puts it on the web app queue. In this loop, we can also try accepting a control instruction to exit:

```
...
        # Check any control instructions
        instruction = get_control_instruction()
        if instruction == "exit":
            print("Stopping")
            return
    ...
```

This will use `return` to stop the behavior when the `exit` instruction is received from the control queue. We then need to start the server and start our behavior. `try` and `finally` ensure that anything in the `finally` part will **always** be run; in this case, it will make sure the web server app is terminated (stopped) too:

```
...
process = start_server_process('control_image_behavior.html')
try:
    controlled_image_server_behavior()
finally:
    process.terminate()
```

You'll see we start the server process with an `control_image_behavior` template. We need to provide that.

The template

This template, in `templates/control_image_behavior.html`, is the same as the one before, but with two important differences, shown here in bold:

```
<html>
    <head>
        <script src="https://code.jquery.com/jquery-3.3.1.min.js"></script>
        <title>Robot Image Server</title>
    </head>
    <body>
        <h1>Robot Image Server</h1>
        <img src="{{ url_for('display') }}"><br>
        <a href="#" onclick="$.get('/control/exit')">Exit</a>
    </body>
</html>
```

In this template, we load a library on the browser called `jquery`, for which documentation is available at `https://api.jquery.com/`. This is handy for interactive web pages. We are using it with an anchor tag (the `a` tag) we saw in the menu earlier, but this has an `onclick` handler. That handler uses `jquery` to send `'/control/exit'` to our web app. Since our web app makes a control instruction from anything after control, this will put `exit` in the control. The `<br>` just creates a line break so that the exit link is shown below the image.

Note that, if you wanted to run this where internet access is difficult, you would need to enhance the server to serve the `jquery` library too. This code tells the browser to download it directly from the internet.

Running the image server

To run the image server, you need to upload all three files: `image_app_core.py`, `control_image_behavior.py` and `templates/control_image_behavior.html`. On your Pi, use `python control_image_behavior.py` to start the process.

You will then need to go to your browser, and point it at `http://myrobot.local:5001` (or the address of your robot). You will see the pictures again. If you then click on the **Exit** link, your app should gracefully quit.

Colors, masking, and filtering – chasing colored objects

Now we have some basics ready, we can use this to build some more interesting behaviors. The next one will be to chase, but not get to close to, a colored object. This requires a few stages. Let's start with a diagram showing an overview of this whole behavior:

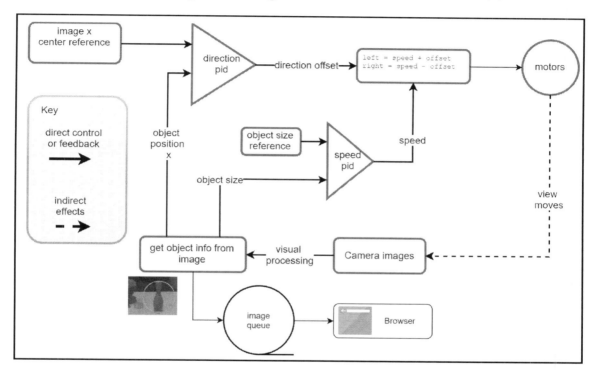

The color-tracking behavior

This behavior contains elements you've seen before: the PID controller and the image queue to the browser. The first thing you'll notice is that there are 2 PIDs. One controls the speed of the motors; the other is an offset, which controls their heading.

The speed PID will take a reference size and the size of an object (based on the radius of a circle around it) processed from the camera, it will then provide a base speed to both motors to try and get that radius close to the reference value. That way, the robot will maintain a distance from an object of a known size.

The heading PID will take a reference center X coordinate, the middle of the image, and the visual processing will produce the X coordinate for the center of an enclosing circle. This PID will produce an output to try and get the difference between these coordinates to zero. By adding to one motor's speed, and reducing the speed of the other, the robot will try to turn to face the object (or, if you swap them for fun, it'll turn away!).

The images are sent, via an image queue using the app core, to the browser. Not shown in the previous diagram is the fact that there is also a control queue with messages to start the motors, stop the motors, and exit the behavior.

The final part of this, and probably the most interesting, is the color tracking. This is controlled by the box labelled **get object info from image**. Let's see how that works next.

Getting information about an object

We are using colored pins from a kid's bowling set. They come in nice, bright, primary colors. I will use green as an example. Let's look at the image processing as a pipeline in the following diagram:

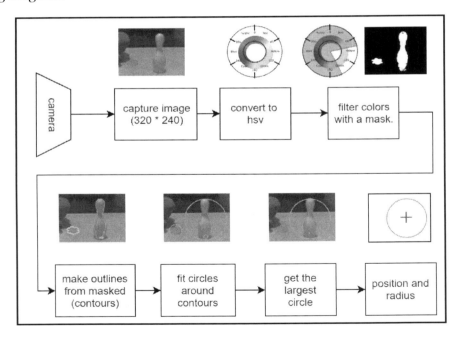

Getting color object information from a camera

The preceding diagram starts from the camera. As mentioned, we work in a low resolution to keep things fast. Next, we convert this to HSV, the colorspace we mentioned in `Chapter 9`, *Programming RGB Strips in Python*. We use HSV because it means we can filter colors in a specific range of hues, by their light (very dark objects may confuse us), and by saturation, so objects that are almost grey are not included. RGB (or BGR) images are tricky to filter, as getting the different light and saturation levels of a particular hue (say, the blues) is not really viable. So, we convert to HSV.

OpenCV has a function, `cv2.cvtColor`, to convert whole images between colorspaces. Note that OpenCV uses 0-179 for the hue range, instead of 0-359. This is so it fits in a byte (0-255), but you can convert hue values by simply dividing by 2 if you know the value you want.

After converting to HSV, we apply a filter (or mask) that will output white if the object is in a known HSV range, or black if it's not. There is a function in OpenCV to do this `cv2.inRange`. This gives us a very easy black and white output, a masked image, to draw around for our system.

Drawing around it is the next thing we do—this means creating outlines, known as contours, which specify only the boundary points of our object. OpenCV again provides a `cv2.findContours` function to do exactly this, which returns a list of shapes, each defined by their outlines.

We can then take the outlines, and ask OpenCV to draw circles around them using `cv2.minEnclosingCircle` for each of the contours. We will then have a bunch of circles, described by a center *x,y* coordinate and radius.

Our object may have highlights, producing more than one circle, and other objects may also produce smaller circles. We are only interested in one, the largest of these, so we can loop through the circles, and keep only the largest.

This largest circle's coordinates and radius give us enough information for our robot to start chasing an object. Let's build this code.

Caveat about red objects

We will use green because red is slightly tricky, as it requires two masks. The hues for red cross a boundary between 179 (the upper limit of our hue range) and 0 (the lower limit), so we would have to mask the image twice and then combine these with an `or` operation. The `cv2.bitwise_or` function can be used for this, if the reader wants to try that.

Enhancing the PID controller

We are going to be using more PID controllers. We still don't require the differential component, but we will develop an issue with our integral component building up while the motors take time to move. The integral has a sum that starts to grow if there is a constant error. It is good to correct for that error, but can result in large overshoot. This overshoot, due to the integral still growing after the robot has started to react, albeit slowly, is called **integral windup**.

To reduce the overshoot from this sum, we can prevent this sum from getting too large by introducing a windup limit to our PID.

Open up the `pidcontroller.py` file and make the changes in bold in the following snippet. First, add the `windup_limit` parameter, which defaults to None if it isn't set:

```
class PIController(object):
    def __init__(self, proportional_constant=0, integral_constant=0,
windup_limit=None):
        self.proportional_constant = proportional_constant
        self.integral_constant = integral_constant
        self.windup_limit = windup_limit
        # Running sums
        self.integral_sum = 0
    ...
```

We then want to prevent our integral growing if we have a limit, and hit it. But we do want to allow changes that reduce the size of the `integral_sum`. The comment in the integral handler explains how it changes:

```
    ...

    def handle_integral(self, error):
        """Integral will change if
            * There is no windup limit
            * We are below the windup limit
            * or the sign of the error would reduce the sum"""
        if self.windup_limit is None or \
                (abs(self.integral_sum) < self.windup_limit) or \
                ((error > 0) != (self.integral_sum > 0)):
            self.integral_sum += error
        return self.integral_constant * self.integral_sum

    ...
```

Another thing is we are able to `start` and `stop` this behavior from the web page. If we start it again, we won't want the PIDs to carry old values. So we should have a `reset` function to zero out the integral sum. Put this after the handle `integral` function:

```
    ...
    def reset(self):
        self.integral_sum = 0
    ...
```

The behavior code

This behavior has two files—a template to pass to our app core with the control buttons, and then the main behavior code.

The template

Copy the template from `templates/control_image_behavior.html` to `templates/color_track_behavior.html`. We will add two further controls to this, `start` and `stop`, displayed here in bold:

```
    ...
            <img src="{{ url_for('display') }}"><br>
            <a href="#" onclick="$.get('/control/start')">Start</a> <a href="#"
    onclick="$.get('/control/stop')">Stop</a><br>
            <a href="#" onclick="$.get('/control/exit')">Exit</a>
    ...
```

We will run the program with the robot stopped first, so we can tune in with our phone or browser and click a **Start** button to see if it is moving.

The behavior

We'll put this in a file called `color_track_behavior.py`. There's no surprise that we start with the imports. Because we are bringing together many elements, there are quite a few, but we have seen them all before:

```
import time

from image_app_core import start_server_process, get_control_instruction,
put_output_image

import cv2
```

```
import numpy as np

import pi_camera_stream
from pid_controller import PIController
from robot import Robot
...
```

Now, we set up our `Behavior` class. We pass this the robot object, and also set up some tunable values for the object size and color:

```
...
class ColorTrackingBehavior(object):
    """Behavior to find and get close to a colored object"""
    def __init__(self, robot):
        self.robot = robot
        # Tuning values
        self.low_range = (25, 70, 25)
        self.high_range = (80, 255, 255)
        self.correct_radius = 120
        self.center = 160
        # Current state
        self.running = False
...
```

The `low_range` and `high_range` values are used for the color filter (as seen in the preceding Pipeline diagram). Colors that lie between these HSV ranges would be white in the masked image. Our hue is 25 to 80, which correspond from 50 to 160 degrees on a hue wheel. Saturation is 70 to 255 – any lower starts to be washed out, or produces grey colors. Light is 25 (very dark) to 255 (fully lit).

The `correct_radius` value is used to set the size we want the object to be in view, and so behaves as a kind of distance setting. The `center` should be half the horizontal resolution of the pictures we capture.

The last member variable set here is `running`. This will be set to `True` when we actually want the robot to be moving. When set to `False`, the processing still occurs, but the motors and PIDs will stop.

The next bit of code is to process any control instructions from the web app:

```
...
    def process_control(self):
        instruction = get_control_instruction()
        if instruction == "start":
            self.running = True
        elif instruction == "stop":
```

```
        self.running = False
    if instruction == "exit":
        print("Stopping")
        exit()
. . .
```

This services the `start`, `stop` and `exit` buttons. It uses the `running` variable to start or stop the robot moving. Next we have the code that will find an object from a frame. This implements the pipeline shown in the preceding snippet. We'll break this function down a bit though:

```
. . .
    def find_object(self, original_frame):
        """Find the largest enclosing circle for all contours in a masked
    image.
        Returns: the masked image, the object coordinates, the object
    radius"""
    . . .
```

Because this code is complex, we have a documentation string (`docstring`) explaining what it does and what it returns. First, let's get the `masked_image` from our frame, converting it to HSV first, then perform the `inRange` filter on it:

```
    . . .
        frame_hsv = cv2.cvtColor(original_frame, cv2.COLOR_BGR2HSV)
        masked = cv2.inRange(frame_hsv, self.low_range, self.high_range)
    . . .
```

Now that we have the masked image, we can draw contours around it:

```
    . . .
        # Find the contours of the image (outline points)
        contour_image = np.copy(masked)
        contours, _ = cv2.findContours(contour_image, cv2.RETR_LIST,
    cv2.CHAIN_APPROX_SIMPLE)
    . . .
```

In this version of OpenCV, the original image is altered by the contours operation. Since we don't want this, we make a copy of our masked image. We find contours and use `RETR_LIST`, as we are not interested in a hierarchy (which is capable of more complicated analysis) and want to keep it fast. `CHAIN_APPROX_SIMPLE` tells `findContours` how we want each contours boundary to be stored. A boundary is a list, or chain of points. Simple asks OpenCV to simplify this to the least number of points; for example, four points for a rectangle.

There are other settings, such as CHAIN_APPROX_NONE, that would return every point along the rectangle's entire outline, but this would make the next part of the pipeline slower, so we use SIMPLE to keep it quick.

The next thing is to find all the enclosing circles for each contour. We use a tiny loop to do this. minEnclosingCircle means to get the smallest circle that entirely encloses all points in a contour:

```
...
        # Find enclosing circles
        circles = [cv2.minEnclosingCircle(cnt) for cnt in contours]
...
```

Each circle is made up of a radius and coordinates—exactly what we want. However, we only want the biggest one:

```
...
        # Filter for the largest one
        largest = (0, 0), 0
        for (x, y), radius in circles:
            if radius > largest[1]:
                largest = (int(x), int(y)), int(radius)
        return masked, largest[0], largest[1]
...
```

We store a largest value of 0, and then we loop through the circles. If the circle has a radius larger than the one we stored, we store the values. It's a little sneaky, but we also convert all the values to int here, as minEnclosingCircle produces non-integer floating point numbers.

We end this function by returning the masked image, the largest coordinates, and the largest radius. Our next function will take an original frame a and processed frame, turn them into a nice dual screen display, and put them on the output queue through to the web app:

```
...
    def make_display(self, frame, processed):
        """Create display output, and put it on the queue"""
        # Make a dualscreen view - two images of the same scale joined
together
        display_frame = np.concatenate((frame, processed), axis=1)
        encoded_bytes =
pi_camera_stream.get_encoded_bytes_for_frame(display_frame)
        put_output_image(encoded_bytes)
...
```

The only new thing here is the `concatenate` function to join the two images. You can change the `axis` parameter to 0 if you wanted screens stacked vertically, instead of horizontally.

The next function processes a frame of data through both of the preceding functions, finding the objects, and setting the display. It then returns the object info as follows:

```
...
    def process_frame(self, frame):
        # Find the largest enclosing circle
        masked, coordinates, radius = self.find_object(frame)
        # Now back to 3 channels for display
        processed = cv2.cvtColor(masked, cv2.COLOR_GRAY2BGR)
        # Draw our circle on the original frame, then display this
        cv2.circle(frame, coordinates, radius, [255, 0, 0])
        self.make_display(frame, processed)
        # Yield the object details
        return coordinates, radius
...
```

Note we use `cvtColor` again here—this is because we need the two images, the original frame and processed frame, to use the same color system in order to be able to join them into a display. We use `cv2.circle` to draw a circle around the tracked object so we can see what our robot has tracked on the web app, too.

The next function is the actual behavior, turning the preceding coordinates and radius into robot movements. When we start our behavior, the pan-and-tilt mechanism may not be pointing straight forward. We should ensure it is with the following commands, and then start the camera:

```
...
    def run(self):
        # Set pan-and-tilt to middle, then clear it.
        self.robot.set_pan(0)
        self.robot.set_tilt(0)
        # Start camera
        camera = pi_camera_stream.setup_camera()
...
```

While these are setting up, we can prepare the two PID controllers we need for speed and direction:

```
        # speed pid - based on the radius we get.
        speed_pid = PIController(proportional_constant=0.8,
            integral_constant=0.1, windup_limit=100)
```

```
        # direction pid - how far from the middle X is.
        direction_pid = PIController(proportional_constant=0.25,
            integral_constant=0.1, windup_limit=400)
  . . .
```

These values I arrived at through much tuning. A section below *Tuning the PID controller settings* will cover how to tune the PIDS.

Now we wait a little time for the camera and pan and tilt servos to settle, then we turn off the servos in the center position:

```
  . . .
        # warm up and servo move time
        time.sleep(0.1)
        # Servo's will be in place - stop them for now.
        self.robot.servos.stop_all()
        print("Setup Complete")
  . . .
```

We can then enter the main loop. First, we get the processed data from the frame. Notice we use brackets to unpack coordinates into x and y:

```
  . . .
        # Main loop
        for frame in pi_camera_stream.start_stream(camera):
            (x, y), radius = self.process_frame(frame)
  . . .
```

We should check our control messages at this point. We then check if we are allowed to move, or if there is any object big enough to be worth looking for. If there is, we can start as follows:

```
  . . .
            self.process_control()
            if self.running and radius > 20:
  . . .
```

Now we know the robot should be moving, so let's start calculating error values to feed the PID controllers. Now is also a good time to print some debug:

```
  . . .
                # The size is the first error
                radius_error = self.correct_radius - radius
                speed_value = speed_pid.get_value(radius_error)
                # And the second error is the based on the center
coordinate.
                direction_error = self.center - x
                direction_value = direction_pid.get_value(direction_error)
```

```
                    print("radius: %d, radius_error: %d, speed_value: %.2f,
        direction_error: %d, direction_value: %.2f" %
                        (radius, radius_error, speed_value, direction_error,
        direction_value))
        ...
```

The speed value and direction value will now contain the values to combine and send to the motors:

```
        ...
                        # Now produce left and right motor speeds
                        self.robot.set_left(speed_value - direction_value)
                        self.robot.set_right(speed_value + direction_value)
        ...
```

We said the preceding code was what we did if the robot is running. If it is not, or there is no object worth examining, then we should stop the motors. If we have actually hit the stop button, we should also reset the PIDs:

```
        ...
                    else:
                        self.robot.stop_motors()
                        if not self.running:
                            speed_pid.reset()
                            direction_pid.reset()
        ...
```

We have now finished that function and the behavior class. Now, all that is left is to set up our behavior and web app core, then start them as follows:

```
...
print("Setting up")
behavior = ColorTrackingBehavior(Robot())
process = start_server_process('color_track_behavior.html')
try:
    behavior.run()
finally:
    process.terminate()
```

Running the behavior

To run this behavior, you will need to upload color_track_behavior.py, the modified pid_controller.py file, and the template at templates/color_track_behavior.html. I'll assume that you already have robot.py and the other supporting files uploaded.

When you start this app with `python color_track_behavior.py`, it will start the web server and wait. At this point, you should use your browser to connect to `http://myrobot.local:5001` and you should be able to see your robot's image feed. You are able to see the object and its circle, along with links to control the robot, as shown in the following screenshot:

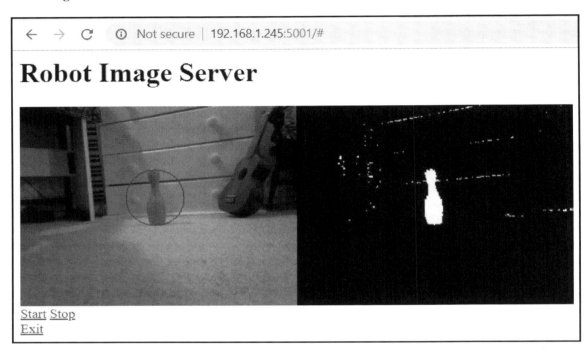

The color tracking web app

To make the robot start moving, press the **Start** button on the web page.

When the robot starts moving, you will see the PID debug output in the console (PuTTY). This will only show when the robot is running. You can press the **Stop** button on the web page to stop the robot moving, or the E**xit** button to exit the behavior.

Tuning the PID controller settings

I start with a proportional constant of 0.1, and raise it, using Nano to make quick edits on the PI, until the robot starts to overshoot—that is, it goes past its target, then returns far back—then I halve this proportional constant value.

It may then have a constant error, so I then start raising the integral constant by about 0.01 until that is smoothed. It is a slow process: start by getting the object close to dead center and by tuning `speed_pid` until it's pretty good, then come back for `direction_pid`.

Do **not** try to tweak all the values at once—rather, change one thing and retry.

For a deeper look at this, see *Tuning A PID Controller* in the *Further Reading* section.

Troubleshooting

If the servo motors stop to slow down, the simplest fix is to use fresh batteries. You may be able to reduce this with a capacitor between the servo power and ground. A capacitor is an electronic component used to smooth out noise. A 470f capacitor will do nicely.

If the code fails to start, remove `_nowait` from the queue operations in the app core—some errors will only show with this taken out. However, leaving it removed can mean the robot behavior will stop when a web client momentarily loses connection.

If there are syntax errors, please check your code carefully.

Please ensure that the previous examples with the web app have worked with the camera, and that you have carried out troubleshooting from any errors.

You may simply need good lighting, as the mask may not pick up poorly lit objects. Also, use the web app to check your robot is in view, and that the mask shows your object mostly in white. If this isn't so, then you may need to tune the upper and lower HSV ranges. The hue is the factor most likely to cause problems, as the saturation and value ranges are quite permissive.

If the robot starts weaving from side to side, you may need to tune the direction PID. Reduce the proportional element somewhat. If the robot barely turns, you can increase the proportional element a little. If the robot is stopped, but not facing the detected object, then increase the integral element for the direction PID by about 0.01. The same tweaks apply if the same problems are seen when the robot moves back and forward.

Enhancements that you could make

This code is fun, but there are many ways the reader could improve this. Here are some suggestions:

- Use the control pipeline to allow a user to tune the color filters, correct radius, and PID values from the web page.
- Perhaps the initial PID values should be close to the other tunable values?
- There is quite a lot of setup code—which could go into a own function/method.
- Could the queues to the web page be used to send the debug data to the page, instead of printing them in the console?
- Perhaps you could find ways to integrate this with the menu app better. Currently, it runs on a separate port as a totally different app.
- The field of view for tracking with the Pi Camera is pretty narrow. A wide-angle lens would improve the field of view a lot, letting the robot see more.

Detecting faces with Haar cascades

Tracking faces (or other objects) by features is a smart behavior. Using different cascade model files, we could pick out objects other than faces. There is a common technique, known as Haar cascades, which are well documented in a paper by Paul Viola and Michael Jones. We will give an overview of this technique, then put it into use on our robot to create a fun behavior.

Finding objects in an image

We will be using an algorithm implemented in OpenCV as a single and useful function, which makes it very easy to use. It provides a simple way to detect objects. There are more advanced and complex methods, involving machine learning, but this one is used in many places, including in camera apps on phones. The images we'll work with will be converted into greyscale (black through grey to white) for this detection method. Each pixel here holds a number for the intensity of light.

Integral images

There are two stages applied in the function. The first is to produce an image **integral**, or **summed area table,** as shown in the following diagram:

Integral images and summed area tables

This creates an array of numbers with the same dimensions as the image. At each coordinate is the sum of the intensities of all the pixels between the current coordinate and (0, 0). Tricks can be used with such an image to quickly find the sum of any rectangle shape in the image, or their difference. See the Viola-Jones paper in the *Further Reading* section for more detail. The cascade stage is able to use this integral image to quickly perform its next powerful trick.

Basic features

The next part of this puzzle is scanning the image for features. The features are extremely simple, involving looking for the difference between two rectangles, so they are quick to apply. The following diagram shows a selection of these basic features:

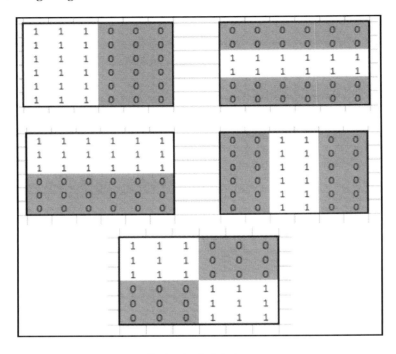

Simple rectangular feature types

The rectangles in the preceding diagram are applied, but the term **cascades** gives a clue as to how they are applied. An object can be described as a set of features that we can try and experiment with. There are face cascades with 16,000 features to apply. Applying every single one to every part of an image would take a long time. So they are applied in groups, starting perhaps with just one. If this fails, that part of the image is not subject to any further feature tests. Instead, they cascade into later group tests. The groups include weighting and applying groups of these features at different angles.

If the features in all the tests pass all the way into the last check, then it is taken as a match. For this to work, we need to find the feature cascade that will work to identify our object. Luckily, OpenCV has such a file designed for face recognition, and we have already installed it on our Raspberry Pi.

This whole operation of applying the summed area, then using the cascade file to look for potential matches, is all available through two OpenCV operations:

- `cv2.CascadeClassifier(cascade_filename)` will open the given cascade file, which describes the features to test, so that these can be used on images. This only needs to be loaded once, and can be used on all the frames. This will return a `CascadeClassifier` object.
- `CascadeClassifier.detectMultiScale(image)` applies the classifier check to an image.

Planning our behavior

We can use code fairly similar to our color tracking behavior to track faces. We'll set our robot up to use the pan-and-tilt mechanism to follow the largest face seen in the camera. The next block diagram shows an overview of the face behavior:

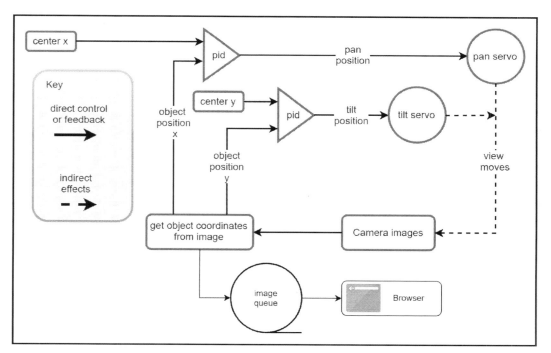

The face tracking behavior

So this will look very familiar. The differences are in the data we are sending to the PID controllers, and that each PID controls a difference servo motor.

The code for face tracking

The code for this behavior will seem very familiar—it started as a copy of the previous behavior, and was adapted for this present purpose. It's possible that refactoring could yield more common code, but it is currently simpler to work with a copy for now. This code will go into the `face_track_behavior.py` file. I've not even created a new template, as the color track template will work just fine for this. The imports are the same as before:

```
import time

from image_app_core import start_server_process, get_control_instruction,
put_output_image

import cv2
import numpy as np

import pi_camera_stream
from pid_controller import PIController
from robot import Robot
...
```

The `init` function for our class is slightly different, and our tuning parameters have center positions and a minimum face size. I've also brought the PID controllers out to the class, so they can be tuned here, and then reset in the control handler (this could be done to the previous behavior too). The Haar cascade we will use is loaded in the constructor. There are a number of other cascade files in the same directory, with which you could try to track things other than a face:

```
...
class FaceTrackBehavior(object):
    """Behavior to find and point at a face."""
    def __init__(self, robot):
        self.robot = robot
        cascade_path =
"/usr/share/opencv/haarcascades/haarcascade_frontalface_default.xml"
        self.cascade = cv2.CascadeClassifier(cascade_path)
        # Tuning values
        self.center_x = 160
        self.center_y = 120
        self.min_size = 20
        self.pan_pid = PIController(proportional_constant=0.1,
integral_constant=0.03)
```

```
            self.tilt_pid = PIController(proportional_constant=-0.1,
integral_constant=-0.03)
            # Current state
            self.running = False
    ...
```

The process control here differs, in that the motors are stopped and PIDs reset when the stop instruction is received, and not in the loop:

```
    ...

    def process_control(self):
        instruction = get_control_instruction()
        if instruction == "start":
            self.running = True
        elif instruction == "stop":
            self.running = False
            self.pan_pid.reset()
            self.tilt_pid.reset()
            self.robot.servos.stop_all()
        elif instruction == "exit":
            print("Stopping")
            exit()
    ...
```

This behavior still has a find object method; however, this has different return values, in that it produces a rectangle instead of a circle. This is where we convert the image to greyscale, then send it through the cascade detectMultiScale method to get a list of matches. We then loop through to find the largest, and return its information as follows:

```
    ...

    def find_object(self, original_frame):
        """Search the frame for an object. Return the rectangle of the
largest by w * h"""
        # Make it greyscale to reduce the data used
        gray_img = cv2.cvtColor(original_frame, cv2.COLOR_BGR2GRAY)
        # Detect all the objects
        objects = self.cascade.detectMultiScale(gray_img)
        largest = 0, (0, 0, 0, 0) # area, x, y, w, h
        for (x, y, w, h) in objects:
            item_area = w * h
            if item_area > largest[0]:
                largest = item_area, (x, y, w, h)
        return largest[1]
    ...
```

The `make_display` and `process_frame` functions are simpler than the color tracking behavior. There is only one image, no mask, and we draw the rectangle onto this before outputting it. The rectangle takes two coordinates: a starting *x,y* and an ending *x,y*. To get the second, we need to add the width and height back in:

```
    . . .
    def make_display(self, display_frame):
        """Create display output, and put it on the queue"""
        encoded_bytes =
pi_camera_stream.get_encoded_bytes_for_frame(display_frame)
        put_output_image(encoded_bytes)

    def process_frame(self, frame):
        # Find the largest matching object
        (x, y, w, h) = self.find_object(frame)
        # Draw a rect on the original frame, then display this
        cv2.rectangle(frame, (x, y), (x + w, y + w), [255, 0, 0])
        self.make_display(frame)
        # Yield the object details
        return x, y, w, h
    . . .
```

Now comes the `run` section. This will need to be broken down. We start with the camera setup and warm-up time:

```
    . . .
    def run(self):
        # start camera
        camera = pi_camera_stream.setup_camera()
        # warm up time
        time.sleep(0.1)
        print("Setup Complete")
    . . .
```

Like the track color behavior, we start the main loop by processing the frame and checking for control instructions:

```
        . . .
        # Main loop
        for frame in pi_camera_stream.start_stream(camera):
            (x, y, w, h) = self.process_frame(frame)
            self.process_control()
        . . .
```

We then only want to be moving if we've detected a large enough object (using height as faces tend to be bigger in this dimension) and if the robot is running:

```
. . .
            if self.running and h > self.min_size:
. . .
```

When we know the robot is are running, for both pan and tilt, we feed the PIDs and send the output values straight to the servo motors. Note that, to find the middle of the object, we take the coordinate, and add half its width or height.

```
. . .
                # Pan
                pan_error = self.center_x - (x + (w / 2))
                pan_value = self.pan_pid.get_value(pan_error)
                self.robot.set_pan(int(pan_value))
                # Tilt
                tilt_error = self.center_y - (y + (h /2))
                tilt_value = self.tilt_pid.get_value(tilt_error)
                self.robot.set_tilt(int(tilt_value))
. . .
```

So that we can track what is going on here, a debug `print` statement is recommended:

```
. . .
                print("x: %d, y: %d, pan_error: %d, tilt_error: %d,
pan_value: %.2f, tilt_value: %.2f" %
                    (x, y, pan_error, tilt_error, pan_value, tilt_value))
. . .
```

Finally, we need to add the code for setup and running our behavior:

```
. . .
print("Setting up")
behavior = FaceTrackBehavior(Robot())
process = start_server_process('color_track_behavior.html')
try:
    behavior.run()
finally:
    process.terminate()
```

Using this behavior

To run this behavior, you will need to have uploaded the files for the color track behavior already. This behavior uses the same library and template code as our face track behavior. So, you need only upload the `face_track_behavior.py` file.

This behavior is started in exactly the same way, by starting $ `python face_track_behavior.py`, and then sending the browser to `http://myrobot.local:5001` . You must press the start button for the robot to move.

Troubleshooting

Start with the troubleshooting steps that we covered for the previous behavior—this should get you most of the way.

If the camera is failing to detect faces in the picture, try making sure the area is well lit. The detection algorithm is only for faces that face the camera straight on, and anything obscuring a part of the face will fool it. Faces only partially in frame are also likely to be missed. Faces that are too far away or small are filtered Reducing the minimum parameter may help with this, but may also generate false positives, as tiny face-like objects can be picked up.

Please do check the indentation matches, as this can change the meaning of where things happen in Python.

Summary

In this chapter, you have seen how to set up the Raspberry Pi Camera module. You then used it to see what your robot is seeing - the robot's view of the world.

You were able to get the robot to display its camera as a web app on a phone or desktop, and then used the camera to drive smart color and face-tracking behaviors. I've suggested ways this could be enhanced, and hopefully given you a taste of what computer vision can do.

In the next chapter, we will create a speech control system for our robot, so you will be able to talk into a handset and the robot will respond to your instructions by launching behaviors.

Questions

1. We used the HSV color system when tracking colored objects. Why would the RGB color system not work for this?
2. PID controllers (or PI control) were used for both behaviors. To the color-tracking behavior, we added an anti-windup measure—what would happen without this limit?
3. When performing computer vision, we use a low resolution for the images. What are some of the reasons for choosing a low resolution?
4. Why do we use queues to send data between the processes in our system?
5. In the color-tracking behavior, what step is needed in between using color filters to make a masked image, and generating enclosing circles for the remaining blobs?

For further learning, I recommend the reader try the other cascade files found in the `/usr/share/opencv/haarcascades` folder on the Raspberry Pi. Perhaps you could try swapping features of the two behaviors, in order to use the servo motors to track the colored object, or chase the faces?

An advanced system with more PID controllers could use the pan-and-tilt mechanism to track the object, then engage the main wheels to chase it and aim to center the pan, while keeping the object in view.

Further reading

- To delve in far greater depth into using the Raspberry Pi Camera, I recommend the PiCamera Documentation, available at `https://picamera.readthedocs.io/`.
- Also, to gain insight into further techniques, the Py Image Search website, at `https://www.pyimagesearch.com`, has great resources.
- OpenCV and visual processing are a complex topic, only briefly covered here. I recommend *OpenCV 3 Computer Vision With Python Cookbook*, available at `https://www.packtpub.com/application-development/opencv-3-computer-vision-python-cookbook`, for more information.
- Streaming video through Flask is a neat trick, and is explored further in Video Streaming With Flask, at `https://blog.miguelgrinberg.com/post/video-streaming-with-flask`.
- I recommend the Flask Books at `https://flaskbook.com/` for other neat ways to use Flask to manage your robot from your phone or laptop.

- Tuning A PID Controller - we touched on this in `Chapter 12`, *Programming Encoders with Python*, and needed more in this chapter. *Robots For Roboticists | PID Control*, available at `http://robotsforroboticists.com/pid-control/`, is a little heavy on the math, but has an excellent section on manually tuning a PID.

- *Rapid Object Detection using a Boosted Cascade of Simple Features*, by Paul Viola and Michael Jones, available at `https://www.cs.cmu.edu/~efros/courses/LBMV07/Papers/viola-cvpr-01.pdf`. This paper, from 2001, discusses in more detail the Haar cascade object-finding technique that we used.

- A good video introducing face tracking is *Detecting Faces (Viola Jones Algorithm) - Computerphile*, available at `https://www.youtube.com/watch?v=uEJ71VlUmMQ`, which dives into the combination of techniques used.

- The Cascade Classification OpenCV Documentation, at `https://docs.opencv.org/2.4/modules/objdetect/doc/cascade_classification.html`, shows the reference for the library functions used in the face tracking behavior.

- OpenCV also has a tutorial on face tracking (for Version 3.0), called *OpenCV: Face Detection using Haar Cascades*, which is available at `https://docs.opencv.org/3.3.0/d7/d8b/tutorial_py_face_detection.html`.

14
Voice Communication with a Robot Using Mycroft

Using our voices to ask a robot to do something and having a voice respond has long been seen as a sign of smarts. Devices around us such as Alexa and Google Assistant have these tools, and being able to program our system to integrate with tools such as these gives us access to this powerful system. Mycroft is a Python-based open source voice system. We will get this running on the Raspberry Pi, by connecting it to a speaker and microphone, and then we will run instructions on our robot based on words we speak.

The following topics will be covered in this chapter:

- What Mycroft is and an overview of how our system will work
- How to add a speaker/microphone board to a Raspberry Pi
- How to install and configure a Raspberry Pi to run Mycroft
- How to create our own skills code to connect the Voice Assistant to our robot

Technical requirements

You will require the following for this chapter:

- An additional Raspberry Pi 3b+ (not the one already in the robot)
- An SD Card
- The Respeaker 2-Mics HAT
- Mini Audio Magnet Raspberry Pi Speaker—a tiny speaker with a JST connector or a speaker with a 3.5 mm jack
- USB power supply
- The robot from the previous chapters (after all, we intend to get this moving)

The code for this chapter is available on GitHub at `https://github.com/PacktPublishing/Learn-Robotics-Programming/tree/master/chapter14`.

Check out the following video to see the Code in Action:

`http://bit.ly/2zpPPxi`

Introducing Mycroft

MyCroft is a software suite known as a **voice assistant**. Once set up, MyCroft will be listening for voice commands. It is then able to determine the actions to perform based on those commands. We'll dig a little deeper into this. MyCroft is based on Python; it is also open source and free. Most of the voice processing is actually done in the cloud (at the time of writing, on the Google system, but a Mozilla system is soon to be available). After commands are processed, Mycroft will then use a voice to respond to the human.

MyCroft is well documented online and has a community of users. There are some interesting alternatives that, when a reader has played with the concepts, they could consider. These are Snips.ai, Snowboy.ai, and Google, to name a few.

What are the concepts of a Voice Assistant?

Speech to text

This generally describes systems that can take audio containing human speech and turn it into a series of words, that a computer can then process.

These can run locally or they can run in the cloud on far more powerful machines.

Wake words

Voice assistants usually have a **wake word**; this is some phrase or word that is spoken before the rest of a command, to *get the attention* of the voice assistant. It would be something such as the *Hey Siri*, *Hi Google*, and *Alexa* utterances. For Mycroft, the word *MyCroft* or the phrase *Hey MyCroft* will suffice.

The voice assistant will usually only be listening for the wake words, and will ignore all audio input until the wake words. The wake word is usually recognized locally on the device, in contrast with the other sounds which are sampled and then sent to a speech-to-text system for recognition.

The MyCroft wake word can be changed.

Utterances

An **utterance** is the general term for something a user will say. These must be somehow matched by the vocabulary that the voice assistants skills define. It is a collection of vocabulary terms that will then result in an intent being invoked.

The vocabulary in MyCroft comprises lists of phrases. A vocabulary file usually contains interchangeable phrases and synonyms.

A good example of an utterance would be asking mycroft about the weather: *Hey Mycroft, what is the weather?*

Intent

An **intent** is a thing that the voice assistant can do—an action—for example, finding what today's weather is like. We will be building intents to interact with our robot. An intent is part of a skill. An intent is defined with some code, for what it does, and then what dialog is used to respond.

An example would be that, in the weather skill, the utterance *What is the weather?* will trigger the intent to go fetch the current weather for the configured location and then speak the details of this back to the user.

An example for our robot would be *ask the robot to drive straight*, with an intent that starts the straight line behavior on the robot.

Skills

Skills define the vocabulary for utterances, then actions or **intents** to carry out on them. Later in this chapter, we will build a myrobot skill with intents to make it move and stop.

Dialog

In MyCroft terminology, **dialog** is anything that Mycroft speaks back to the user. A skill can have a collection of dialogs with a known name. These can then have different sets of synonymous actual words to speak and can have different languages.

Vocabulary

As mentioned, utterances, once converted into text are matched to **vocabulary**. Vocabulary files, like dialogs, are logical parts of an intent, helping match what was said to some action. The vocabulary files contain synonymous phrases, and can also be organized into language and locale sets to make your skill multi-lingual.

Adding sound input and output to the Raspberry Pi

Before we can use a voice processing/voice assistant, we need to get the basic setup of giving the Raspberry Pi some speakers and a microphone. At the time of writing, there are a number of Raspberry Pi add-ons that can provide this. One simple one, with a microphone array (for better recognition) and a connection to speakers is the Seeed Studio Respeaker 2 HAT, which is widely available.

We will be creating a separate voice assistant board that will communicate with our robot, but we won't be putting it directly on the robot. This is for a few good reasons:

- **Noise**: A robot with motors will be a noisy environment. Having a microphone anywhere near the motors will make it close to useless.
- **Power**: The voice assistant is listening constantly. The robot has enough demands for power already with the other sensors that are running on it. This applies both in terms of battery power and the CPU power needed.
- **Size and physical location**: The speaker and voice HAT sit on top of the robot. While separate PCM (I2s) amplifiers and mics could be fitted on to the robot, they would add far more complication to an already busy robot.

So, for these practical reasons, this will be a second Raspberry Pi, set up just as a voice assistant.

The next photograph shows the Respeaker 2-Mics Pi HAT:

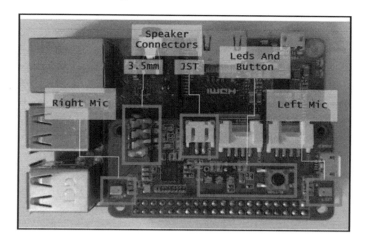

The Respeaker 2-Mics Pi HAT (Seeed Voicecard)

The hat has two microphones, which are two tiny rectangle metal parts on each side of the Respeaker HAT. Speakers must be connected to it to hear output from it. The Respeaker 2 HAT has a button connected to a GPIO pin, and an array of three RGB LEDs, which our apa102 LED class could drive. The reader could consider these to enhance the code.

Physical installation

Take the new Raspberry Pi 3b+. The Respeaker 2 HAT will sit directly on the Pi headers, and the board overhang must be over the Pi, not sticking out.

The speakers will have either a tiny two pin connector (JST) type that fits snugly in a single two-pin socket on the board, or you may have speakers that plug into the 3.5 mm jack on the Respeaker 2. The next photograph shows the speaker plugged into it:

The Mycroft Voice Assistant Respeaker set up on my desk

I've left mine bare on a desk as shown in the previous photograph. However, a Raspberry Pi case or project box could be used—be sure to ensure that there is somewhere to secure the speaker and that the microphones are not covered up.

The only other hardware needed is an SD card and power supply. For the next few sections, I strongly recommend using a mains power supply. Do not plug it in and power it up yet.

Installing Raspbian for the voice assist Pi

First, we need a new Raspberry Pi SD setup; for this I recommend the same procedures from Chapter 3, *Introducing the Raspberry Pi - Starting with Raspbian*, and Chapter 4, *Preparing a Raspberry Pi for a Robot - Headless by Default*. When coming to the hostname section, I chose VoiceAssist. It must be different from the name used for the Pi on the robot. Ensure it is connected to Wi-Fi and you can reach it via SSH (PuTTY).

When in the `raspi-config` section, make these additional settings:

- Go to **5-Interfacing Options | SPI |Enable**.
- Go to **7-Advanced Options | A4 Audio| Force 3.5MM Jack** and press *Enter*.

Please continue through `Chapter 4`, *Preparing a Raspberry Pi for a Robot - Headless by Default*, including rebooting and updating the Pi. We also need the Git tool, PulseAudio, and Mplayer:

```
$ sudo apt-get install -y git pulseaudio mplayer
```

Installing the Respeaker software

The Respeaker HAT has software and drivers to enable it. These are installed from a GitHub repository owned by Seeed Studio (yes there really are 3 e's!), who created the Respeaker 2 HAT. This will take about 10-15 minutes to perform:

```
git clone https://github.com/respeaker/seeed-voicecard.git
cd seeed-voicecard
sudo ./install.sh
sudo reboot
```

After a reboot, it's time to see if the Raspberry Pi has set up the sound card. In a PuTTY session type `aplay -l` to list playback devices. In the output, it should contain a line saying `card 1: seeed2micvoicec` if the card has been picked up.

Similarly, we can check the recording devices by typing `arecord -l` and, in the output, you should find a line containing the microphone array: `card 1: seeed2micvoicec` `[seeed-2mic-voicecard]`. There may be more on this line, but this shows the device has been set up.

We can now test this card. We will make a small recording from the microphones to a voice file by typing the following:

```
$ arecord -f CD >/tmp/test.wav
```

`-f` tells arecord (alsa recording tool) to use a CD standard for the audio. `>` is sending the recorded data to the `/tmp/test.wav` file. You can speak to the mics and then press *Ctrl* + *C* to finish the recording.

If you are using the 3.5 mm jack, you will need to raise the headphone volume. Type `alsamixer -c 1` to start it on card 1. This will show you a number of level meters. The first will be headphone. Use the up arrow on your keyboard to increase its volume (perhaps to full) and then *Esc* to finish.

We can now play that file back on our speaker:

```
$ aplay -f CD -Dhw:1 /tmp/atest.wav
```

You should now hear that recording. The `-D` flag is selecting the output device 1, which would be the Respeaker HAT.

Installing Mycroft on the Raspberry Pi

In this section, we will install and begin to interact with the MyCroft system on our Pi; by the end of this section, we will have had some small dialog with it and be ready to create our own skill for MyCroft.

MyCroft has a prebuilt SD card image for a Raspberry Pi called PiCroft. However, this image does not always support the recent Raspberry Pi types (such as the Pi3) or different sound cards. We already have an image that can play and record audio on our Raspberry Pi, so we are going to install this the same way that a PiCroft SD card image is made from a standard Raspbian.

This will require some command-line work and file editing to connect it up to our sound hat (or sound card) as the initial installation doesn't yet connect it to the sound output.

Base installation

First, we get a script from GitHub that will perform this installation:

```
$ wget
https://rawgit.com/MycroftAI/enclosure-picroft/stretch/home/pi/update.sh
```

The `wget` command fetches an `update.sh` file from the internet, a shell script that contains commands to install the Mcyroft system.

It will take a long time—be prepared to leave it for 30 minutes to an hour. It will occasionally require responses too. Run it with the following:

```
$ bash update.sh
```

You will be asked if you want to install, please type Y to get the installation started. Towards the end of the installation, it will ask you to press a key and take you into Nano (a text editor on board the Raspberry Pi). Press *Ctrl + X* to finish.

We will need to let Mycroft start up and prepare everything; the simplest way here is to reboot the Pi using `sudo reboot` and wait for it to come back. Mycroft will start up, but won't yet be able to output audio.

SSH in (log in with PuTTY) and you will see Mycroft starting. Let it run for five minutes or so while it sets up its handlers and devices.

Getting Mycroft to talk to the sound card

Now you need to connect Mycroft and the sound card.

We need the PulseAudio service to start when the Pi starts, so to do this we will create a `systemd` service file for it. Press *Ctrl + C* to exit Mycroft so you can type commands again.

We can use the Nano editor already in the Pi to create this file with the `$ sudo nano /etc/systemd/system/pulseaudio.service` command.

When the editor window appears, type the following into it:

```
[Unit]
Description=PulseAudio Service

[Install]
WantedBy=multi-user.target

[Service]
Type=simple
PrivateTmp=true
ExecStart=/usr/bin/pulseaudio --system --realtime --disallow-exit
```

The service file starts with `Description` of `Unit` (units can be things other than services). This is human-friendly text, so you can put what you like. It's probably sensible to say `Pulseaudio Service` here.

The `[Install]` section contains a `WantedBy` statement, which says at what stage during boot up the service configured must start. We say `multi-user.target`, which targets the point at which users can log into the Pi.

The last section of this file is [Service], which details what and how to run. We say Type=simple because we just want to start the process and leave it. PrivateTmp=true tells systemd that we want this service to have it's own private /tmp directory. ExecStart is critical; it specifies the pulseaudio program with /usr/bin/pulseaudio and the parameters to run it with. The parameters together mean to run as a system service, to stay running until we reboot.

Press *Ctrl + X* to exit Nano, answer Y when asked to save (write the buffer), and then *Enter* to accept the filename. We need to enable that service with $ sudo systemctl enable pulseaudio.

We also need the pi user, which we log in as and Mycroft runs as, to have access to PulseAudio. To do this, we need to add this user into the PulseAudio security groups. The usermod command adds a user into groups. -a means add and -G means to groups. Case is important here. We list the groups that are needed with commas (no spaces) and the pi user:

```
$ sudo usermod -a -G pulse,pulse-access pi
```

We also need to tell PulseAudio to let us connect from another user. To do this, use $ sudo nano /etc/pulse/system.pa. Go to the bottom of the file and add the following:

```
...
#allow localhost connections
load-module module-native-protocol-tcp auth-ip-acl=127.0.0.1
```

Save and close this file.

Now we need to get details of our card, so we can set those up for Mycroft. In pulseaudio terminology, a sink is a device that you can send audio data to—an output device. We want to list those. However, pulseaudio has quite verbose output, so we use the egrep tool to filter it to the lines with the card index (number) and the card type to ensure we find our Seeed studio Respeaker card. To filter those, we tell egrep to filter for lines that have index or alsa.card_name. The | character allows either/or operators on search filters.

```
$ pacmd list-sinks | egrep "index|alsa.card_name"
```

This should show something like the following:

```
* index: 0
            alsa.card_name = "bcm2835 ALSA"
  index: 1
            alsa.card_name = "seeed-2mic-voicecard"
```

This tells me that the bcm device is my default, but at device 1 is the HAT—`2mic-voicecard`.

We can now edit the file to configure Mycroft's sound output, `$ sudo nano /etc/mycroft/mycroft.conf`, and edit the similar lines to match:

```
...
  "play_wav_cmdline": "paplay -d 1 %1",
  "play_mp3_cmdline": "mplayer -ao pulse::1 %1"
...
```

Note that the number 1 in `-d 1` and `pulse::1` should be the card index number you found above. Press *Ctrl + X* to write this out and reboot one more time; your Pi should start talking to you.

Starting to use Mycroft

It's worth connecting with ssh (putty) or leaving a monitor connected to see when Mycroft is ready to accept input. When it is, you should be able to speak to it. Say clearly *Mycroft say hello* within a meter of the microphones on the Pi. It may respond *please wait a moment while I finish booting up*. Give it a minute, and try again.

Mycroft will then tell you it needs to be paired at `mycroft.ai` now. You will need to register the device using the code it gives you. You will need to create an account there to do so (or log in if this is a second device/attempt).

Once you have done so, you can then try speaking *mycroft say hello* and it should respond with *hello*. You will hear a sound when Mycroft has heard its wake up word and is listening. You will need to speak as clearly as you can—I've found that it needs you to clearly pronounce each syllable; those *t* and *n* sounds are not optional.

Other things you can say include the following:

- *mycroft weather*: This will use the weather skill and tell you the weather. It may be for the wrong location; use the mycroft.ai website to configure your device to your own location.
- *mycroft what is 23 times 76*: This will use the wolfram skill, which can handle mathematical questions.
- *mycroft wiki banana*: This will use a wikipedia skill and Mycroft will tell you what it has found about the banana.

Try these out to get used to talking to Mycroft so it responds. It may say *I don't understand* and the log will tell you what it heard, which can help you try to tune how you pronounce things for it.

We can now create a skill to connect Mycroft to our robot.

Troubleshooting

If you are not able to get Mycroft to speak or recognise talking, try the following:

- Ensure you have a good network connection from your Raspberry Pi. Mycroft is only going to work where you can reach the the internet. See the Mycroft documentation for handling proxies.
- Attaching a monitor while the Pi is booting may reveal error messages.
- Please consult the Seeed documentation for the Respeaker 2 Voicecard (`https://github.com/respeaker/seeed-voicecard`).
- Mycroft has a troubleshooting system starting with: **Troubleshooting and Known errors** (`https://mycroft.ai/documentation/troubleshooting/`).
- Mycroft is under active development. Taking the latest PiCroft image and applying the Respeaker and PulseAudi may help—although, at the time of writing, the Raspberry Pi 3b+ was not supported by the PiCroft image, so it had to be built on the Raspbian Stretch image. In short, getting this installed and running is subject to change.
- Mycroft can fail to boot properly if the internet connection isn't great and rebooting it can help.
- PulseAudio can be tricky to debug, requiring diving into the internet to diagnose problems. The `/var/log/messages` file on the Raspberry Pi can tell you about system problems. Also, `systemctl status pulseaudio` will tell you if the service is dead or in some way broken. Do make sure the Pi user has been added to the previous pulse groups.

Programming Mycroft skills for the robot functions

The robot backend provided by the flask menu is good enough to create a Mycroft skill for. The next diagram shows an overview of our voice system:

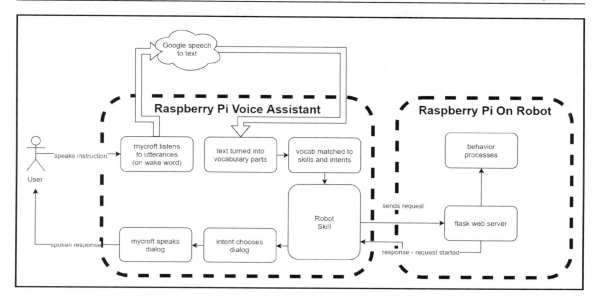

Overview of the robot skill

From the previous diagram, you can see that after you say something with the wake word, upon waking, MyCroft will transmit the next utterance to the Google speech to text system. This will then return the text that Google interpreted.

MyCroft will then match this against vocabulary files for the region you are in and match that with intents set up in the skills. Once matched, an intent in a skill will be invoked. Our robot skill has intents that will mostly make network (HTTP) requests to the Flask Menu server we created for our robot in Chapter 11, *Programming Distance Sensors with Python*. When the flask server responds to say that the request has been processed (perhaps the behavior is started), the robot skill will choose a dialog to speak back to the user, perhaps to confirm that the request has been carried out or if there was a problem.

To build this, we will not need to change our menu server, except perhaps to add more behaviors from later chapters in; please refer to Chapter 11, *Programming Distance Sensors with Python* if you want to do this.

We'll start with a simple skill, with a basic intent, and then the reader can expand this to perform more. I've picked the Drive Forward (behavior_line from Chapter 7, *Drive and Turn - Moving Motors with Python*) because it is simple.

It's worth noting that the time taken to get the speech processed at Google means that this is not suitable for stopping in a hurry; the voice recognition can take some time. Using the stop button on the menu server (from Chapter 12, *Programming Encoders with Python*) will be more effective. A reader could consider using GPIOZero in the intent, and a when_pressed handler to trigger the stop handler on the menu server.

Building the intent

We can start with the intent, then look at some vocabulary. To build it, we will use a library built into MyCroft named adapt.

Create a folder called my-robot-skill, which we will work in to build the MyCroft skill. The main intent file will be an __init__.py file in this folder. This means that Python in Mycroft will treat the whole folder like it is a Python library, called a package. Let's start putting some code in my-robot-skill/__init__.py:

```
from adapt.intent import IntentBuilder
from mycroft import MycroftSkill, intent_handler
from mycroft.util.log import LOG

import requests
...
```

The imports have IntentBuilder to allow us to build and define intents around vocabulary. MyCroftSkill is a base class that we will use; our code will use this base to plug into the Mycroft system. intent_handler allows us to mark which parts of our code are actually intents, associating the code with IntentBuilder. By importing LOG, we are able to write information out to the MyCroft console and see problems there.

The final import, requests, is a tool to let us make requests to web servers from in Python. This means we can use it to activate menu options on our robots menu server remotely:

```
...
class MyRobot(MycroftSkill):
    def __init__(self):
        MycroftSkill.__init__(self)
        self.settings.load_skill_settings_from_file()
        self.base_url = self.settings.get("base_url")
...
```

In this section, we've started creating our skill class, from the base, `MyCroftSkill`. As we set up our class, call `__init__` on the base class, so it can perform any further set up needed by a base skill. Loading the base class would have prepared some settings; we then ask for one of these, `base_url`. This will be the address of our Flask server on our other Raspberry Pi, as we've named it or as it appears on a network. We'll see a settings file later—this allows us to separate the configuration there from the code:

```
. . .
@intent_handler(IntentBuilder("").require("robot").require("DriveForward"))
    def handle_drive_forward(self, message):
        try:
            requests.get(self.base_url + "/run/behavior_line")
            self.speak_dialog('Robot')
            self.speak_dialog('Starting')
        except:
            self.speak_dialog("UnableToReach")
            LOG.exception("Unable to reach the robot")
. . .
```

For proper code indentation, kindly refer to the GitHub link: `https://github.com/PacktPublishing/Learn-Robotics-Programming/tree/master/chapter14/my-robot-skill`.

This code defines an intent such as *Mycroft Robot drive forward*. We have a method named `handle_drive_forward`, which is decorated with `intent_handler` by the @ sign; decorating means to wrap a method in some further handling as it is defined. This `intent_handler` defines what language would activate the handler in its parameter; here, we use `IntentBuilder` with a set of required vocabulary. Since all of our robot intents will have the word `robot` in it, we require this bit of vocabulary, then we also require the specific `DriveForward` vocabulary. We will later set up what actual words can be interpreted to mean those bits of vocabulary.

The inside of the function has a `try`/`except` statement. This will attempt to contact the robot and speak some `UnableToReach` dialog if it fails to do so. We will put something in the dialog files to make that clear to the user. We use `LOG.exception` to show the actual exception to the user; there may be other reasons that this code failed. You can use `LOG` with `.error` or `.info` to add debug to these skills.

The function will use `requests.get` on the whole address (URL) of the menu option, constructed with a `/run/line_following` part (this could be another behavior). This will be sent to the Flask server on the robot to run, behaving as if you had clicked that option in the menu. After this request, Mycroft will speak *Robot starting* to notify the user that it has been contacted.

As we build more such intents, we could try to generalize this into some inner method. We are also treating many error types as *unable to reach the robot*, while not inspecting the result code from the server other than it was contacted.

This file then needs to profile a `create_skill` function outside of the class, which Mycroft expects to find in skills:

```
...
def create_skill():
  return MyRobot()
```

The settings file

Our intent started by loading a setting. We put this in `my-robot-skill/settings.json` and it defines the one URL we use.

A URL, or uniform resource locator, defines how to reach some kind of resource; it starts with a protocol specification—in this case, `http` for a web (hypertext) service. This is followed by a colon (`:`) and then two slashes (`//`) with a hostname or host address—the network address of the computer/server/Raspberry Pi the resource will be on. As a host can have many services running, we can then have port number, with a colon as a separator—in our case, `:5000`. After this, you could add a slash (`/`) then select a specific resource in the service; we don't do so in these settings, but we append specific resources in the previous intent.

Please use the hostname/address of your robot Raspberry Pi if it is different:

```
{
    "base_url": "http://myrobot.local:5000"
}
```

The requirements file

Our skill uses the `requests` library. When Mycroft encounters our skill, we should tell it to expect this. In Python, requirements files are the normal way to do this. Put the following in `my-robot-skill/requirements.txt`:

```
requests
```

Creating the vocabulary files

We next need to create a folder inside the skill folder for the vocabulary. This should be `my-robot-skill/vocab/<IETF language and locale>`. A language/locale means we should be able to define vocabulary for variants such as `en-us` for American English and `zn-cn` for simplified Chinese; however, at the time of writing, `en-us` is the most supported Mycroft language, with other language support being developed. Further reading on the Mycroft forums may be needed to support other languages.

Each intent has its language defined in one or more vocabulary pieces, each of which go into a vocabulary file, with each separate line in the file holding a different phrase meaning the same as all of the others. These allow a human to naturally vary the way they say things, something people normally only notice they do when a machine fails to respond to their slightly different way of asking for something.

So, for our intent, we need two vocabulary files. There is a bit of a trick in thinking up useful similar phrases for the vocabulary files. Let's start off with `my-robot-skill/vocab/en-us/robot.voc`:

```
robot
my robot
ask robot to
tell the robot to
```

So any of those phrases will be used where we have said `robot` in our previous intent builders. Next is `my-robot-skill/vocab/en-us/DriveForward.voc`:

```
drive forward
drive in a line
drive
go forward
move forward
go go go
```

Note the capitalization of the vocabulary file name must match the intent builder; I've then used my own convention of capitalizing the non-shared vocab parts.

Inevitably, when you test this, you will eventually try to say a sensible sounding phrase that isn't there. Mycroft will tell you *Sorry, I don't understand,* and you will add another similar phrase to the vocabularies above.

Dialog files

We also want to define the phrases Mycroft will say back to you. We have three that our intent requires so far. These go into a `my-robot-skill/dialog/en-us` folder. It's the same as the vocabulary files mostly. The first is the common word `robot` in `my-robot-skill/dialog/en-us/Robot.dialog`:

```
The Robot
Robot
```

Then, we can define `my-robot-skill/dialog/en-us/UnableToReach.dialog` as follows:

```
Sorry I cannot reach the robot.
The robot is unreachable.
Have you turned the robot on?
Is the menu server running on the robot?
```

By defining multiple possible dialogs, Mycroft will randomly pick one to make itself less repetitive. We need `my-robot-skill/dialog/en-us/Starting.dialog`:

```
Starting
is Starting
will Start
```

Current skill folder

Our `skills` folder should look like this now:

- `my-robot-skill`
    - `__init__.py`
    - `requirements.txt`
    - `settings.json`
    - `vocab`
        - `en-us`
            - `robot.voc`
            - `DriveForward.voc`

- dialog
  - en-us
    - Robot.dialog
    - Starting.dialog
    - UnableToReach.dialog

We are going to now need to upload this whole folder structure to our robot, using SFTP (FileZilla) to your Mycroft Pi, at the /opt/mycroft/skills folder and Mycroft will automatically load this skill. If you need to update the code, uploading the files to this location again will cause Mycroft to reload it.

Any problems loading or using the skill will be shown on the Mycroft output—either on a monitor or an ssh session into the Voice Assistant Pi. The output can also be found in /var/log/mycroft/skills.log—the less Linux tool is useful for looking at log output like this, using *Shift + G* to jump to the end of the file or typing /myrobot to jump to its output.

You then need to power up the robot, ssh in and start the menu server with python menu_server.py.

You can then try out your skill with *Mycroft tell the robot to drive forward*. Mycroft should beep to show the user it's awake and, once it has got the words from speech to text, it should send /run/behavior_line to the menu server on the robot. You should hear Mycroft say one of the dialog phrases, such as *The robot Is starting* and see the robot drive forward.

Troubleshooting

If you encounter problems making intent respond please try the following:

- First check the syntax and indenting of the previous Python code.
- Ensure that your robot and the voice assistant Raspberry Pi are on the same network; I've found this to be problematic with some Wi-Fi extenders and IP addresses are needed instead of myrobot.local—you can use the settings.json file to configure this.

Adding another intent

Now we have our skill, adding a second intent becomes fairly easy, using another of the modes in our robots menu server. For this, I will pick the line following behavior. You may need to calibrate the line sensors again, and prepare the line for following if it has been put away. You may also notice that, since introducing the servo motors, the motors seem slower for the same settings, so I suggesting increasing the speed factors on the line following behavior; I doubled these to 60 and -60 on my robot.

Vocabulary

We will need to create some line following vocabulary; we can put this in `my-robot-skill/vocab/en-us/FollowLine.voc`:

```
follow a line
follow the line
follow lines
line following
line following behavior
```

Code

In the `my-robot-skill/__init__.py` file, add the following to the `MyRobot` skill:

```
...
@intent_handler(IntentBuilder("").require("robot").require("FollowLine"))
    def handle_follow_line(self, message):
        try:
            requests.get(self.base_url + "/run/line_following")
            self.speak_dialog('Robot')
            self.speak_dialog('Starting')
        except:
            self.speak_dialog("UnableToReach")
            LOG.exception("Unable to reach the robot")
...
```

This is almost identical to the Drive forward intent, with only the `FollowLine` vocabulary included, the name of the handler (which could be anything, but must not be the same as another handler), and the URL endpoint. This is ripe for refactor. Refactoring is changing the appearance of code, without affecting what it does. This is useful for dealing with common/repeating code sections or improving how readable code is.

In the same file, add the following:

```
. . .

    def handle_start_behavior(self, mode_name):
        try:
            requests.get(self.base_url + "/run/" + mode_name)
            self.speak_dialog('Robot')
            self.speak_dialog('Starting')
        except:
            self.speak_dialog("UnableToReach")
            LOG.exception("Can't reach the robot")
. . .
```

This will be a common start behavior handler. It takes `mode_name` as a parameter and uses that in its request. All of the dialog and error handling we saw before is here. The two intents now become far simpler. Change them to the following:

```
. . .
@intent_handler(IntentBuilder("").require("robot").require("DriveForward"))
    def handle_drive_forward(self, message):
        self.handle_start_behavior("behavior_line")

@intent_handler(IntentBuilder("").require("robot").require("FollowLine"))
    def handle_follow_line(self, message):
        self.handle_start_behavior("line_following")
. . .
```

Adding new intents is now easier as we can reuse `handle_start_behavior`.

Running with the new intent

You can now upload the folder structure again—since the `vocab` and `__init__` files have changed. When you do so, note that Mycroft will automatically reload the changed skill so it is immediately ready to use.

Summary

In this chapter, you've seen how to get a Raspberry Pi to run the Mycroft environment and you've connected it to a speaker/microphone combination. You've been able to play with Mycroft and get it to respond to different voice commands.

You've learned about the terminology of voice assistants, intents, skills, utterances, vocabulary, and dialog. You've been able to put that into practice by creating a skill that communicates with the robot, starting a skill on the robot.

In the next chapter, we will connect a Joypad to our second Raspberry Pi and use this to remotely drive or trigger behaviors on our robot. We will also set up another `systemctl` file to start `menuserver` when the robot starts.

Questions

Try these assessment questions to check your understanding:

- Why would the user define multiple variations for each vocabulary part?
- Similarly, why would they do this for the dialog?
- Why did we wrap our intent with `try`/`catch`?
- What is the significance of the `en-us` string in the vocabulary/dialog file structures?
- How did we make the Pi start the `pulseaudio` system when it boots?

Suggested enhancement task: Add more intents to the skill, for example, wall avoiding. You could add a stop intent although the response time may make this less than ideal. Also, could the RGB LEDs on the Mycroft be used?

Further reading

MyCroft has a large community that supports and discusses the technology at `https://community.mycroft.ai/`. It is strongly recommended that the troubleshooting information at this community is used as, at the time of writing, MyCroft is under active development and has both many quirks and many new features. It's also a good place to share skills you build for it.

Seeed Studio, the creators of the Respeaker 2-Mics HAT host documentation and code for this device, along with bigger four-and six-microphone versions at `https://github.com/respeaker/seeed-voicecard`.

15
Programming a Gamepad on Raspberry Pi with Python

The robot we've been programming and making has many behaviors, but some end up with the robot on the other side of the room. We've also got a neat camera with some visual feedback available on what the robot is doing. Wouldn't it be neat to take control and drive the robot sometimes? In this chapter, we will see how. We will build a control system that includes our visual control for the robot.

The following topics will be covered in this chapter:

- When speech control won't work – why we need to drive
- Choosing a control pad – what we are going to use to drive the robot, and why
- Preparing the Raspberry Pi for remote driving – how to get the basic driving system going
- Upgrading the menu and display code for full headless – integrating the driving with display and menu
- Making it start when the Pi starts – using systemd to get our menu system to start automatically

Technical requirements

For this chapter you will need the following items:

- Your Raspberry Pi robot with the camera set up and code
- A touch screen device like a phone with Wi-Fi.
- A wireless network

The GitHub code for this chapter is at https://github.com/PacktPublishing/Learn-Robotics-Fundamentals-of-Robotics-Programming/tree/master/chapter15.

Use the `0_starting_point` folder to find the complete code from the previous chapters and the `full_system` folder on GitHub for the full code of this chapter.

Check out the following video to see the Code in Action:

`http://bit.ly/2DQkt6b`

When speech control won't work - why we need to drive

So in the last chapter, we built a Mycroft system to launch behaviors. If you tried to build intents to make the robot stop in time, or drive left or right, you will probably have noticed that even with the clearest speaking, it takes some time to respond.

Speech control also only really works in a quiet room. Any time a robot is out (you would like to drive it somewhere), this is not so useful.

Mycroft is also utterly dependent on having access to the internet. It is one thing to have a small shared network for a robot and a controller, it's another to always require internet access, which can become tricky when not at your home, school, or lab.

An external controller can be responsive, giving you fast control over the robot's movements. With a local network, it won't need external internet access. It can be used to drive a robot back to you after a behavior has run and you've stopped it, and be used to stop errant behavior. And with a bit of thought, it can be used to deliver useful, or plain interesting, feedback on what your robot is doing.

Choosing a controller

We want to be able to control our robot with something that is handheld and wireless. Trailing a wire to our robot would make little sense. Having seen how our robot drives in Chapter 7, *Drive and Turn - Moving Motors with Python*, we will want a control system that affects the wheels in a direct way.

One way to do this would be to use a Bluetooth joypad. There are a large number of these on the market, which may require specialist drivers to read. Bluetooth has a habit of dropping pairings at inopportune times.

However, you already have a handheld device, in your pocket, your phone. It has a touch screen, capable of reading finger movements. With a bit of the right code, you can display the video between controller bars, creating a kind of robotic *periscope* you can drive around and see (it's quite tricky to drive on camera - harder than overhead). We've already been building web applications for our robot, that we can access over Wi-Fi, and most phones can connect to that. So instead of going out and buying a new joypad, we will make a web app that your phone can access, like an app, to drive the robot and see a robot's-eye-view of the world.

Design and overview

So, to make a phone web app, a little bit of design on how we would expect this to work is needed. This could be as simple as a pen drawing on a scrap of paper, or using a drawing tool to get professional-looking results. The next image shows a screen mockup of this:

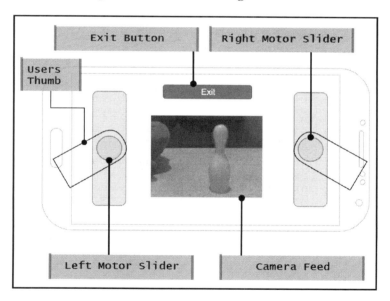

Screen mockup of driving web app

The mockup shows a mobile phone screen in landscape mode. The top of the screen has an exit button, and we can set this up to go to our menu after instructing the app to exit.

The middle of the screen has a video feed from the robot, using the mechanism described in the previous chapter. The left and right have sliders. The sliders, like an analog joystick, can be dragged to any position on their track with touches, and when let go will spring back to the middle. The next image shows how this works:

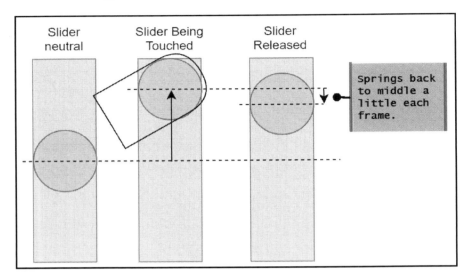

Slider return to middle behavior

Note that they don't immediately drop to the middle when let go, but animate back to this over a few frames. We'll need a little math to make that happen in our code.

These sliders let you drive the robot tank-style (with a joypad, the two analog sticks would be set up to perform the same way). Each slider controls the speed of a motor. While this sounds tricky (not like driving a car), with a little practice it is a very sensitive way to drive a two-wheeled robot. The further away from the middle you slide a slider, the faster the associated motor will go. We will also ensure that in the case of a loss of communications, the robot motors will stop after a second.

This is exactly the same control system your behaviors have been using throughout the book, but made interactive. The next diagram shows some of the motions needed for common moves:

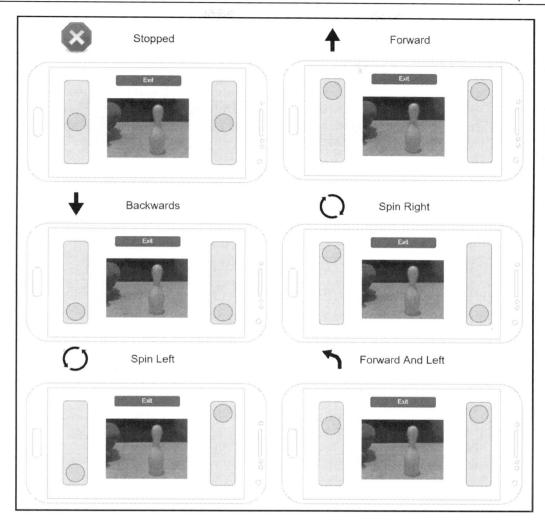

Common moves on two sliders

The red dots represent where your thumb is touching the screen. By sliding both forward, the robot will drive forward, and the further you slide them, the faster it will go. Backwards is sliding them both back. To spin the robot, slide them in opposite directions. To drive forward and a little left, or right, you slide both forward but bring the right slider a little higher than the left. You are also able to compensate for veer this way.

Preparing the Raspberry Pi for our controller and driving with it

Our Raspberry Pi has already been able to run web services, using Flask to create a menu server and video servers. We can use image and control queues to make a behavior interact with a web server. We are going to reuse these capabilities. In the phone app, the slider controls will need to be smart. The next diagram shows the parts of our manual drive system:

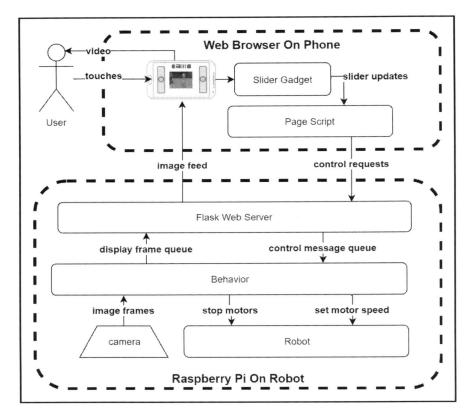

The system overview of a manual drive app

At the bottom layer, the **stop motors** and **set motor speed** calls are made to the robot. These are from the behavior based on timeouts or on the **control message queue** from the server. Meanwhile, the behavior loop will also be taking **image frames** from the camera, encoding them, and pushing them onto the **display frame queue**.

The next layer up is the Flask web server. This consumes the **display frame queue** supplying frames to the multi-part **image feed**. The Flask server will handle **control requests** and push them onto the **control message queue**.

On the phone, there is a page script, which will handle **slider updates** and turn those into **control requests** using the jQuery library. The slider gadget turns **touch** events into **slider updates** (it will be doing animation and converting for this).

The page itself uses an `img` tag to display the **video** feed like before, and places the slider widgets. The exit button is really just a simple link here.

The page script and slider widget will require JavaScript and CSS programming.

Enhancing the image app core

To build this, we will start by extending and reusing the image app core we used in the previous chapters. We'll add a few features:

- Serving static files: Our JavaScript and CSS files will be served here, along with a local copy of the jQuery library. Flask does this automatically, but we need cache headers so it stays fresh.
- Extending control to allow a whole path: Currently it only allows a single word, we need a bit more than that now. This way we can tell `/control/set_left/100` to put `set_left/100` on the control message queue.
- Add an exit handler that redirects to the menu server and puts an `exit` message on the control queue.

First, we will need a few more helpers imported from Flask. We are editing the `image_app_core.py` file:

```
...
from multiprocessing import Process, Queue

from flask import (Flask, render_template,
    Response, redirect, request)
...
```

Note that I've surrounded the import with brackets, this is so we can spill the imports to a new line. We will be using the `redirect` and `request` helpers for our exit handling.

To stop things we don't want being cached, we can instruct Flask to add no-cache headers after every request:

```
...
@app.after_request
def add_header(response):
    response.headers['Cache-Control'] = "no-cache, no-store, must-
revalidate"
    return response
...
```

Next, we need to modify our control system to handle longer control messages. We use the `path:` prefix, so the longer message can be just a path in the URL. The prefix with the colon tells Flask the type of data to expect. By saying it is a path, slash characters are expected in this string:

```
...
@app.route('/control/<path:control_name>')
def control(control_name):
    control_queue.put(control_name)
    return Response('queued')
...
```

The last extension to this is the `exit` handler. This will put an exit on the queue and redirect. This image app core system runs on port `5001`, but our menu server runs on port `5000`, so we replace the port in the current `url_root` to get there:

```
...
@app.route('/exit')
def handle_exit():
    control_queue.put('exit')
    menu_server = request.url_root.replace('5001', '5000')
    return redirect(menu_server, code=302)
...
```

`code=302` will mean the response to the browser shows this exit redirection is temporary, so that if an exit is asked for again, it should still come and make the request here first. Browsers on phones can be tricky in that they try to minimize the number of requests, mostly to avoid unnecessary traffic. This is usually handled through various caching (keeping results local on the phone), but for us this will mean requests don't get to our robot, or arrive in a strange order. We intend to ensure that this doesn't happen, here by saying the redirection is temporary, and we will use other ways later to prevent caching.

Create the `static` folder. We will put JavaScript and CSS code in this `static` folder. We will also make a local copy of the jQuery library. Make a `lib` directory under `static`, then download jQuery (the minimum version at the time of writing is at `https://code.jquery.com/jquery-3.3.1.min.js`) and store it in the `lib` folder. You should have a `static/lib/jquery-3.3.1.min.js` file.

Writing the behavior

The next part we will need is the behavior. This will not be that complex and use code seen before in the visual processing chapters, with a small bit of additional code in the control message area. I'll put this in `manual_drive.py`, starting with the imports we've seen for visual processing:

```
import time
from robot import Robot
from image_app_core import start_server_process, get_control_instruction,
put_output_image
import pi_camera_stream
...
```

We'll make a `ManualDriveBehavior` class. In this, we'll store a robot object, and keep track of timeouts. The timeout will stop the robot if there are no more control messages:

```
...
class ManualDriveBehavior(object):
    def __init__(self, robot):
        self.robot = robot
        self.timeout = time.time() + 1
...
```

The control section may need a little breaking down. This code is in the context of our `Behavior` class. We look for a control instruction, and if there is one, we can keep looking for more by looping. Before processing the instruction, we will reset the timeout:

```
...
    def process_control(self):
        instruction = get_control_instruction()
        while instruction:
            self.timeout = time.time() + 1
            parts = instruction.split('/')
...
```

We will now process the instruction. We now split this into a command, and parameters, by the / character that is used for URLs. We can take the parts; the first part will be the command. We can check if this command is `set_left` or `set_right`:

```
    ...
            if parts[0] == "set_left":
                self.robot.set_left(int(parts[1]))
            elif parts[0] == "set_right":
                self.robot.set_right(int(parts[1]))
    ...
```

We check for the command matching, and then set the robot motor speed to the next part of the instruction, the speed. This will currently be a string, so we use `int` to convert it into an integer number for our motors.

We also need to handle the `exit` command:

```
    ...
            elif parts[0] == "exit":
                print "Stopping"
                exit()
        instruction = get_control_instruction()
    ...
```

The `exit` command will exit our application. If this list of command handlers exceeds five, this could be improved by using a dictionary (like `menu_modes`) and then calling different handler methods.

Note that we then get another instruction. This is the end of the `while` loop; the instruction is used to come back into the loop. The reason we will do this is our phone app may have queued a number of instructions for both motors, so we should try to any queued instructions and deal with them immediately. We are now done with processing control.

The next method in our behavior is to make the display. Since the video feed is simply what the camera sees, we just get the frame, encode it, and put it on the server image queue:

```
    ...
    def make_display(self, frame):
        """Create display output, and put it on the queue"""
        encoded_bytes = pi_camera_stream.get_encoded_bytes_for_frame(frame)
        put_output_image(encoded_bytes)
    ...
```

We then need our behavior's `run` method, along with our method's main loop. This starts with some setup, similar to the color tracking:

```
. . .
    def run(self):
        # Set pan and tilt to middle, then clear it.
        self.robot.set_pan(0)
        self.robot.set_tilt(0)
        # start camera
        camera = pi_camera_stream.setup_camera()
        # warm up and servo move time
        time.sleep(0.1)
        # Servo's will be in place - stop them for now.
        self.robot.servos.stop_all()
        print("Setup Complete")
. . .
```

We then enter into our main loop, around feeding camera frames through to the display:

```
. . .
        # Main loop
        for frame in pi_camera_stream.start_stream(camera):
            self.make_display(frame)
. . .
```

The other things our main loop needs to deal with are control instructions and the automatic stop. It can be quite frustrating to watch a robot drive off into the distance or off a desk, so it will revert to stopping if nothing is making sense. This is still in the `for` loop.

```
. . .
            self.process_control()
            # Auto stop
            if time.time() > self.timeout:
                self.robot.stop_motors()
. . .
```

We now finish our behavior with the top-level code to create and start the components:

```
print "Setting up"
behavior = ManualDriveBehavior(Robot())
process = start_server_process('manual_drive.html')
behavior.run()
```

The template (web page)

So, our server has been asked to show the `templates/manual_drive.html` template. This will have the code to render our widgets:

```html
<html>
    <head>
...
```

Now, that we are in our head section, we are targeting a phone, and we want the system to render the display to fit a phone, ensuring that it adapts to the display size. The display is mostly visual, with little text, so we don't want the user's touch interactions to accidentally scale the display. The next line tells the browser that this is our intention:

```html
...
        <meta name="viewport" content="width=device-width, initial-scale=1.0, user-scalable=no">
...
```

We are going to give our display some particular looks and style. With more sophisticated pages, the style is kept in a separate sheet, in our case `display.css`. But this could be used in multiple pages to give them a similar style. We are also going to use the jQuery library, and a touch-slider system that we will build. These are the HTML equivalent of imports. Putting a question mark after the library path for these will cause our phone to reload this every time; it's intended again to stop a cache preventing us from reloading fixed code. There's a title to go on the top of the tab:

```html
...
        <link rel="stylesheet" type="text/css" href="/static/display.css?">
        <script src="/static/lib/jquery-3.3.1.min.js"></script>
        <script src="/static/touch-slider.js?"></script>
        <title>Manually Drive The Robot</title>
    </head>
...
```

We are done with the head section, and we will then use the body to define the drawn parts of our page:

```html
...
    <body>
        <svg id="left_slider" class="slider_track">
            <circle cy="50%" cx="50%" r="15%" class="slider_tick"/>
        </svg>
...
```

The first part of our body is a slider track. We use an `svg` object for the track. SVG-scalable vector graphics can be used directly within an HTML page in all current smart phone browsers. Here, we create an `svg` container, but give it a class of `slider_track` which we can use to style both tracks, and an ID of `left_slider` which we can use both to position it, and to attach it to the touch events. As a general guide, a class is used to attribute many objects with the same properties, and an ID is intended to identify a particular object. These identifiers can be used for CSS, or in the JavaScript, to create code behaviors for those objects.

In the `svg`, we have a circle element. We set the center x, center y, and radius of our circle. The width and height percentages are in relation to the slider track it's contained in, putting the circle in the middle of the track. The radius % is slightly complex, it's based on the diagonal size of the `svg` element; suffice to say you may need to adjust this if it's looking too big or too small. The circle's color will come from the stylesheet:

```
. . .
        <a class="button" id="exitbutton" href="/exit">Exit</a>
. . .
```

This will give us a link to exit the app, but it also has a class and ID. The `button` class will be associated with fonts, colors, and styles that could be used for other buttons (for example to enhance the menu app), but the `exitbutton` ID is used in the stylesheet to position this in the place we designed before.

Next, we have our video block. This time, the `img` tag for the video is contained inside a `div`. We want our video to keep its ratio (4:3) on any size screen, and the `div` tag helps us to preserve the ratio while letting it fill to fit the space:

```
. . .
        <div id="video"><img src="{{ url_for('display') }}" /></div>
. . .
```

The next element in our body will be the right slider. This is a repeat of the left, with only the ID being different. You could copy and paste the left code, changing the ID:

```
. . .
        <svg id="right_slider" class="slider_track">
            <circle cy="50%" cx="50%" r="15%" class="slider_tick"/>
        </svg>
. . .
```

Now we have the elements that are drawn on our page, we need some JavaScript code to connect things together. JavaScript is different in syntax from Python; you normally declare variables with `var` instead of just naming them, you use semicolons `;` to end lines, and use curly brackets `{ }` to delimit blocks, so the indentation is more out of convention and keeping it readable than for the computer. JavaScript has many concepts that are common with Python; it uses classes/objects in a different syntax, but for the same reasons.

In our page, we will need a function to send motor speed data as control messages. To put JavaScript on our page, we need to enclose it in `<script>` tags. First, we create a sequence, this is changed and sent for every message. It serves to prevent the page cache giving us strange results:

```
...
        <script type="text/javascript">
            var sequence = 0;
            function set_motor(name, speed) {
                $.get('/control/set_' + name + '/' + speed, sequence);
                sequence ++;
            }
...
```

The speed is combined with a motor name (left or right) and then sent to the server to put on the control queue. We are using `$.get` to send this, a jQuery function that performs an HTTP `GET` request. `GET` usually means to request information, there is an alternative POST type to send information (like POSTing a letter), but in this case `GET` is easier to link up with our existing control queue system and not rewrite other behaviors using it.

An important idea in JavaScript is that a function can be a bit of data. We've used it before in Python in our square driving system when we swapped which motor was on the inside of a curve. In JavaScript, passing a function in as a parameter to another function is a common way to do things. Because this is done often, functions used that way are not even given names; they are anonymous functions, or can be called lambdas.

Now, we need to set up the sliders and link them with `set_motor` so they will update this every time they change. jQuery has a special function, `$()`, which will run any function passed to it when the page has completed loading:

```
...
            $(function () {
                var leftSlider = new Slider('left_slider', function(speed)
{set_motor('left', speed);});
                leftSlider.setup();
                var rightSlider = new Slider('right_slider',
function(speed) {set_motor('right', speed);});
```

```
        rightSlider.setup();
    });
```
. . .

We gave the page load system an anonymous function. In this, we start by creating a new Slider object (we'll see how these are made in the library). The Slider objects constructor looks like `Slider(id, when_updated)` where `id` is the id of the object we are turning into a slider (an `svg` track), and `when_updated` will be a function to call when the slider has changed.

We construct a `leftSlider` and a `rightSlider`, setting their IDs to the page element Ids. We then give an anonymous function to make make a further call with the speed of the left or right motor to `set_motor`.

We now end our page by closing all the tags:

. . .
```
        </script>
    </body>
</html>
```
. . .

You can start to run this now to see how it looks. Upload the whole folder (including templates) to the robot, and then run `python manual_drive.py`. Point a browser at `http://myrobot.local:5001/` , substituting your robot's hostname or address to see it. At this point, I strongly suggest using the desktop browser to discover errors in the HTML or JavaScript. At the time of writing, Firefox, Safari, and Chrome have support for emulating mobile devices in the browser and touch events too, so these seem like the best candidates.

It probably looks a bit flat, with things totally flat or in the wrong place, nothing like the mockup. The video works though. We've yet to tell the browser where we want things on the page, or what colors to make them. We also don't have the slider code yet.

The stylesheet

So, we can now give it some style. Stylesheets can take up a lot of time in tuning and getting them just right, visually. Create the `static/display.css` file to hold this style information. If you think my color choices are terrible, please feel free to substitute your own; search `w3c colors` to find suitable colors to use. Names or hex (#1ab3c5) colors can be used.

CSS styles sections start with a selector, a way to match objects in the HTML page. These can be made from tag names, class names prefixed with a full stop, or ids prefixed with a # mark. For a comprehensive look at css selectors, see the additional reading. Each section uses braces { } to delimit a section of style. The styles in that section are made of a property name, a colon :, and then a setting for it. These are followed by a semicolon ; to end each setting.

We'll start by making our slider track 10% of the viewport width, that is, 10% as big as the screen. CSS has a special unit, vw, for this, along with vh for percentage of the viewport height. See additional reading for notes on CSS units:

```
.slider_track {
    width: 10vw;
...
```

We'll also give the slider track a solid line border, in the color blue, and a light blue background. This will match our mockups:

```
...
    height: 90vh;
    border: 1px solid blue;
    background-color: lightblue;
}
...
```

This uses a CSS **selector** `.slider_track`, which says this style applies to all objects with that as their class. Both of our sliders have this class, so changes here affect both of them.

We also need to style the tick, the circle we see on the sliders. Let's just give it a light pinkish fill color, like our mockups:

```
...
.slider_tick {
    fill: mistyrose;
}
...
```

Now we've described the general properties of our sliders, we need to tell our browser to put these left and right. When making a display match closely to the screen mock up, we can use **absolute positioning** with viewport percentages to say exactly where things should be. Here, we use `#left_slider` with the # mark meaning an id instead of a class, identifying a single specific object. Let's put the left slider on the left, and the right on the right:

```
. . .
#left_slider {
    position: absolute;
    left: 5vw;
    top: 5vh;
}
#right_slider {
    position: absolute;
    right: 5vw;
    top: 5vh;
}
. . .
```

You can try this by uploading it, stopping the running behavior and starting it again, then reloading. You'll see the exit button and video are in the wrong place. In fact, the exit button doesn't look like a button at all, so let's make it a nice big touch button with some styling. We will combine a class selector and an id selector, so you can reuse the button to enhance the menu and make that more touch friendly later.

First, we make button a `block` type. As it's just a link, it usually expects to be just a bit of text, but as we want a rectangular block, we'll give this 10% of the viewport height to make it pretty big. We'll leave width to be more specific later:

```
. . .
.button {
    display: block;
    height: 10vh;
. . .
```

We want the text to be in the center both vertically and horizontally for a block. There is a style for the text alignment horizontally. By setting the line height to the height of the block, the text will be centered by default. We will make the text twice as large using `2em`:

```
. . .
    text-align: center;
    font-size: 2em;
    line-height: 10vh;
. . .
```

We want to take the underline of the button text, which you normally get with a link. We'll also give it some color, a blue background with white text:

```
    ...
    text-decoration: none;
    background-color: blue;
    color: white;
}
    ...
```

This class can be used on other buttons, but this is specifically an exit button. So, we want to position it exactly on our layout. Yet again, we use absolute positioning, and set the width to keep it centered. If our `left` is 30vw, we want the `right` to be 30vw too. So *100vw-60vw* = *40vw*, and we make the `width` to be *40vw*:

```
    ...
#exitbutton {
    position: absolute;
    width: 40vw;
    left: 30vw;
    top: 5vh;
}
    ...
```

Trying this out you will now see the exit button in the right place, but the video is still in the top left. Depending on the screen you use, it may also be too big or small. We need to do a little trickery to get it the right size and position.

If you recall from the previous chapter, we've chosen to keep our video at 320 x 240 to reduce how much data is being used for it. This has a ratio of 4:3, which we will want to preserve. Video can look strange if this ratio, the **aspect ratio**, is changed. If you check the HTML page, we actually have a `video` container div, with the `img` tag pointing at the feed inside. This is so we can combine them to get the shape we want. First, we want that container to be a block. We want it to be 20% from the top of the screen. The `vmin` unit is a percentage of the minimum dimension of the screen, so it ensures that this block is never so large it would obscure the two slider bars:

```
    ...
#video {
    display: block;
    margin-top: 20vh;
    width: 80vmin;
    height: 80vmin;
    ...
```

We want this to be centered. We can't use absolute positioning because we actually don't know if `vmin` is width or height. Setting the left and right margins to auto will instruct the browser to try and make those the same, automatically positioning the object in the horizontal middle of the screen:

```
. . .
    margin-left: auto;
    margin-right: auto;
}
. . .
```

Our outer container is in the middle, and constrained to not be too big.

The inner object (`img`) should fill the outer container horizontally (100%), but be constrained so its height is the 4:3 ratio, or 75% of the width. The padding instructions use a container width for their percentage, so a cheeky (but documented) trick is to set padding-bottom to this percentage, which will keep the inner video feed object at the right shape. By selecting `#video img`, we are applying this style to the `img` object inside the object with the `video` id:

```
. . .
#video img {
    width: 100%;
    padding-bottom: 75%;
}
```

Apply this and our page is fully styled. It should now look a lot like the mock up in your browser, with the video. The slider bars still don't do anything yet though. Note that you may need to force your browser to reload the stylesheet.

We now need to add the slider code.

Creating the code for the sliders

The sliders are going to be slightly smart. They will need to respond to touch events, moving the circle to match the touch location, and sending an update message to show how far this movement is from the middle. The sliders will automatically return to the center when the touch events stop, so they are somewhat animated. We will use JavaScript for these, and create a JavaScript Slider object definition (equivalent of a Python class) that we can make the two sliders with.

As defined in our HTML, we will put this in `static/touch-slider.js`. As we are in a `.js` file, the `<script>` tags are not needed. We'll start with a constructor for our object, storing the `id` as a selector, and using the `when_updated` function to call back when the slider changes:

```
function Slider(id, when_updated) {
    this.selector = '#' + id;
    this.when_updated = when_updated;
};
...
```

This is the constructor; in JavaScript, the class prototype is defined separately from this constructor. We'll start that prototype with a method for handling touch events (`touchMove`). We will keep a member variable, `touch`, set to true if the screen is currently being touched. Note that a comma (`,`) is used to separate items in the prototype definition:

```
...
Slider.prototype = {
    touched: false, // is a touch still occuring
    touchmove: function(event) {
...
```

When this `touchmove` function is bound to an event, it is called with the event detail as a parameter. These JavaScript event handlers are a lot like the functions we've used in Python when writing the line follower code. We read the `targetTouches` member of that event to find out the places the screen is being touched. When we look at the first item, it is a list, but we assume there is only one touch for the target (a slider track). We then get the relative position of this touch from the top of the slider:

```
...
        var touch = event.targetTouches[0];
        // Get the touch relative to the top of the slider
        var from_top = touch.pageY - $(this.selector).offset().top;
...
```

Now we have a relative position, we can convert it into a percentage of the total track's length and call another method to handle the change (we'll figure out what to put there later; for now, we just want the touches):

```
...
        // height of track in pixels
        var trackheight = $(this.selector).height();
        // Convert this to twice a percentage of the track. (0 is the
middle)
```

```
        var relative_touch = (from_top/trackheight) * 100;
        this.set_position(relative_touch);
...
```

Now we know that the track is being touched, we will set that variable. We will also make sure that this event stops here, as we do not want the touches to the track being used to scroll or zoom the page, so we prevent the default event handler:

```
...
        this.touched = true;
        event.preventDefault();
    },
...
```

The next handler is to tell our system that the touches have stopped on this target:

```
...
    touchend: function(event) {
        this.touched = false;
    },
...
```

Our system will be animating moving back to the center when it's not touched. The animation should be quite responsive. We also want it to send updates to our robot, but not too many as it would fill the control queue. So our slider will have two timers, one to animate/update it, and another to call the page code when things have changed. In the setup function, we will bind the handlers and prepare these timers. JavaScript uses interval timers to repeatedly call bits of code. The timings are in milliseconds:

```
...

    setup: function() {
        $(this.selector).on('touchmove', this.touchmove.bind(this));
        $(this.selector).on('touchend', this.touchend.bind(this));
        setInterval(this.update.bind(this), 50);
        setInterval(this.update_if_changed.bind(this), 200);
    },
...
```

In this snippet, all of our methods are passed to these events with a .bind(this) suffix. This ensures that when this is used in those functions, it is our Slider object.

The next method our Slider will need is setting the position, used in our `touchmove` handler, and we will also use it when animating back to zero. This method will set the position, ensuring it is a whole number, log this to the JavaScript console (useful for debugging), update the slider track, and set a `changed` variable so the slower timer can check for differences. The `position` starts off at 50 percent, which is the middle of the track:

```
    . . .
    changed: false,
    position : 50,
    set_position: function(new_position) {
        this.position = Math.round(new_position);
        console.log(this.id + " - " + this.position);
        $(this.selector).find('.slider_tick')[0].setAttribute('cy',
this.position + '%');
        this.changed = true;
    },
    . . .
```

We update the track by using the selector we made, then finding the slider tick inside it. This find produces a list, even if in our specific case there is only one; you could have multiple child items. We use `setAttribute` to modify the center X property of the circle, which will cause it to move to the right place on the track.

The next method we will need should perform the animation of the track, making it spring back to the 50% mark if it is pulled away. This will look a little like our PID controller code, with a slight trick.

First, we calculate an error; this is how far away we are from the 50% mark:

```
    . . .
    update: function() {
        var error = 50 - this.position;
    . . .
```

Now, we get a change value by scaling the error proportionally, with a factor of `0.3`, and add/subtract an extra `0.5` to ensure the movement rounds up to at least 1%:

```
    . . .
        var change = (0.3 * error) + (Math.sign(error) * 0.5)
    . . .
```

Now, we only want to actually change the movement if we are not touching the track, so it stays where you keep your thumb. The animation should also only be changing if the current position is not at the neutral 50% mark:

```
. . .
        if(!this.touched && this.position != 50) {
. . .
```

We now use our update position function, adding the current position to the change amount we've set. This will finish the `if` statement, and the update method:

```
        this.set_position(this.position + change);
    }
},
```

The last method we need in our touch slider is the target of our slower updates, which will check our changed flag, and if it is different, call the `when_changed` handler with the new number.

Here we need to convert from the values used by the slider to display the circle as a percentage from 0 (top of the slider) and 100% (bottom of the slider), to values for setting our motor speeds, from 100 (full forward), to 0 (stopped), and down to -100 (full reverse). The next image illustrates this conversion:

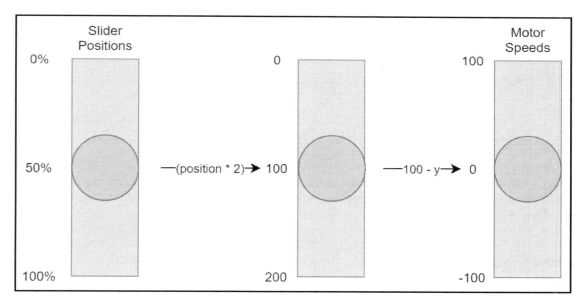

Slider positions illustrated

The previous image should assist in understanding the conversion done in this next section of code:

```
...
    update_if_changed: function() {
        if(this.changed) {
            this.changed = false;
            this.when_updated(100 - this.position * 2);
        }
    }
};
```

Running this

You can now upload the whole set of files to a folder on your robot. As before, you can use `python manual_drive.py` to run this.

You can use developer mode on a browser to view the web page before trying it on a phone, by right-clicking on your page and clicking **Inspect element**. In the developer tools, there will be buttons for emulating phone devices and touch events. You can check that dragging the sliders has the desired results, and click on the **Console** button to see if there are errors from the JavaScript. Point it at `http://myrobot.local:5001` (using your robot's hostname or address).

Common problems in JavaScript and CSS are missing punctuation such as semicolons, commas, or brackets. Having class or ID selectors that do not match (or are missing the required dot/hash mark syntax) will make styles fail to apply, or element lookups in JavaScript produce no results.

It can be difficult to get phones to reload code, so try to shake out any problems in a desktop browser first, then start your phone's internet browser and point it at the same location. With the phone, you should be able to use your thumbs to drive the robot.

If your robot seems to be pausing, and then spending a while catching up with your events, you could adjust the `update_if_changed` interval time to something longer.

It will take some practice to drive the robot manually. I suggest practicing overhead driving first, and when you have got the hang of that, try driving through the camera. The frame rate on the camera is not very high, and the driving loop is currently constrained by this frame rate.

Upgrading the menu and displaying code for full headless

We are now able to drive our robot from the phone, but the menu doesn't seem very touch friendly. It also will not successfully run any of the behaviors with displays using Flask. We will make the menu buttons bigger and more touch friendly, using styles similar to our manual drive behavior. The menu can also load our server page after clicking a behavior with a server like this one, or the visual tracking behaviors from the last chapter.

Making menu modes compatible with Flask behaviors

If you've already tried running the Flask-based behaviors (any of the visual processing, and the manual drive) in the menu, you will have noticed some very odd behavior indeed. Your behavior will appear to be doing the right thing with sensors on the robot, but the web service fails to do anything useful on port 5001.

This is due to Flask operating in a way that uses its own subprocesses to manage itself when in debug mode, which allows it to reload changed code. We won't be using it in debug mode, so the fix for this is to remove debug when it's run. Edit the last few lines of menu_server.py, noting that debug=True is removed from the run line:

```
# Start the app running
# if you enable debug, disable the reloader here.
app.run(host="0.0.0.0")
```

You can now add the manual drive, color tracking, and face tracking behaviors to the menu and they will start properly.

Loading video services

When we click on a menu option for one of the video server-based behaviors, they start, but then we need to send our browser to port 5001 on our robot manually. It would be kind of neat if we performed a redirect to one of these behaviors when we start them. We know how to redirect, as we've done it in the manual drive behavior when handling the exit button. However, we only want the menu system to do this for a mode that has such a service. To do this, we can update our mode config, which was a simple list, changing it into dictionaries containing a script to run, and optionally a true/false server value to say we need to redirect.

So first in `robot_modes.py`, we'll change the `mode_config` to have this option. I've skipped the middle options, but they will follow the same pattern of changes:

```
    ...
    mode_config = {
        "avoid_behavior": {"script": "avoid_behavior.py"},
        "circle_head": {"script": "circle_pan_tilt_behavior.py"},
        ...
        "color_track": {"script": "color_track_behavior.py", "server":
True},
        "face_track": {"script": "face_track_behavior.py", "server": True},
        "manual_drive": {"script": "manual_drive.py", "server": True}
    }
    ...
```

The new manual drive behavior has been added here. (You will need to follow the pattern in `menu_config` to get new options to show).

In the previous example code, the last three behaviors have the `"server": True` setting. We now need to modify the `.run` method to use this changed structure and pick out the script. While there, we'll also make it stop any still running process when a new one starts; the return value is also redundant, so I've removed it:

```
    ...
    def run(self, mode_name):
        """Run the mode as a subprocess, and stop any we still have one
running"""
        while self.is_running():
            self.stop()
        script = self.mode_config[mode_name]['script']
        self.current_process = subprocess.Popen(["python", script])
    ...
```

Next, we need a method to check whether we should redirect, based on the flag of the mode being `True`, and the current process still being alive. Note the explicit `is True`, this makes it clearer that the value is a `True/False` flag:

```
    ...
    def should_redirect(self, mode_name):
        return self.mode_config[mode_name].get('server') is True and
self.is_running()
    ...
```

We have prepared `robot_modes.py`; the `menu_server.py` file is where the menu flask app runs, which will need to perform the redirect. We will use the `request` object, modifying the port on `url_root` again, but we will also wait a few seconds so the child app has a chance to start running. Add these imports to `menu_server.py`:

```
. . .
import time
from flask import Flask, render_template, redirect, request
from robot_modes import RobotModes
. . .
```

Now, we can set up our `run` handler to redirect when the mode intends:

```
. . .
@app.route("/run/<mode_name>")
def run(mode_name):
    # Use our robot app to run something with this mode_name
    mode_manager.run(mode_name)
    if mode_manager.should_redirect(mode_name):
        # Give the other process time to start
        time.sleep(3)
. . .
```

The 3-second sleep is so our child service can be running before we direct a user there. You may need to make this longer if it's not fast enough. Before redirecting, it's worth checking that the child process is actually running. It's possible that for some reason it failed to run, so we should not redirect to it. We can ask our `mode_manager` if the process is running:

```
. . .
        # If it's not broken
        if mode_manager.is_running():
. . .
```

Now, we can perform the redirect, replacing the port number:

```
. . .
            # Now redirect
            new_url = request.url_root.replace('5000', '5001')
            return redirect(new_url)
. . .
```

This leaves the question of what to do if it failed. The answer is to show our menu again, but with a message to signal the failure. At the end is the fallback to our normal, non-server behavior, which says that the process is now running:

```
    ...
        else:
            return render_menu(message="%s dead." % mode_name)
        return render_menu(message="%s running" % mode_name)
    ...
```

Styling the menu

Our menu now works, but if we are driving this with a phone, the links are not very phone/touch-friendly. We suggested we might be able to reuse the stylesheet in the menu. Before we start, add the following cache behavior so we see fresh styles as we did in `image_app_core.py`. Add the following to `menu_server.py`:

```
...
@app.after_request
def add_header(response):
    response.headers['Cache-Control'] = "no-cache, no-store, must-
revalidate"
    return response
...
```

Making the menu template into buttons

Before we change anything in the menu template, we should load our stylesheet into it. Open up `templates/menu.html` and add the link to that file. We can add a `charset` definition too:

```
...
<head>
    <meta charset="UTF-8">
    <title>My Robot Menu</title>
    <link rel="stylesheet" type="text/css" href="/static/display.css">
</head>
...
```

The menu template currently uses a list of items for the menu. We can add a class to that list to make it a `menu` type list, and the `button` class to the links so we can style them:

```
. . .
  <ul class="menu">
    {% for item in menu %}
      <li><a class="button" href="/run/{{ item.mode_name }}">{{ item.text
}}</a></li>
    {% endfor %}
    <li><a class="button" href="/stop">Stop</a></li>
  </ul>
. . .
```

Save this, and we will then need to open up the `static/display.css` stylesheet to define what a list with the `menu` class looks like. The `.button` selector is already covered. We will make the list container fill the screen width, but without any extra margins (space around the outside of the item) or padding (space between the inside of the item and its child list items):

```
. . .
.menu {
    width: 100%;
    margin-top: 0;
    margin-bottom: 0;
    padding: 0;
}
. . .
```

Our menu consists of list items. Although it is a list of buttons, the default way it's displayed is with a dot, a bullet point. We want to set this to none (no shape), and not position based on the bullet point either. We can use CSS `list-style` properties to change that. The selector here applies to list items (`li`) that are children of a `.menu` class object:

```
. . .
.menu li {
    list-style-type: none;
    list-style-position: initial;
}
. . .
```

Finally, to make this nice and touch friendly, we can make the buttons a little wider, at the same width. `60vw` (60 percent of the viewport width) should do it. We use the margin auto trick to center this. The buttons are `.button` class children. Finally, so we can see the separate items, we add a 1-pixel light blue border to them:

```
. . .
.menu .button {
    margin-left: auto;
    margin-right: auto;
```

```
    width: 60vw;
    border: 1px solid lightblue;
}
```

Upload the whole directory again, and start the menu server with `python menu_server.py`. You could embellish the CSS by adding round buttons or putting spacing between the buttons. You should be able to click on the tracking or driving behaviors and after 3 seconds be redirected to their page. Clicking the exit buttons or link should take you back to the menu.

Once you have tested this out on a desktop, you are ready to try it on your phone.

Making it start when the Pi starts

You now have a menu system to launch your robot behaviors, and a set of compatible behaviors in it. Although using ssh to log in is great to debug, see problems, and fix them, if you want to demonstrate your robot, it is even better to turn on your robot, point your phone browser at it once the lights stop blinking, and go.

We are going to do two things to make this useful:

- Use an LED to indicate that it's ready (in menu mode) to allow the robot to tell us before our phone has linked to the page
- Use systemd to automatically start the menu Flask server when the robot is switched on

Adding lights to the menu server

We won't want the whole robot system added to our menu, but the lights alone can be used to indicate our robot is now ready. We will import the LED system, turn it on as the server starts, and then turn it off/release it when the first mode/run request arrives.

Open the `menu_server.py` file, and we can import the LEDs:

```
...
from robot_modes import RobotModes
from leds_8_apa102c import Leds
...
```

We need to set up our LEDs and turn one LED green:

```
...
# Prepare our robot modes for use
mode_manager = RobotModes()

leds = Leds()
leds.set_one(1, [0, 255, 0])
leds.show()
...
```

In our `run` method, we need to clear the LED. Since we only want to do it once, we can set the global LEDs to `None`, and then check this next time:

```
...
def run(mode_name):
    global leds
    if leds:
        leds.clear()
        leds.show()
        leds = None
...
```

You can test this by uploading the menu server code and running it again. The LED should light when it starts, then when you select another behavior, it will go out. It should work perfectly to move from the menu to the LED test behavior.

Using systemd to automatically start the robot

We encountered systemd in the voice control chapter as a way to automatically start the PulseAudio system. Here, you can use systemd to start the menu when the Raspberry Pi is ready. See additional reading for more information about Raspberry Pi systemd.

This is done by creating a unit file, which we will copy into place on our Pi.

Call this file `menu_server.service`. First we give it a description, and tell systemd to start our service after we have networking on our Raspberry Pi:

```
[Unit]
Description=Robot Menu Web Service
After=network.target
...
```

Now, we tell systemd we want this to start as the Pi is ready for users to log in:

```
...
[Install]
WantedBy=multi-user.target
...
```

The next section configures how to run our menu. The working directory should be the place you have copied your robot files into. In my case, this is `/home/pi/full_system`. The `ExecStart` statement tells systemd the command to run the service. However, it does not assume a path the way a shell would, so prefix the `python` command with `/usr/bin/env`:

```
...
[Service]
WorkingDirectory=/home/pi/full_system
ExecStart=/usr/bin/env python menu_server.py
User=pi
```

You will now need to set this up on the Raspberry Pi. First, upload it to your Raspberry Pi home directory, then you'll need `sudo` to copy it into the system configuration. Type this via SSH on the Pi. Note you will see permission errors if you miss the `sudo`:

```
$ sudo cp menu_server.service /etc/systemd/system/
```

We should now ask systemd to load our configuration, and then enable our service:

```
$ sudo systemctl daemon-reload
$ sudo systemctl enable menu-server
```

The system will confirm it is enabled with this:

```
Created symlink /etc/systemd/system/multi-
user.target.wants/menu_server.service →
/etc/systemd/system/menu_server.service.
```

You can then try starting your service with this:

```
$ sudo systemctl start menu_server
```

This may fail, and you will see `Unit menu_server.service is not loaded properly: Invalid argument` if there are problems with the unit file. Please correct them, copy it back over, and rerun the sudo commands to install the new file.

If starting this server is successful, you will see the green light go on, showing it is ready. You will then be able to point your browser at the robot and control it.

If you want to see more of what the server is doing, you can use this command:

```
$ systemctl status menu_server
```

And the Pi will respond with something like this:

```
● menu_server.service - Robot Menu Web Service
   Loaded: loaded (/etc/systemd/system/menu_server.service; enabled; vendor
preset: enabled)
   Active: active (running) since Wed 2018-11-07 21:59:26 UTC; 10s ago
 Main PID: 16006 (python)
   CGroup: /system.slice/menu_server.service
           └─16006 python menu_server.py

Nov 07 21:59:26 myrobot systemd[1]: Started Robot Menu Web Service.
Nov 07 21:59:26 myrobot env[16006]: * Serving Flask app "menu_server" (lazy
loading)
Nov 07 21:59:26 myrobot env[16006]: * Environment: production
Nov 07 21:59:26 myrobot env[16006]: WARNING: Do not use the development
server in a production environment.
Nov 07 21:59:26 myrobot env[16006]: Use a production WSGI server instead.
Nov 07 21:59:26 myrobot env[16006]: * Debug mode: off
Nov 07 21:59:26 myrobot env[16006]: * Running on http://0.0.0.0:5000/
(Press CTRL+C to quit)
```

This can show some recent activity, but you may want to follow the output of behaviors as they run. To do this, you will need to use the `journalctl` command. Use `-u` to specify the service we created, and then `-f` to follow the log:

```
$ journalctl -u menu_server -f
```

We will then be able to see servers as they run. Perhaps not as convenient for debugging, but handy for launching services. Use *Ctrl + C* to stop following.

You can now reboot the robot, wait for the green light, and start driving it. The green light will also mean that your Mycroft Voice Assistant can send requests to the robot too.

If you upload new code, you will need to restart the service. You can use the following command to do so:

```
$ sudo systemctl restart menu_server
```

Congratulations, your robot is now truly headless! It doesn't even need a PC or laptop to start it doing things.

Enhancement Ideas

You could enhance the system in many ways. Adding a **shutdown** menu link will mean you could more gracefully shut down the Pi, where it would start the command `sudo poweroff`.

You could consider changing the menu to a grid, by using the menu space differently, as you may need to scroll to get there.

For desktop compatibility, the manual driving system could be enhanced with keyboard interactions to drive the robot, which are not quite as fun as the phone, but a handy fallback.

Summary

Your robot has now gained the ability to be driven manually. It may take you a while to get used to handling it, and manually correcting for veer (motors behaving slightly differently) is harder than when the PID systems correct themselves, but you will gain skills at driving it with your phone. You can use the camera on the front of the robot to get a robot's-eye-view of the world.

You've also seen how to connect your menu server up to the video server apps such as manually driving, color tracking, or face tracking. By making the buttons more touch friendly on the menu server, you can use a phone to launch most behaviors.

Finally, we gave the menu server a way to indicate being ready on the robot with an LED, and then set it up to start automatically when the robot is turned on. If your robot and phone can connect to the same network (perhaps you can set up your phone hotspot in a `wpa_supplicant.conf` file), you will be able to launch the behaviors from places outside your lab and demonstrate them to people.

In the next chapter, we will look at meeting the robot-making community, where to find further skills in robot building, and programming so you can continue building.

Questions

These questions should help you check your understanding:

1. What is a static file?
2. What does the `path:` prefix mean for a section of a Flask route?
3. What is the unit `vw` in CSS, and why do we use it?
4. How do you get events when a screen is touched in JavaScript?
5. What do the selectors `.button` and `#video` mean for CSS/jQuery?
6. In the systemd service file, what does the statement `After=network.target` intend?

Further reading

To find out more about the topics covered in this chapter:

- The Flask API documentation (`http://flask.pocoo.org/docs/1.0/api/`) is highly recommended, both to help understand the Flask functions we've used, and to see other ways this flexible web server library can be used.
- For a more guided look at the Flask web server, I suggest reading *Flask By Example*, by Gareth Dwyer, showing you how to build more involved web applications using Flask.
- CSS selectors are used throughout HTML, CSS, and JavaScript applications. A good combination of reference and tutorial can be found at the W3C Schools CSS Selectors (`https://www.w3schools.com/cssref/css_selectors.asp`) website. I would recommend exploring the site for its information on most web application technologies. For CSS units, see W3C Schools CSS Units (`https://www.w3schools.com/cssref/css_units.asp`) to practice and find more types of units to use.
- For getting more familiar with the JavaScript, CSS, and HTML technologies used here, freeCodeCamp (`https://www.freecodecamp.org/`) is a valuable resource, with self-learning modules.
- Raspberry Pi has handy documentation on user systemd files at `https://www.raspberrypi.org/documentation/linux/usage/systemd.md`. *The Redhat Administrators Guide - Creating And Modifying systemd Unit Files* (`https://access.redhat.com/documentation/en-us/red_hat_enterprise_linux/7/HTML/system_administrators_guide/sect-Managing_Services_with_systemd-Unit_Files`) is a very comprehensive reference on the different sections and statements.

16
Taking Your Robot Programming Skills Further

You've now learned some of the basic building skills and some of the more interesting programming tricks with robotics. But this robot is only really suitable for a lab, it's not really ready for competitions or touring, and this is only the start of a robotics journey. There is also a large community of robot builders and makers, coming from many angles. How can you be part of this?

In this chapter, you will learn about the following:

- Where to find other people building robots online and become part of communities
- Where to actually join and share spaces with other robot builders and demonstrate or build with them
- Further building skills and where to continue learning about robot construction
- Places to develop knowledge about OpenCV and computer vision
- Where further study is available on machine learning and AI

Online robot building communities – forums and social media

Robot building is a topic that shares space with the general community of makers. Makers are everywhere. There are ham radio and electronics enthusiasts who are more connected with the electronics side of the robot building; there are artists who are using devices such as the Arduino and Raspberry Pi to bring their creations to life. Teachers are using these devices to show children the world of technology, or to assist in teaching other subjects to them. There are also people with problems to solve, and brilliant and sometimes crazy ideas to try out.

Robotics can be part of the maker community, which has a very strong presence on social media such as Twitter, Instagram and YouTube. Searching them for tags such as `#raspberrypi` (`https://twitter.com/hashtag/RaspberryPi`), `#arduino` (`https://twitter.com/hashtag/Arduino`), and `#makersgonnamake` (`https://twitter.com/hashtag/makersgonnamake`) will reveal many of these conversations going on. A rallying point is the `@GuildOfMakers` (`https://twitter.com/guildofmakers`) account on Twitter. I talk about robotics making on my own account, `@Orionrobots` (`https://twitter.com/orionrobots`), from which I follow many robot communities and share what that I myself have been making.

Another part of the robotics community is far more focused on the AI side of robotics, with specialist groups in visual processing, speech recognition with the various implementations, and more advanced topics such as neural networks and deep learning, or genetic algorithms. These communities may be close to universities and company research bodies. For speech processing, the Twitter tags `#mycroft` (`https://twitter.com/hashtag/mycroft`) and `#voiceassistant` (`https://twitter.com/hashtag/voiceassistant?f=tweetsvertical=default`) will find these. For visual processing, the tags `#computervision` (`https://twitter.com/hashtag/computervision?f=tweetsvertical=default`) and `#opencv` (`https://twitter.com/hashtag/opencv?f=tweetsvertical=default`) will find relevant conversations and blogs. Searching for TensorFlow and machine learning will help. The YouTube channel ComputerPhile (`https://www.youtube.com/user/Computerphile`) has some great videos on the concepts and theory.

Finding Twitter feeds from universities involved, such as MIT Robotics (`https://twitter.com/MITRobotics?lang=en`), CMU Robotics Institute (`https://twitter.com/cmu_robotics?lang=en`), and The *Standford Vision and Learning Lab* at `http://svl.stanford.edu/` will reveal some amazing projects. Industrial robotics companies tend to be less helpful to makers, but can be a source of inspiration.

Robot parts vendors online often have great projects along with community influence. In the UK, we have Pimoroni (`https://blog.pimoroni.com/`), 4Tronix (`http://4tronix.co.uk/blog/`), and coolcomponents (`https://coolcomponents.co.uk/blogs/news`), to name only a few. In the US, there is Adafruit (`https://blog.adafruit.com/`) and Sparkfun (`https://www.sparkfun.com/news`). Finding these vendors on social media will often reveal robotics and maker discussion, as well as sources for parts and projects.

The online Instructables (`https://www.instructables.com/`) community shares many projects, including robotics builds and other things to make that will help a robot maker, either in experience or tooling. The Hackaday (`https://hackaday.com/`) website also has many great stories and tutorials.

YouTube channels to get to know

First, my own: orionrobots (`https://www.youtube.com/orionrobots`). I share many of my robot builds, experiments with sensors, and code on the channel. I put the code on GitHub with the intent that people can learn from and build on my ideas.

The maker James Bruton (`https://www.youtube.com/user/jamesbruton`), aka XRobots, makes very complicated and large 3D printed robotic builds, making in his own home creations that rival the great university robots, robotic costumes with real functionality, and self-balancing walkers.

The Ben Heck show (`https://www.youtube.com/playlist?list=PLwO8CTSLTkijtGC2zFzQVbFnbmLY3AkIa`) is less robotics, more general making, including robotics. This is far more focused on the maker side than the coding side, but is an extremely inspiring resource.

Computerphile (`https://www.youtube.com/user/Computerphile`) is a YouTube channel that has great videos on programming, including aspects of robotics, visual processing, and artificial intelligence. It includes interviews with some of the great figures still around in computing.

The Tested channel (`https://www.youtube.com/user/testedcom`) features Adam Savage of the Mythbusters team, with very skilled makers doing in-depth builds and sharing their work and techniques.

The vendors Makezine (`https://www.youtube.com/user/makemagazine`), Adafruit (`https://www.youtube.com/user/adafruit`), Sparkfun (`https://www.youtube.com/user/sparkfun`), and Pimoroni (`https://www.youtube.com/channel/UCuiDNTaTdPTGZZzHm0iriGQ`) have YouTube channels (and websites) that are very tutorial-based, and can help in getting to know what is available.

Technical questions – where to get help

For technical questions, Stack Overflow can help, with specialist areas for Raspberry Pi (`https://raspberrypi.stackexchange.com/`), Electronics (`https://electronics.stackexchange.com/`), and Robotics (`https://robotics.stackexchange.com/`). Quora (`https://hi.quora.com/`) offers another question and answer community for technical questions. Raspberry Pi has a forum at `https://www.raspberrypi.org/forums/`. MyCroft has a community forum at `https://community.mycroft.ai/`.

OpenCV has a forum for technical questions following the Stack Overflow style at `http://answers.opencv.org/questions/`.

Twitter is a more open format, where you can ask technical questions. To do so, be sure to use hashtags for the subject matter, and perhaps tag some influential twitter robotics people to help.

Video channels on the subject are good places to ask; of course, do watch the video to see if the answer is there.

A trick for finding alternative tech and solutions on search engines is to type the first technology you think of, then vs (as in versus) and see what completions are suggested. This will give you new options and ways to solve problems.

Meeting robot builders – competitions, makerspaces, and meetups

As you start to build more, meeting up with other makers is a must. First, you will gain from the experience and knowledge in the community, but also there is a great social aspect. Some events are free, but the larger ones will have fees associated with them, with the best mix being free and regular local groups, with travel to larger gatherings occasionally.

Makerspaces

Makerspaces – these spaces are for any kind of maker, be it robotics, crafting, arts, or radio specialists. They serve as tool collectives with a collection of the tools a maker may need, along with space to use them.

It is in these spaces you can expect to find a collection of 3D printers, laser cutters, lathes, a full electronics bench, CnC machines (computer controller tools to cut material), and all kinds of hand tools.

Some have the materials for making your own printed circuit boards (PCB's). Makerspaces also have a community of people using the tools for their projects. People are there for the community and are happy to share their experience and knowledge with anyone.

Makerspaces are a great place to learn about making and practice skills. Some, such as the Cambridge Makerspace (https://twitter.com/cammakespace), have robot clubs. Around me, I have the London Hackspace (https://london.hackspace.org.uk/), Richmond Makerlabs (https://richmondmakerlabs.uk/), and South London Makerspace (https://southlondonmakerspace.org/). Examples can be found in most major cities, for example, in Mumbai there is the Makers Asylum (https://www.makersasylum.com/). *Make* magazine has a Directory Of Makerspaces (https://spaces.makerspace.com/), although searching Google Maps for makerspace and hackspace near you will probably yield results.

There are Makerspaces in many cities and towns around the world. They are also known as maker collectives, Hackerspaces, and fab labs. They tend to want to be found on search engines and social media, so should be easy to search for. If there are none in your area, reaching out via social media to other makers may find like minds to organize small groups like this yourself; just be clear on what a venue allows, as, for instance, soldering can be a problem until a dedicated space is found with a large enough collective.

Maker Faires, Raspberry Jams, and Dojos

Maker Faires (https://makerfaire.com/)—many countries host these festivals of making, where people gather to show and build things together, robotics often being a part of such festivals. These can be one-day events, or camping festivals like the EmfCamp (https://www.emfcamp.org/) in the UK. These are places to get started on new skills, show and tell things you've made, and see what others have been making.

Raspberry Jams (https://www.raspberrypi.org/jam/) and Coder Dojos (https://coderdojo.com/) are groups that get together to regularly exercise their programming and, sometimes, maker skills. A Coder Dojo is a community programming workshop. A Raspberry Jam is a similar event, closely related to Raspberry Pi. They can be aimed at adults and kids, so do find out what there is locally and what they are aiming at. Becoming a mentor for kids at a Dojo or Jam is a great way to get to know other interested makers and programmers.

They also tend to have quite inspiring Twitter feeds.

Competitions

Robotics competitions are still fairly rare outside of academia. The FIRST (`https://www.firstinspires.org/robotics/frc`) engineering initiative in the US is about getting schools and colleges to build robots and compete, with a few sporadic FIRST teams outside the US. FIRST challenges can be autonomous and manually driven. Most countries do have some kind of **Science Technology Engineering and Mathematics (STEM)** available at `https://www.stem.org.uk/` a robotics competition which you will be able to find out about on the internet; be sure to see if they are open to the general public or just schools.

In the UK, the PiWars (`https://piwars.org/`) competition is run annually and involves many autonomous and manual challenges set around the Cambridge University School of computing. It has a strong community element and is a great place to meet robot builders as a competitor or spectator. The `#piwars` (`https://twitter.com/hashtag/PiWars`) Twitter tag has quite an active community discussing this, particularly when robot makers are gathering to build and test robots before the event too. Another competition in the UK is Micromouse, `http://www.micromouseonline.com/`, which is all about maze-solving robots with other kinds of robots exhibited by makers too. Both also have small robot markets. The annual Raspberry Pi parties are a fun get-together, but the focus is much more on meeting and less on building together.

The Robotex (`https://twitter.com/hashtag/PiWars`) international robotics exhibition is held in Estonia, and combines lots of show and tell with days of competitions and serious prizes. They welcome robot builders working with electronics and Pis alongside Lego and other materials.

As these require travel, you should probably consider a large-enough box, with bubble wrap or packing foam, to safely transport your robot(s) to and from such events. I advise that you remove the batteries to reduce the possibility of a stray wire causing a short and packing them into a plastic bag to insulate them from any metal. I also recommend a field repair kit with a breadboard, wires, spare batteries, a charger, all the screwdriver types, replacement components for logic-level shifters, hook and loop tape, a standoff kit, and possibly a multimeter. Robots often need a little tuning and repair when arriving at an event.

Suggestions for further skills – 3D printing, soldering, PCB, and CnC

As you build more robots, you will want to create more elaborate or customized systems.

So, to build a robot that is competition grade, you will need some additional skills in the hardware building aspect—which are worth spending time on.

Design skills

We've used block diagrams and simple drawings. However, to become more serious about robot building you'll want to design your own parts, or look further into how bought parts will integrate. You will want to create cases, chassis, sensor mounts, brackets, wheel types, and any number of parts. CAD (Computer aided design) is key.

2D design for illustration and diagrams

For 2D design and illustration, I recommend Inkscape (`https://inkscape.org/`). This is more artistic than CAD-oriented, but if you want to make logos and other designs it is quite handy. *The Book of Inkscape: The Definitive Guide to the Free Graphics Editor* by Dmitry Kirsanov is highly recommended, and shows the principles of the system from the perspective of a main developer on the project.

Draw.io (`https://www.draw.io/`) is useful for creating diagrams like the ones in this book. You can combine these two systems using Inkscape to make new shapes to use in Draw.io. Inkscape allows more freedom in terms of shape manipulation, but Draw.io is better for placing shapes and connecting things.

3D CAD

It is thoroughly worth getting to know 3D CAD systems such as Fusion 360 (`https://www.autodesk.com/campaigns/fusion-360-for-hobbyists`), OnShape (`https://www.onshape.com/products/free`), and OpenSCAD (`http://www.openscad.org/`). **OpenSCAD** is totally free, the others tend to have free entry-level CAD systems for makers.

3D CAD systems will let you design parts, and then create further designs to test assembling them.

All of them will take some investment in time, and I recommend using tutorials and YouTube videos to get to grips with them. The Makers Muse channel (`https://www.youtube.com/channel/UCxQbYGpbdrh-b2ND-AfIybg`) is a good place to start on this.

The following are book recommendations for 3D CAD:

- *Fusion 360 for Makers* by O'Reilly
- *OpenSCAD for 3D Printing* by Al Williams

The Thingiverse (`https://www.thingiverse.com/`) community share 3D designs for printing and making, and one very effective technique can be to either draw inspiration from, reuse, or repurpose creations seen there. If you can, import a bracket into Fusion 360, add the particular holes/base or connectors you need; it could save hours of work trying to model a mount for a sensor from scratch. The community will also have tips on printing these. Alternatives are Pinshape (`https://pinshape.com/`) and GrabCad (`https://grabcad.com/`).

Skills for shaping and building

Now you have CAD drawings of parts, you can send them to places to have them made, or learn techniques for manufacturing them yourself.

As a general recommendation, the MIT **How To Make Almost Anything** (`http://fab.cba.mit.edu/classes/863.14/`) course materials (which are updated annually) are a fantastic resource for finding ways to put things together—although they look plain, the links there are very useful. As mentioned in the social media section above, YouTube and other channels are rich now with practical examples and hands-on tutorials for making things.

Machine skills and tools

CnC Milling and 3D printing allow you create solid parts and can give great results, however, each are a field of their own with many skills to learn on the way. Laser cutting allows you to make flat parts, but with some ingenuity flat parts can be assembled (like so many types of furniture) into sophisticated, solid 3D objects.

The Youtube channel NYC CNC (`https://www.youtube.com/user/saunixcomp`) covers a lot of CnC tips and usage; however, the online book *Guerrilla guide to CNC machining, mold making, and resin casting* by Michal Zalewski is also a brilliant resource.

For all of these machining techniques, I would not suggest going out and buying your own to start, but to find out more about the local-community Makerspaces mentioned previously and use the facilities they have there. Some libraries are also getting into this with 3D printers and simple maker materials. Using these will be cheaper than buying your own, you will be among a community of others with experience, and it will be far easier than trying to go it alone.

If you just want the 3D printed, or laser cut parts, there are places online that will make things for you. Ponoko (`https://www.ponoko.com/`), RazorLAB (`http://www.razorlab.co.uk/`), 3DIng (`https://www.3ding.in/`), Protolabs (`https://www.protolabs.co.uk/`), Shapeways (`https://www.shapeways.com/`), and 3D Hubs (`https://www.3dhubs.com/`) are some of the companies that offer such services. Looking for 3D printing and laser cut services in your region in a search engine will not be difficult, but it will still help to have gained some experience through a Makerspace to understand what is and isn't possible with these machines. Using the wrong machine for a job, or making the wrong design decisions, could lead to huge costs.

3D printers, laser cutters, and CnC machines require routine maintenance and upkeep tasks; for example, levelling a 3D print bed or tramelling the CnC chuck. They also require consumables such as stock (plastic filament, wood to mill ,or laser cut), replacement components, and bed adhesive materials. Unless you are printing a lot, it is rarely an economy to own your own when you have access to another via a Makerspace or an online market.

Hand skills and tools

Some basic woodworking and crafting skills are always handy. Practicing these at a Makerspace will help you see how things can go together. With this comes knowing how to choose wood that is suitable, as much wood is too soft, too heavy, or too irregular. Wood can be carved by hand, or used in the aforementioned CnC machine.

Learning modelling skills, such as using plasticard, creating molds, and casting, are other ways to make 3D parts. Plasticard is an inexpensive flexible material of varying thickness, that can be easily cut by hand, perhaps using a printed template, and then assembled.

Woodworking can be used to create molds and makeshift robot chassis. Molds allow you to make multiple copies or use materials in high quality parts. Casting can be tricky, especially dealing with bubbles, but there are good books on the subject. For this, I recommend the book *Secrets of Expert Mold Making and Resin Casting* by Karl K. Juelch, and the *Guerilla Guide To CnC* mentioned in the machine tools section.

Further interesting material skills, such as working with metal, allow for even bigger robots. This means learning how to cut, shape, and weld metal parts. This is not needed for most smaller robots.

Carbon fiber or Kevlar materials are really useful in fighting robots, but not the autonomous kind we have been building in this book.

This is a place where the Instructables (`https://www.instructables.com/`) community (briefly mentioned previously) will really help, with practical instructions and tutorials on building things. You can either follow along complete projects, or just skim read for techniques to borrow from them. As well as looking for robots, look at modelling techniques (often similar), plasticard builds, woodwork, or metal work tutorials.

Electronics skills

The next thing is to extend your electronic skills. We have been using Raspberry Pi hats, and modules to build our robots. This is fine when beginning, but starts to feel clumsy when there are a lot of parts, with demands on space or fragile wiring making it far from ideal. You'll note our wiring on the robot is very crowded.

Electronics principles

Learning more about the functions of the electronic components and common circuits will help you understand your robot further, expand it, find ways to reduce the size, or eliminate problems on the robot.

Power electronics will give you a better understanding of the motor controller and battery regulation circuits in your robot. Digital electronics will let you connect other logic devices, use new sensors, or aggregate them in useful ways. Analog electronics will also open up new types of sensors and actuators, and give you tools to diagnose many electrical problems that can crop up.

Learn how to draw, and read schematic circuits for the common parts. Online courses and YouTube channels teach electronics step by step, with books such as *Make: Electronics* by Charles Platt giving a very hands-on learning path.

The EEvBlog (`https://www.eevblog.com/episodes/`) channel is less step by step, but offers more general immersion in electronic engineering concerns.

Taking soldering further

Many more parts are available if you learn more soldering. Although we've done a little soldering, it's just the bare minimum. Soldering is a skill that many makers use daily.

Good places to start are the Raspberry Pi guide to soldering (`https://www.raspberrypi.org/blog/getting-started-soldering/`), *The Adafruit Guide To Excellent Soldering* (`https://learn.adafruit.com/adafruit-guide-excellent-soldering`), and the *EEVBlog Soldering* tutorial (`https://www.youtube.com/watch?v=J5Sb21qbpEQ`).

I recommend starting in a local Makerspace, where you will be able to benefit from others, and doing simple soldering projects. Soldering headers onto a module is a pretty basic way to start, along with kits such as those made by Boltportclub (`https://www.boldport.club/`) to stretch those skills a bit further. Soldering allows you to start thinking about creating your own boards or Raspberry Pi hats.

You will start off soldering simple headers, and what are known as "through hole" components, because they go through a hole in the board. This is the right type of construction to gain confidence with the technique.

As you become more confident, you will find kits that use Surface Mount soldering. Surface mount components do not have legs that go through holes, but simple metal pads that are soldered directly onto copper pads on the board. They take up far less space, so allow for smaller constructions, but they are also quite a lot more fiddly, and eventually require fairly professional tools to do. The more simple surface mount components, such as LEDs, resistors, and capacitors, can be soldered by hand. See the *EEVBlog Surface Mount* tutorial (`https://www.youtube.com/watch?v=b9FC9fAlfQE`) for a starting point.

Devices with tens of pins may not work, and would require solder ovens and solder paste. At that point, you may be making custom circuits and a PCBA (Printed Circuit Board and Assembly) service might be the correct path.

Custom circuits

As you gain confidence with electronics and soldering, you will want to create more of your own circuits, and transfer them onto more professional-looking PCBs, to save space and perhaps make them easier to wire. Breadboards are good for learning and experimenting, but they are not ideal for competing, and quickly become bulky and untidy, while point-to-point wiring is fragile and prone to mistakes.

The first stage of custom, more-permanent circuits is using stripboard or perfboard and soldering components onto them. This is definitely a good further step from breadboards, and will save space. They can still be a little bulky and messy, though. You may also want to use parts that are surface mounted, or have irregularly laid out legs of different sizes, and don't fit conveniently on perfboard or stripboard.

To take your circuits to the next level, learning to design PCBs is the next path. You will be able to save yet more space, have more robust circuits, and can now use tiny surface mount parts. You could even design PCBs that are for light structural placement too.

Although for breadboards you can use Fritzing (`http://fritzing.org/home/`. It has been used extensively in this book), I don't recommend it for schematic or PCB work. To design these, software such as KiCad (`http://kicad-pcb.org/`) or Eagle (`https://www.autodesk.com/products/eagle/overview`) are good hobbyist tools. I recommend the book *KiCad Like a Pro* by Peter Dalmaris.

You can use facilities at local Makerspaces to make PCBs or send them to board houses to have them beautifully made, with fine tracks, lettering, and fancy colored soldermasks (you'll see more such terminology in the field). Custom PCBs allow you to really tune the layout to avoid any point-to-point wiring, work with tiny surface mount parts, add helpful text right on the board for some wiring, and get a really professional look. Some even use this to make other parts for the robot, structural parts, or front panels in PCB.

Finding more information on computer vision

You've now started to see computer vision in `Chapter 13`, *Robot Vision - Using a Pi Camera and OpenCV*. We used OpenCV to track colored objects and faces, but barely scratched the surface of computer vision.

Books

To continue learning OpenCV, I recommend the book *OpenCV with Python By Example* by Prateek Joshi, Packt Publishing. This uses computer vision to build augmented reality tools, and to identify and track objects, and takes you through different image transformations and checks, showing screenshots for each of them. It is also quite fun with lots of hands-on code.

Computer vision can be extended to 3D computer vision with the Kinect, which are tricky to find as they are no longer made, but they have a 3D sensing system that make them valuable for use in robots. They may still be found on eBay or at pre-owned game shops. The O'Reilly book, *Making Things See*, is more oriented at desktop computers (it predates the Raspberry Pi), but is a great place to become familiar with this awesome sensor.

Online courses

I have already recommended PyImageSearch (https://www.pyimagesearch.com/) in Chapter 13, *Robot Vision - Using a Pi Camera and OpenCV* as it contains some of the best resources for learning OpenCV and experimenting with machine vision. It is a free resource, but the maintainer of the website, Adrian Rosebrock, also has a book called *Deep Learning for Computer Vision with Python*.

Learn Computer Vision with Python and OpenCV (https://india.packtpub.com/in/application-development/learn-computer-vision-python-and-opencv-video) – a Packt video that is a 1 hour and 20 minute-long course by Kathiravan Natarajan – dives in some depth into many aspects, using the excellent Jupyter tool to experiment with image transformations.

The TensorFlow Tutorials (https://www.tensorflow.org/tutorials/) website (a machine learning framework) has tutorials specifically aimed at using it in computer vision. It is certainly an interesting idea, but there may be simpler OpenCV pipelines. Training up machine learning systems to perform visual recognition can take a lot of time and sample data. It's worth noting that the Haar Cascade files we used have probably been optimized with machine learning systems.

A further video course—Advanced Computer Vision Projects by Matthew Rever (https://www.packtpub.com/big-data-and-business-intelligence/advanced-computer-vision-projects-video)—has further computer vision projects, culminating in using the TensorFlow machine learning system to analyze human poses from camera input.

Social media

The twitter tags #computervision and #opencv were mentioned in the Online robot building communities section, and they are a good place to ask questions or share your work about the subject.

Computerphile has a small Computer Vision playlist (`https://www.youtube.com/watch?v=C_zFhWdM4i&list=PLzH6n4zXuckoRdljSlM2k35BufTYXNNeF`) explaining the concepts and theory of some visual processing algorithms, but does not tend to dive into hands-on implementation.

Extending into machine Learning

Some of the smartest sounding types of robotics are those involved in machine learning. The code used throughout this book has not used machine learning, instead using well-known algorithms. The PID controller is a system that makes adjustments to read a value, but it is not machine learning. However, optimizing PID values might come from a machine learning algorithm. We used Haar Cascades to detect faces; this was also not machine learning, but a machine learning system was probably used to generate the Cascades. Machine learning tends to be great at optimizing tasks and discovering and matching patterns, but poor at making fully-formed intelligent-seeming behavior.

The basic overall idea with many machine learning systems involves having a set of starting examples, with some information on which are matches and which are not. The machine is expected to determine or learn rules on what is or is not a match. This may be a fitness score, based on learning rules to maximise such a score. This aspect is known as training the system.

For PID control system, fitness would be based on settling to the set point in the fewest steps with little or no overshoot, based on training values from data – like machine variations, response times, and speed.

Once again, I recommend the Computerphile AI Video playlist (`https://www.youtube.com/watch?v=tlS5Y2vm02&list=PLzH6n4zXuckquVnQ0KlMDxyT5YE-sA8Ps`) video series for getting to know the concepts around machine learning; it's not hands-on, but is more focused on the ideas.

Machine learning can be quite focused on data and statistics, but the techniques learned can be applied to sensor data to make this more relevant to robotics. There are many examples of the TensorFlow system being used to build object recognition systems. Genetic algorithms evolving solutions have been used to great effect for robot gaits in multi-legged systems or finding fast ways to navigate a space.

Robot Operating System

Some of the robotics community make use of the **Robot Operating System (ROS)**, refer to—http://www.ros.org/. This is used to build common, cross-programming language abstractions between robot hardware, and behaviors. It's intended to encourage common reusable code layers for robot builders. AI systems built on top of this can be mixed and matched with lower level systems. The behaviors/robot layers we have built allow some reuse, but are very simplified compared with ROS.

The book *ROS Programming: Building Powerful Robots* by Lentin Joseph, et al covers linking the TensorFlow AI system with ROS-based robotics.

For a simpler introduction, *Robot Operating System (ROS) for Absolute Beginners: Robotics Programming Made Easy* by Lentin Joseph uses a combination of the Python and C++ programming languages to build a smart AI robot.

Summary

In this chapter, you learned about finding out who else and where else robots like this are being made, and how to be part of those communities. You've also seen where to compete with a robot, where to get more advice, and how to find information to progress the different skills you've started building much further. In the next chapter, we will be summarizing everything that we have learned throughout the book, with a view towards building your next robot.

Further reading

The following are further practical robotics books available that I enjoy:

- 123 *Robotics Experiments for the Evil Genius* by Myke Predko: This is perhaps a little dated, but spends time on the construction and workshop techniques along with building electronics circuits. It doesn't really dig into code.
- *Robot Programming: A Guide to Controlling Autonomous Robot*s by Tracey Hughes and Cameron Hughes: A code-based investigation into robotic programming techniques, based on the Java programming language. A colorful and well-illustrated book. You will find the robot built in this book fits the criteria to start programming in that book pretty well, with only a gripper needed to complete it.

- *Robot Building for Beginners* by David Cook: This book leads you through building "sandwich", a scratch-built robot based on a lunchbox. It is a little more maker- and electronics-based but is quite a fun project to follow.
- *Robot Builder's Bonanza (4th Edition)* by Gordon McComb: This was an influencial book and is quite extensive in covering the ways to make a robot. This is the best book for going beyond buying kits and into the construction of bigger and more mechanically complicated robots.

17
Planning Your Next Robot Project - Putting It All Together

You've now seen throughout this book how to plan, design, build, and program a robot. We've covered many of the starting topics with some hands-on experience in them, an example demonstrating the basics, and some ideas of how those could be improved. In this chapter, we will think about your next robot. How would you plan and design it? What skills might you need to research and experiment with? What would you build?

The following topics will be covered in this chapter:

- Visualizing your next robot – what will it look like?
- Making a block diagram – identify the inputs/outputs and parts it would need.
- Choosing the parts – what trade-offs will you think about to choose parts for the robot?
- Planning the code – what software layers and components might this robot need, what behaviors would be fun?
- Let the world know - how would you share your plans, or your robot, with interested people?

Technical requirements

For this chapter, I recommend having some diagramming tools, a pen, and some paper. The online tool Draw.io would be a good recommendation.

- Pen/pencils
- Paper – a sketchbook, like graph paper, is great, but the back of an envelope will do
- A computer with internet and access to Draw.io

Visualizing your next robot

When we started this book, in Chapter 2, *Exploring Robot Building Blocks - Code and Electronics*, we first learned how to look at robots as a sketch. I suggested that you make quick drawings, as rough as you such as, with a pen, and then move on to more formal block and layout diagrams later.

Every robot starts with a bit of inspiration. Perhaps there is a competition you want to try, maybe you've seen something like another robot or an animal you want to mimic (crabs are fascinating!). Other inspirations may come from seeing an amazing new part or sensor, or wanting to learn/play with a new skill. You may even have made a list of amazing robots you want to try and build.

Before building a robot, make a short bullet-point list of what it will do, what sensors/outputs it will have, and what it might have to deal with. This lets you focus your efforts. This is an example, which I made for my Spiderbot project (inspired by being sent a six-legged robot chassis):

- It will have six legs (yes, an insect, not a spider)
- I will use it to experiment with legs and gaits
- It will be able to avoid walls

Your quick sketches could first be a basic six-legged stick drawing, with some squares at one end to represent the ultrasonic sensor, and perhaps a few arrows with notes to depict what they mean. You've seen this technique in detail in Chapter 2, *Exploring Robot Building Blocks - Code and Electronics*. My preferred first sketches are with a biro on graph paper, but I'll use any paper I have, as shown in the following photo:

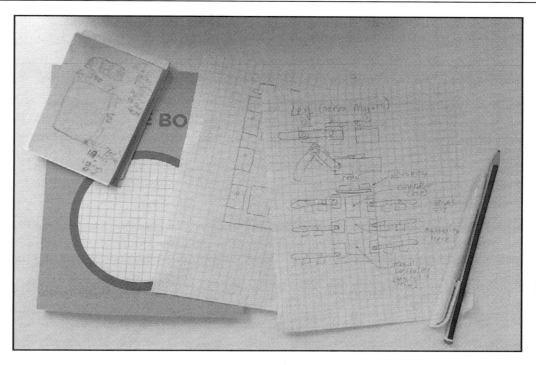

Sketching your ideas on paper

Visualizing the robot can be made with 2D, 3D or profile sketches. Here are a few tips:

- Draw lightly, then follow through with firmer strokes when you are more confident with the design.
- Annotate it a lot with anything that comes to mind.
- Don't worry about being to scale, dimensioning, or being a perfect drawing; this is simply to capture your own ideas to flesh out.
- It can be a good idea to date it, and put a working name on it, even if you have a better name later.
- Feel free to combine block style representations with sketchy visual versions.
- Keep a biro/pencil and notepad/scrap paper with you somewhere so you can quickly jot down ideas. A whiteboard is great if you are near one. A pencil can let you erase and rewrite, and a ballpoint pen is easy to keep in a bag or pocket.
- Get the big ideas down first, come back for detail. It's easy to get bogged down in detail on one aspect, forget the other parts, and run out of time. You can always make a tiny note to remind yourself.

This process can be revisited at any time during the robot build, perhaps when you have further ideas, when you have a problem you are solving, or want to refine it. Most ideas start with some bullet points and a scribbled sketch; waiting for access to a computer or trying to draw it perfectly will detract from the next amazing idea you already have in your mind—get it down first.

Making a block diagram

Now you have a sketch of roughly what it will look like, recall how in Chapter 2, *Exploring Robot Building Blocks - Code and Electronics* and throughout the book we created block diagrams showing the robot we built there. Any robot can be represented this way. This is where you would have a block for each input and output, and then create controller and interface blocks to connect them to. Don't worry at this stage about the diagram being perfect, the main point is it conveys an idea of what will probably be connected to what. It's also quite likely that the initial diagram will need some change as you build a robot and come across constraints that you were not aware of.

Here are two stages of a block diagram for SpiderBot. I knew going in that each leg had three motors, but not a lot else. The next image shows the diagram showing rough connections, thrown together in a short time with Draw.io, from a biro-on-graph paper sketch:

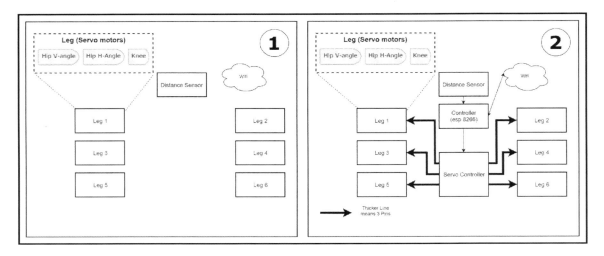

Spiderbot block diagram

The other block diagram to consider is software, which we will visit in the *Planning the code for the robot* section.

Choosing the parts

Now you have a rough sketch of the robot and the block diagram, you are ready to start choosing the parts you would use to build a robot. Throughout this book, we have looked at the trade-offs between different kinds of sensors, different chassis kits, controllers, and so on. These are trade-offs on weight, complexity, availability (you don't want a part that is irreplaceable), and cost, which were covered in detail in `Chapter 6`, *Building Robot Basics - Wheels, Power, and Wiring*.

If the robot has been inspired by a particular kit—for example, Spiderbot was inspired by me being sent such a kit—then this will possibly constrain the other part choices you need to make. It is clear that I'd need to support 18 servo motors, however, at the time of writing, a 16-motor controller was available, so I elected to use two IO pins of my controller to deal with it.

Another tradeoff was the controller. I knew that I'd want Spiderbot to be Wi-Fi enabled, but it wasn't going to be doing visual processing, so a small, cheap, and low-power controller like the ESP8266 was a great choice for it.

For power, I knew that it would require a lot of current for all those servos, but it wouldn't be able to carry a great deal of weight, so a more specialist LiPo battery would be needed, along with a charger/protection circuit.

When choosing the parts, consider how they will fit together: is there a clear path to interfacing the choice of motor controller with your choice of main controller? Have these two components been used together or are you prepared for the complexity of making a new interface? Based on the parts you think you will buy, collect their dimensions, and try making a test-fit diagram, as we did in `Chapter 6`, *Building Robot Basics - Wheels, Power, and Wiring*. This is best done before buying new parts.

It was then a matter of finding stockists to buy it. I do have some local favorites (such as CoolComponents, Pimoroni, and ThePiHut), and you will find those in your region as you build more. Looking for local Pimoroni, Sparkfun, Raspberry Pi, and Adafruit stockists will help you find the right kind of store.

Amazon, Alibaba, and eBay can also be used to find modules on their markets, but be very clear what it is you are buying and how much support you will get. Individual parts can be found at large stockists such as Element14, Mouser, RS, and Digikey; although they tend not to have many prebuilt modules, they are reliable and have large catalogs.

This is mostly online. There may be high street sellers of electronics and mechanical parts, but this is becoming rarer.

Another thing you may do is use parts from an existing stock, which you will build up as you build robots. Toys can be hacked into robot chassis, motors can be salvaged from old printers and electromechanical systems (with care). In this case, the test-fit diagram will help you see what you may need to change to make things work with the salvaged parts.

Now, you are ready to assemble your new robot. The building guides in Chapter 6, Building Robot Basics - Wheels, Power, and Wiring, and Chapter 7, *Drive and Turn - Moving Motors with Python*, along with the basic soldering guide in Chapter 9, *Programming RGB Strips in Python*, will get you started, although the additional reading and skills suggested in Chapter 16, *Taking Your Robot Programming Skills. Further* will give you many more options for assembling the robot.

Planning the code for the robot

Now you have the parts, and you've starting building the robot. The next thing to consider is the code for the robot. We started planning code in layers in Chapter 2, *Exploring Robot Building Blocks - Code and Electronics*, and then explored this further in Chapter 7, *Drive and Turn - Moving Motors with Python* under the *Robot object* heading.

The general idea is to create layers of code in the system. For a basic robot, these layers could be just functions or classes, and for a more complicated one, these may be different software components talking on a shared software bus (like a message queue or as connected services). The library we have already built will work for many small-wheeled robots, with some refining as you gain experience with it, and behaviors can be adapted for new sensors and outputs if you have kept the behavior separate from the hardware concerns.

Use diagrams to draw the blocks and layers to express where those boundaries lie. Expect to write code in modules and blocks that you link together, so each individual part can be reasoned about. It should not be necessary to get lost in the details of an SPI databus transaction when thinking about how to make pleasing LED patterns.

Then you can also use diagrams to explore the behavior from a data-flow perspective, like the PID and feedback diagrams used to express the behaviors in `Chapter 13`, *Robot Vision - Using a Pi Camera and OpenCV*, for the color object and face tracking behaviors, or as data pipelines such as those in the same chapter showing the image transformations. Don't expect to capture the whole story in one diagram; sometimes a few are needed to approach the different aspects of the behavior.

Spend time to consider the tricky areas here, such as additional math that might be needed if the sensor/movement relationship is complicated. You might not get it right the first time, so building it and reasoning about why it behaved differently from your expectations will be needed. This is where going and finding similar works on the internet, or reading one of the may recommended books will yield a deeper understanding of what you are attempting. In most cases, persistence will pay off.

There are formal representations for diagrams like flowcharts or the UML (Unified Modelling Language) types. These are worth finding out about and learning as a resource to draw upon for drawing. The Draw.io software has a nice library of diagram elements. The most important aspect of a diagram is to convey the information—what is in your head as you explore an idea must be expressed in a way that makes sense to you six months later, or your team if you build a robot with a team.

Sometimes, building simple behaviors gives you a library to use for more complicated and interesting ones, like our straight-line drive behavior was a building block to start on the driving in a square behavior.

You can now program the robot, but be prepared to go around a few planning, implementing, testing, and learning loops. Do not be disheartened by testing failures as these are the best opportunities to learn. The most learning is done in planning and determining test failures. If it all works first time, it's far less likely to stick with you. Each behavior in this book took multiple attempts to get right, and tuning them is a trial and error process.

Letting the world know

Your robot is now being built. You are bound to have questions about how to proceed and problems to be solved – perhaps you've already encountered them before building. This is the right time to get online and start linking with the robotics communities.

Use Twitter and Stack overflow to ask questions, or even answer questions from other robot builders. Use YouTube to share your creation, or the story of your build, and to see other people's builds. You do not need to wait until you have a perfect polished product, share the steps you've taken, the frustrations you have encountered, and even the failures you've learned from—these make for some of the best stories, and as you fill find with others, can be just the right motivation for someone else to keep on persisting with difficult builds.

Use a combination of YouTube, Instructables, and blogs online to practice new skills, or, better yet, get to a nearby Makerspace, Coder Dojo, or Raspberry Jam to practice new skills with others who are also making and learning.

Being a robot builder will make you always a student, there is always more to learn in the subject, not least because it is still an area of much research. There are people pushing the boundaries of human knowledge in robotics, and you can push the boundaries of your own skills and knowledge, while becoming a mentor and helper to extend the boundaries of what others can do. Perhaps you will come up with kits, modules, and code to lower barriers to entry, and you may also find new novel ways to use robotics or build a sensor that pushes the boundaries of human knowledge. Whichever way it is, engaging with the robot community is exciting, refreshing, and keeps you hunting for new stuff to try.

Testing your robot in lab conditions is okay, but the most rigorous testing happens outside, at competitions and demonstrations. You will shake out new bugs, find new problems to solve in these cases, as well as create a network of robot-building friends and peers. Robotics has a stereotype of being a very solitary hobby or profession, but this need not be the case as there are plenty of people making something, so go make with them.

Building with a team can be very rewarding and challenging. It will allow you to create more ambitious builds than going alone. Getting involved in any of the communities, especially local ones, will probably represent your best chance of finding team members.

Summary

You've now seen throughout this book how to build and program your first robot. You've seen where to find out more and how to extend your knowledge. In this final chapter, we've summarized what you've learned, and suggested how to use this to plan, build, and program your next robot, as well as taking it on tour and being a member of the robotics community.

You have reached the end of this book (other than the *Appendix*), but I hope this is just the start of your robotics journey.

Appendix

Here you will find any extra information to help build your robot, or deal with some problems that can crop up. It also has information on converting the robot code to run on Python 3.

Finding parts

The parts in this book have been chosen because they are available in many locations and, where possible, on the most common websites. You may have to try variations of the search terms to find a part similar to the ones used – do cross-reference pictures to ensure the part is the right type before ordering it.

The following is a starting point for searching for these (and other robot parts):

- Amazon: Most countries have a local Amazon, and many parts can be found there.
- Alibaba/AliExpress: There are worldwide outlets for this, with electronics parts from China easily available.
- eBay: eBay has many components and maker modules, although they can take some time to arrive, and you need to read and check carefully what you are ordering. Make sure you know that it will work, how much postage will be, and when it should arrive.
- Mouser & Digikey: Major global electronics stockists. They occasionally have maker modules of the type we've used in this book, but more often have plain components.
- To find local retailers, look for stockists of Raspberry Pi, Arduino, Pimoroni, Sparkfun, and Adafruit parts.
- As a last resort, you can look to import these yourself directly from the aforementioned brands.

Converting this code to Python 3

The code in this book is written in Python 2 and OpenCV 2.4.9. At the time of writing, these were the defaults on Raspbian and provided the path of least resistance for getting the reader up and running with building behaviors on the robot. OpenCV for Python 3 was a many-hour compilation, although since the majority of the chapters were proofed, Piwheels provides a less painful path to getting that working. This is with the exception of the Mycroft section, for which Python 3 on the MyCroft assistant is the default and the path of least resistance.

However, all the code on the robot can be adapted for Python 3, and has been tested with it. The OpenCV parts do change a little, too.

Code could be backported and made polyglot, but it was felt that explaining this polyglot code along with the behavior would obscure the code and make it harder to explain. So, I have made sure it is in this Appendix; Python 3 is not being ignored, and when it is the path of least resistance default, perhaps a further edition of the book with Python 3 as the default would be likely.

The Python 3 code will be added to a Python 3 branch on the GitHub repository for this book.

The rest of this section shows the major changes needed.

Integer division

In Python 2, using the single slash (/) division operator results in integers even if the result is non integer, by rounding them. In Python 3, this is not the case. Since we are talking about hardware, most hardware is being sent bytes of data that must be in integer form. So, in places where we were relying on that integer division the code could be made explicit with the double slash (//) operator, or better yet converting values to integers with `int(<some result>)` where that is needed.

Using `int(<some result>)` around an operation is compatible with both Python 2 and Python 3.

Print function

In Python 2, `print` is a keyword. It is used without parentheses, and introducing these will lead to Python treating the parameters as a type of list (a tuple) and printing it like a list (the way `repr()` behaves).

In Python 3, `print` has been made a function. The parameters will work the same way, but must be wrapped in parentheses. Those that are already in parenthesis will now chain together the parts of the list.

In the GitHub repository, I've added this: `from __future__ import print_function`, which means that the converted Python 3 code is multi-language and will work in Python 2 as well.

In the book code, `print` is mostly used for setup and debug. The `print` function actually makes for more readable code, in that the \ line continuation character is not needed to put many items in a print. It also allows print to be used as a callback, although I don't think this is made use of this in the book.

Input/raw input

In one behavior, we test the servo motors and calibrate them by typing in angles. This is done using the `raw_input()` Python 2 built-in.

In Python 2, the `raw_input()` built-in exists because an older form, `input()`, actually executed code typed in, and is considered a bit of a security risk. It's strongly discouraged in Python 2.

In Python 3, the `input()` built-in function now does what `raw_input()` did, and the `raw_input()` symbol no longer exists. So, code needs to change to use that.

Python 2 compatibility

There is a Python library that can be installed with pip, called `futures`. In its features, you can use `from builtins import input`.

This will work in Python 2 and Python 3, making both treat `input()` the way Python 3 does, for making multi-language code.

Ranges have become generators

When we setup LEDs in `Chapter 9`, *Programming RGB Strips in Python*, we pass ranges to the LED setting functions, and we reuse these ranges multiple times to set the same bunch of LEDs. For an example of this, look at the line-following behavior with LED debug in `Chapter 9`, *Programming RGB Strips in Python*.

In Python 2, the `range()` function creates a list. This is a list spanning all the numbers in the range, which you can loop over multiple times without affecting the content. For example, `range(5)` will create the `[0, 1, 2, 3, 4]` list.

In Python 3 the `range()` function creates generators. These are *lists waiting to happen*. We used generators in the chapter on visual processing to get frames from a camera as they came. However, in this context, if we store that range, then loop through it, it will be exhausted, so couldn't be used multiple times. However, we actually want to use it multiple times, so we want to create a list.

This is relatively easy, even in a way that works in both languages. Creating a `list` with `range` as its source of items is the main strategy:

```
>>> range(5)
range(0, 5)        # this is a generator, it's not a list yet.
>>> list(range(5))
[0, 1, 2, 3, 4]    # this is now actually a list
```

OpenCV versions

Closely related to using Python 3 is using a more recent version of OpenCV. This may perform better but, at the time of writing, it is quite long-winded to install for Python 2.7. It installs easily in Python 3 by using a PiWheel (prebuilt packages for Python on the Raspberry Pi).

I'll assume that `pip3` is the Python 3 pip installer:

```
$ sudo pip3 install picamera[array] numpy opencv-python
```

Following this, only one OpenCV function appears to have changed enough to require our code to change.

Find contours

In OpenCV 2.4.9 this function has the signature (arrangement of parameters and return values) of:

```
contours, hierarchy = cv.findContours(image, mode, method[, contours[, hierarchy[, offset]]] ).
```

We copy the image because this function will modify the image with outlines as it finds the contours in it.

In OpenCV 3, findContours now has a different return value:

```
image, contours, hierarchy = cv.findContours(image, mode, method[, contours[, hierarchy[, offset]]]).
```

The original image is not altered. An additional image (which can be ignored if you don't want it: Python will dispose of it) is returned, which has the same changes the old OpenCV version would have made.

With this changed, the code should now function well with OpenCV 3.

Power smoothing capacitor

When less-than-fresh batteries are used, power drawn for the wheel motors can cause the servo motor to droop. While this may make for cute-looking behavior as though it's shaking its head when reversing away from things or changing direction, it's not ideal and means there are voltage drops as the motors pull lots of current. This is especially noticeable if you have used alkaline batteries, that are not able to deliver as much current as LiPo batteries can.

A **capacitor** is a component used to store power, almost like a battery. Using a large capacitor between a ground pin and voltage pin on the servo motor pins can prevent this voltage drop. I recommend a minimum for 470 uF, if not bigger, using an electrolytic capacitor.

The pattern is to use a jumper wire from the servo V-pin to the breadboard. At the breadboard, wire this into an empty column. Then place the capacitor on the empty column, with the leg painted with the "-" signs in one of the available ground rails. The following screenshot shows how to do this:

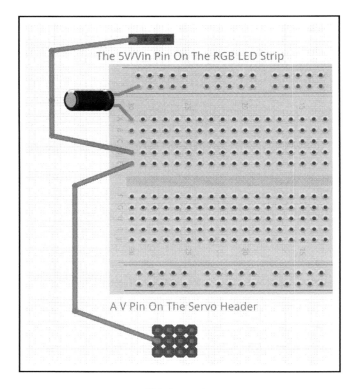

Wiring in a capacitor

A capacitor smooths things by storing up some power, and then whenever there is a shortfall, it will discharge this power, topping things up a little. The larger the capacitor value, the higher the capacity it has to make up for a drop. Capacitors rate in Farads, with the scientific suffixes denoting the scale of the number. So 470 uF or 470 microfarads is 470×10^{-6}. This is a reasonably large capacitor. The servo drop caused by voltage drop off should now be far less pronounced.

Assessments

Chapter 1, Introduction to Robotics

- What element of a robot is used to monitor its environment?
    - Sensors
- What type of robot element do motors represent?
    - Outputs
- What are the three elements of a robotic system?
    - Sensors, outputs, and controller
    - Or electronics, mechanical parts, and code
- Where have robots been operating the longest in regular usage?
    - In industry
- Why are wheels used more often than legs?
    - They are more stable, simpler, and less can go wrong.
- What is the principle connecting output, input, and control in a loop?
    - Feedback
- Why might a household washing machine be considered more robotic than a UK Robot Wars entry?
    - A washing machine uses sensors and feedback with code for autonomous behavior. Robot Wars competitors are entirely manually driven.

Chapter 2, Exploring Robot Building Blocks - Code and Electronics

- What is an I/O pin?
    - A pin you can connect inputs and outputs to on a controller – an input/output pin
- What tools do you need to make a block diagram?
    - A pen and paper

- What are the drawbacks of the laser ranging sensor versus the ultrasonic distance sensor?
  - The laser ranging sensor is sensitive to light conditions and more expensive.
- What type of system is a microphone?
  - A sensor or an input
- What kind of I/O pin is correct for measuring a varying resistance?
  - An analog pin
- What type of I/O pin would be suitable for detecting an on/off signal?
  - A digital pin

Chapter 3, Introducing the Raspberry Pi - Starting with Raspbian

- What is the name of the software we will be using on our Raspberry Pi?
  - Raspbian (it is a Linux distribution and an operating system)
- What did we use to make the SD card?
  - The Etcher spftware
- What is the CSI connector on the Raspberry Pi for?
  - The Pi Camera module
- Which versions of the Raspberry Pi are recommended for use in this book?
  - 3, 3B+, and possibly future versions

Chapter 4, Preparing a Raspberry Pi for a Robot - Headless by Default

- What are the major items you would not leave attached to a **headless** computer?
  - You would not leave a **screen** and a **keyboard** attached.
- If you gave your robot the hostname `awesomegiantrobot`, what address would you use to reach it in PuTTY?
  - `awesomegiantrobot.local`
- Why is it advisable to expand the filesystem on your Raspberry Pi?
  - So that the whole of the SD card is used. The image from Raspbian starts off using only a tiny fraction of the available space.

- How do you properly shut down the Raspberry Pi?
  - Type `sudo shutdown -h now` and wait for the lights to stop flashing, then remove power.

Chapter 5, Backing Up the Code with Git and SD Card Copies

- For what reasons would you use source control?
  - To keep your code for later
  - To go back in history
  - To try ideas
- What would you use branching for?
  - To try out ideas
  - To go back to a working branch
- Why keep SD card copies?
  - So you can restore the whole system, including configuration
- What reasons are there for editing files on another computer and uploading them to the Raspberry Pi?
  - You can choose your own editor
  - You now have a copy of code in more than one place

Chapter 6, Building Robot Basics - Wheels, Power, and Wiring

- Why is it a good idea when using multiple Raspberry Pi "hats" or bonnets to look at their pin use?
  - Hats may use the same I/O pins for different purposes, making them incompatible.
- Why have we chosen to power the Pi separately from the motors?
  - To avoid brown outs, resets caused by noise or voltage drops from the motors

- What are the consequences of too small a motor controller?
    - It will overheat, causing it damage or to shut down.
- Why do I recommend test fitting before buying any parts?
    - To ensure the parts will fit together on the chosen chassis

Chapter 7, Drive and Turn - Moving Motors with Python

- Why do we use the `atexit.register` mechanism?
    - To register a stop function, so the robot's motors will stop when the code stops, even if there is an error
- How can we correct a motor going the wrong way?
    - We can swap the two motor-lead connections for that motor at the screw terminals.
- What are the main advantages of a common interface for a Robot object?
    - We can build new behaviors on top of the object without writing setup and translation code repeatedly.
    - We can move our behaviors onto other motor controllers by wrapping them in the same interface.
- How must the motors move (left and right) to make this robot turn?
    - To turn, one motor must be going at a different speed from the other.
    - To spin, one motor should be going in the opposite direction from the other.

Chapter 8, Programming Line-Following Sensors Using Python

- What can happen if the test track is too shiny or not dark enough?
    - The robot will fail to detect the track and may drive straight over it or jitter as it partially detects it.
- What are the other names for GND or G pin?
    - Ground, "-", negative, and "-ve"

- Why would strong sunlight interfere with this sensor?
    - Sunlight can flood the sensor with IR light, drowning out the sensors' own beam.
- In event-driven programming, such as we've used in this chapter, what do you call the section of code that will be called when an event is triggered?
    - Code triggered by an event is known as a **handler**.

Chapter 9, Programming RGB Strips in Python

- When soldering, do you heat the pad, the pin, or the solder?
    - You heat the pad and pin first, so the solder melts and flows into them.
- Why do you not connect the LED strip directly to the Raspberry Pi?
    - The LED strip requires 5V and the Pi is running 3.3V. At best, it will communicate poorly; at worst, it could damage the Pi. Use the logic-level shifter.
- Why are we using fractions of the number of LEDs in the LED class for our ranges?
    - The number of LEDs in different strips and configurations can change, for example, the LED Shim has 24 LEDs. This means one behavior will work with different LED setups.
- What is the difference between a HSV color with a saturation of 0 and a saturation at the full range?
    - At saturation 0, the color will be gray or have nearly no color. At the full range, the color will be very vivid.

Chapter 10, Using Python to Control Servo Motors

- What does the acronym PWM stand for?
    - Pulse Width Modulation: the means of controlling a device by varying the size (or width in time) of pulses sent to the device

- In terms of the Servo motor's internal mechanism, from what components is the error calculated?
  - The difference between the actual current position of the motor and the requested position of the motor
- What is a servo "horn"?
  - A small collar with arms to attach to a servo motor spindle to convert its output into motion
- What could result from a servo being impeded when trying to reach a requested position?
  - It can lead to overheating and damage to the servo motor.

Chapter 11, Programming Distance Sensors with Python

- What might interfere with a light-based distance sensor?
  - Sunlight, florescent lighting, and other light based sensors – such timing sensors used on tracks
- Why do we divide our speed of sound number by 2?
  - Because the sound pulse has travelled from our robot to the object and then back – twice the distance
- Why in the more complicated behavior has a variable delay been introduced?
  - To ensure the robot drives back for some time and doesn't jitter
- Why could the robot still reverse into things?
  - There are no rear sensors and the robot is not moving accurately enough to construct a map.

Chapter 12, Programming Encoders with Python

- What are the edge types we are counting with our encoder code?
  - **Rising** and **falling** edge types, when signal goes up and goes down
- Why should we not drive motors at 100% for these control systems?
  - Because there will then be no unused capacity for adjustments: there would be clipping

- What are some factors that encoders on the wheels/motors like this not account for?
    - Slipping/skidding
    - Variations in the wheels themselves

Chapter 13, Robot Vision - Using a Pi Camera and OpenCV

- We used the HSV color system when tracking colored objects. Why would the RGB color system not work for this?
    - When tracking color, the ranges used to filter are looking for a range of hues; for example, greens or reds. Tracking this in relation to the green and blue elements on RGB colors is tricky and perhaps not really viable.
- PID controllers (or PI control) were used for both behaviors. On the color track behavior we added an anti-windup measure, what would happen without this limit?
    - The integral sum would grow too high, which can cause the robot to overshoot if the response takes time.
- When performing computer vision, we use a low resolution for the images. What are some of the reasons for choosing a low resolution?
    - Less data to move around the system keeps the web app responsive
    - Faster processing times for the visual processing operations
    - Reduces noise to the visual processing algorithms, otherwise additional filters (for example, a Gaussian blur) may have to be introduced
- Why do we use Queues to send data between the processes in our system?
    - Having multiple processes accessing the same data at the same time can lead to unpredictable problems.
    - The Python Multiprocess Queue structure is designed to be a safe way to send data between processes.
- What step is needed between using color filters to make a masked image and generating enclosing circles for the remaining blobs?
    - We generate "contours", outlines around the "blobs" of color found in the image. These give lists of coordinates for each shape found.

Chapter 14, Voice Communication with a Robot Using Mycroft

- Why would the user define multiple variations for each vocabulary part?
  - When you talk, you naturally use synonyms: different ways to say the same thing. Without expressing those in the vocabulary file, Mycroft is not able to pick them up.
- Similarly, why would they do this for the dialogs?
  - To make Mycroft's responses seem more natural, as it will randomly pick synonymous phrases from the dialog
- Why did we wrap our intent with a `try/catch`?
  - So we can ensure that Mycroft speaks to us if it fails to contact the robot, and logs the problem somewhere
- What is the significance of the `en-us` string in the vocab/dialog file structures?
  - This is a language code. Mycroft will be allowing other language codes so it can be customized to many languages.
- How did we make the Pi start the pulseaudio system when it boots?
  - We used systemd with service, targeted to start before the multiuser level.

Chapter 15, Programming a Gamepad on Raspberry Pi with Python

- What is a "static" file?
  - A static file is a file served by a webserver that is not generated or changed, but just delivered as is to the browser. This is perfect for JS, CSS files, or library files.

- What does the `path:` prefix mean for a section of a Flask route?
    - This can be used to denote that the route section matches a string that may contain slash / separator characters, to put into a variable, like the following example:

    ```
    . . .
    @app.route('/control/<path:control_name>')
    def control(control_name):

    . . .
    ```

- What is the unit `vw` in CSS, and why do we use it?
    - vw is an abbreviation for viewport width. It specifies things as a percentage of viewport width. It is used so things can scale in proportion to size of the screen we are looking at them with.

- How do you get events when a screen is touched in JavaScript?
    - You pass a function or method to `$(<target selector>).on('touchmove', <function or method>)`. You probably need to `.bind` the method.

- What do the `.button` and `#video` selectors mean for CSS/jQuery?
    - `.button` selects objects with `class="button"`.
    - `#video` selects an object with `id="video"`.

- In the systemd service file, what does the `After=network.target` statement intend?
    - The service described will only be started after the network target is reached, that is, networking is up and running on the Raspberry Pi.

Other Books You May Enjoy

If you enjoyed this book, you may be interested in these other books by Packt:

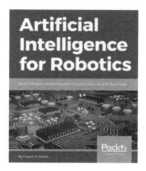

Artificial Intelligence for Robotics
Francis X. Govers

ISBN: 978-1-78883-544-2

- Get started with robotics and artificial intelligence
- Apply simulation techniques to give your robot an artificial personality
- Understand object recognition using neural networks and supervised learning techniques
- Pick up objects using genetic algorithms for manipulation
- Teach your robot to listen using NLP via an expert system
- Use machine learning and computer vision to teach your robot how to avoid obstacles
- Understand path planning, decision trees, and search algorithms in order to enhance your robot

Python Robotics Projects
Prof. Diwakar Vaish

ISBN: 978-1-78883-292-2

- Get to know the basics of robotics and its functions
- Walk through Interface components with microcontrollers
- Integrate robotics with the IoT environment
- Build projects using machine learning
- Implement path planning and vision processing
- Interface your robots with Bluetooth

Leave a review - let other readers know what you think

Please share your thoughts on this book with others by leaving a review on the site that you bought it from. If you purchased the book from Amazon, please leave us an honest review on this book's Amazon page. This is vital so that other potential readers can see and use your unbiased opinion to make purchasing decisions, we can understand what our customers think about our products, and our authors can see your feedback on the title that they have worked with Packt to create. It will only take a few minutes of your time, but is valuable to other potential customers, our authors, and Packt. Thank you!

Index